3/94

 St. Louis Community College

Forest Park
Florissant Valley
Meramec

Instructional Resources
St. Louis, Missouri

GAYLORD

UNTAMED
and
UNABASHED

UNTAMED
and
UNABASHED

Essays on Women and Humor
in British Literature

REGINA BARRECA

 Wayne State University Press   Detroit

Library of Congress Cataloging-in-Publication Data
Barreca, Regina.
    Untamed and unabashed : essays on women and humor in British
literature / Regina Barreca.
       p.   cm. — (Humor in life and letters series)
    Includes bibliographical references and index.
    ISBN 0-8143-2136-4 (alk. paper)
    1. Humorous stories, English—Women authors—History and criti-
cism. 2. English wit and humor—Women authors—History and
criticism. 3. English fiction—Women authors—History and criticism. 4. Women in literature—Great Britain. I. Title. II. Series:
Humor in life and letters.
PR830.H85B37   1994
823.009'9287—dc20   93-30645

Designer: Mary Krzewinski

Special Acknowledgment: Portions of a number of these chapters have
been previously published, in different form, in the following: *Last
Laughs: Perspectives on Women and Comedy*; *New Perspectives on
Women and Comedy*; *LIT: Literature, Interpretation, Theory.* I am
grateful to the publishers, Gordon and Breach, for permission to include this material.

*This book is
dedicated to my
brother, Hugo
Barreca, who
always told me to
listen to the words.*

Contents

Acknowledgments

My thanks to my research assistants Rose Quiello, Allison Hild, Julie Nash, Kendra Hansis, and Leslie Hjeldness, all of whom worked with diligence, energy, and patience—without forfeiting their senses of humor—to help me put this book together. Colleagues and friends Margaret Higonnet, Nancy Walker, James Kincaid, John Glavin, Pam Katz, Brenda Gross, Lee Jacobus, Gerhard Joseph, Mary Ann Caws, Michael Timko, Jane Marcus, Bonnie Januszewski, Rachel Brownstein, Sarah Blacher Cohen, Robert Polhemus, Elisabeth Bronfen, Jack Hall, Nancy Lager, Tim Taylor, and Mary Anne Yanulis all contributed support, encouragement, and perspective; they deserve and have my sincere gratitude, as do my undergraduate and graduate students at the University of Connecticut. My thanks, too, go to Dean Thomas Giolas and Susan Benedict at the Research Foundation of the University of Connecticut, and to Kim Schleicher and Helen Smith at the English department of the University of Connecticut. Finally, thanks to my husband and colleague Michael Meyer, who keeps asking "Do you really think this stuff is funny?" and so helps me define exactly why I *do* find it funny, after all.

1

Introduction

"Untamed and Unabashed": Towards a Theory of Women and Humor in Literature

Lydia was Lydia still; untamed, unabashed, wild, noisy and fearless.

Jane Austen, Pride and Prejudice

Be truthful, one would say, and the result is bound to be amazingly interesting. Comedy is bound to be enriched. New facts are bound to be discovered.

Virginia Woolf, A Room of One's Own

Until very recently there existed the mostly unassailed conviction that those few women who wrote comedies wrote them only with a desire to provide mild entertainment, a textual flirtation, a batting of the rhetorical eyelashes. Without being defined as such, studies of humor have traditionally studied male humor. Even relatively recent collections claim to deal with material "from Woody Allen to Philip Roth"—not an astonishingly diverse crowd if these two represent the poles of experience. Oxford's most current volume of humor has on its jacket a picture of the map of the United States with a cigar protruding from a mouth drawn across the country. These collections contain one or two selections by women, and, unnervingly, often offer the same selection by women, as if only Dorothy Parker ever told a funny story, and as if *she* could only tell the same funny story over and over again.

Most books on comedy in literature ignore writings by women authors, making passing (if not parenthetical) reference to Jane Austen, implying that she was the sole female writer ever to employ any form of humor. (A friend recently gave me the frontspiece to a 1918 book series titled *English Men Of Letters: Jane Austen*. Nobody seemed to have found the idea of Austen as a "man of letters" funny in 1918). Women writers have recognized that this sort of split in perceptions of comedy can cause a number of problems. George Eliot comments, with her signature understatement, that "a difference of taste in jokes is a great strain on the affections" (*Daniel Deronda* 201).

Women must recognize fully that we have always had a joke of our own, despite the fact that men, who decide what is universally applicable and empirically true, have declared that women do not have a sense of humor because women do not laugh at what men find funny. Women are usually no more thrilled by Norman Mailer's humor than we are by the Three Stooges. We are not usually tickled by the bad luck of the fool or by the embarrassment of the underling. But we do laugh—and laugh with a vengeance. Much of women's comic play has to do with power and its systematic misappropriation. Women's humor is about our reclamation of certain forms of control over our own lives. Humor allows us to gain perspective by ridiculing the implicit insanities of a patriarchal culture.

Why "male" and "female" comedy? Why make it gender-specific? Why not see comedy as the last frontier of the universal, humor as that glorious patch of hallowed ground where we all meet and laugh with equal joy? A charming thought, but dangerous in its attempt to seduce the reader into a belief that we all laugh at the same things, even when we happen to laugh at the same time; that we all see the same thing when we stand next to one another. Comedy, out of all the textual territories explored, is the least universal. It is rigidly mapped and marked by subjectivity. Almost every detail of our lives affects the way we create and respond to humor; age, race, ethnic background, and class are all significant factors in the production and reception of humor.

Your aged aunt, for example, might still chuckle over a joke about an Edsel, but your niece probably won't be able to join in. Your friend from Alabama might not enjoy your set of "redneck" jokes; your old roommate from New York might think they are terrific. Your Italian sister-in-law might not appreciate Mafia jokes, and your Jewish mother-in-law might be offended by JAP jokes. This set of in-laws might even reserve the right to make fun of their own immediate families without extending you that privilege. In other words, while "we" can laugh at jokes made by "us" about "us," we might deeply resent it if "they" tell the same story about "us." It would seem more than self-evident, then, that gender would be as great an issue for the discussion of humor as any of these other factors, but gender remains one of the last issues to be addressed. While it would be regarded as outrageous to tell a racist joke to a person of color, for example, many men rarely hesitate to tell a sexist joke to a woman. Such story-tellers then accuse women of being humorless if they do not laugh.

An emeritus professor unwittingly illustrated this principle for me when I gave an academic talk at a small northeastern college in 1991. My paper concerned, not surprisingly, the way that women and men respond differently to certain forms of humor. This gentleman raised his hand the moment I stopped speaking in protest at what he believed was my role in the loss of humor in contemporary society. "I used to be able to tell wonderful, hilarious jokes in my introductory course in archeology," he growled, "But by the time I retired, I couldn't say anything anymore for fear of offending a female student. We used to be able to laugh at ourselves and to laugh together, and now we have lost that." I was quick to explain that I was all for laughter in the classroom, and that I thought a discussion of difference in humor would have the effect of allowing more people to have access to comic forms of expression. Perhaps, I suggested, he was just being oversensitive —heaven knows we all need to laugh at ourselves. He said that he had the perfect example of a joke which made us all laugh at ourselves, but which, unfortunately, he could no longer tell because the "feminist humor police" would be after him. "Here is this wonderful joke," he announced, "I will tell it to you. How do you know if a skeleton was a male or female?" I cringed slightly, but smiled in what I hoped looked like encouragement; it didn't seem promising, but I wanted to give him the benefit of the doubt. "How can you tell? If the mouth is open, it's a woman. They never stop talking! Get it?" The hundred or so people in the audience coughed, there were some nervous guffaws, but few—if any—laughs. "So?" he asked, "What do you say?" I said that, with all due respect, the woman's movement has earned its keep if it prevented him from telling that joke.

"Can I help you see," I asked, "that your joke doesn't sound, to an eighteen-year-old woman, like a joke about 'us' laughing at 'ourselves'—but instead sounds like a joke told by an authorative male professor about silly, prattling women? And can't you see that the first time this young woman wants to raise her hand to ask a question or make a point, she might hesitate because she doesn't want to appear to you like one of the non-stop talking bag-of-bones you described earlier? Your joke isn't about 'all of us'" I explained, "Because *you* aren't included in the group you're targeting." He came up to speak to me afterward and was as charming a gentleman as anyone's best grandfather, but I was glad that he was not in the front of the room when he made his joke. If he had been my professor, I might not have made it to the front of the room myself.

This blindness towards gender-response in humor appears ubiquitous, even for those scholars who take comedy seriously. For example, Peter Farb wrote an article called "Speaking Seriously About Humor," which was

published by *The Massachusetts Review* in 1981. Farb, in a standard scholarly explanation of the forms and effects of various types of humor, offers
without apology or embarrassment, as an example of the "Spooneristic Co-
nundrum," the following: "What's the difference between a pygmy village
and an all-female track team? The pygmy village is a cunning bunch of
runts" (773). If this is such a terrific example of a certain form of word play,
then (as the graduate student who photocopied Farb's article for me wrote
in its margin), "how come I'm not laughing?" Farb's joke should perhaps be
praised for its economy, since it manages to be both sexist and racist at the
same time. But Farb's example is most useful in illustrating that a joke is
not, in fact, always a joke. A joke depends on the teller and the told, and if
something is not funny it does not mean the person listening has no sense of
humor. It might be that the person creating the humor is not funny. The
summary remark that I have often used to delineate traditional critical ap-
proaches to women's comedy was made by Reginald Horace Blyth in his
book *Humour in English Literature*: "The truth is . . . that women have not
only no humor in themselves but are the cause of the extinction of it in
others" (14). Blyth goes on to argue that the proof that women have no sense
of humor lies in the following argument:

> This is almost too cruel to be true, but in every way women cor-
> respond to and are representative of nature. Is there any humour
> in nature? A glance at the zoo will answer this question, and
> even the animals, let alone primitive men, must have always felt
> the contrast between what they wanted and what they got. But
> women are the undifferentiated mass of nature from which the
> contradictions of the real and ideal arose, and they are the un-
> laughing at which men laugh. (15)

That this comment now usually provokes laughter when, no doubt, it was
meant to provoke only a sympathetic nod of agreement indicates that the
study of comedy and humor is ready for feminist exploration.

As may already be apparent, any one critic's definition of comedy simply cuts a swatch from a larger fabric and proclaims it whole cloth. I cannot
claim to do otherwise; I can merely make my pattern available to the reader.
Indeed, I would not want to argue that male critics have not contributed
useful insights concerning theories of comedy. In fact, a number of these
critics raise issues which, when applied to texts by women, seem to find
their most appropriate venue. When James Kincaid, for example, speaks
about comedy as the most "powerful narratives of illumination and libera-
tion we have," and argues that "when we say that comedy is inferior to tragedy, we join hands with Phyllis Schlafley, Castlereagh, Pat Buchanan, Mar-
ie Antoinette, Caligula, and Orin Hatch," we are clearly in the presence of a

critic who embraces the idea of comedy as subversive and gleefully threatening to the dominant order. Nevertheless, critics such as Kincaid, Eco, Bakhtin, Polhemus, and a handful of others are up against a central, longstanding, deeply-embedded, and ultimately conservative belief that the serious study of comedy does not concern women.[1]

The necessity to explore women's creation of comedy becomes further complicated by the need for constant qualification, rebuttal, and redefinition of these positions. The texts under discussion, then, are not meant to represent the full-flowering of all women's writing; rather, they were chosen to illustrate particular forms of comedy and humor. The following discussion of women writers does not seek to prove that every woman who ever wrote, wrote comedy; it does not seek to prove that everything every female character in every text every woman ever wrote speaks satirically, sarcastically, ironically or with intent to subvert (although I do intend to argue that there are more trouble-makers than has been previously noted); it does not intend to argue that the ending of *The Mill on the Floss*, for example, is really a slapstick take-off on traditional couplings or that Elizabeth Bowen should have done stand-up routines. Instead, I want to argue for the acknowledgment of, and identify the patterns of, women's humor in some works of English literature because it is of the utmost importance to see gender-specific traditions (since they do, indeed, exist). In *On Lies, Secrets, and Silence*, Adrienne Rich has identified a "serious cultural obstacle encountered by any feminist writer" in that "each feminist work has tended to be received as if it emerged from nowhere; as if each of us has lived, thought, and worked without any historical past or contextual present" (11). We need to chart, not to invent or create, a tradition of women's humor.

While it is true that traditional forms of masculine humor have recorded their revolt against certain inequities in a given social system, there remains a difference between how men and women approach the subject of their irreverence. Women have been outsiders in this culture, but when they use humor, they become outlaws. Even the existentialist male writer will write from within the dominant discourse in terms of his gender. The most economically oppressed of male writers nevertheless writes from a position of privilege awarded to him by a culture that equates value with maleness in much the same way that an Anglo writer writes from a position of privilege in the Western world. Although these observations may cause discomfort to the existentialist, economically depressed Anglo male writer—or critic—who regards his own oppression as unique, they remain valid. Nancy Walker, in her study of American women's humor, explains that "[e]ven when the white male humorist adopts for his own purposes the stance of the outsider . . . he writes with the authority of the insider, the person who is potentially in a position to change what he finds wrong, whether it is the law or the cut of a dinner jacket" (*A Very Serious Thing*, 11).

The difference, then, between men's humor and women's humor, is the difference between revolt and revolution. When women's laughter is directed towards authority, it can bring down the house. Is it still necessary to assert that feminist humor differs from traditional, masculinist humor? Yes, because we must map gender difference in humor in light of the fact that when women do not laugh at humor whose sole function is to degrade or discredit, we are still told that something is wrong with us. We are told that we cannot appreciate comedy. When a man in our company asserts that women lack humor, that line should alert us that things are not going in our favor—the way the horn of a Peterbuilt truck alerts you that it's turning into your lane too fast for you to move out of the way. If a woman reader responds by saying "I don't think that's funny" what she probably will hear as a reply is "What's the matter? Don't you have a sense of humor?" or "See, women can't take a joke," both of which translate into—as Joanna Russ has told us in "Dear Colleague, I am not an honorary male"—"I find jokes about you funny. Why don't you find jokes about you funny?" (182).

Despite the cliche of the unlaughing woman, women's texts are full of humor, and the comic heroine is often triumphant. As Rachel Brownstein tells us in *Becoming a Heroine*, "The comic heroine has it all over the tragic: she is applauded for venting a lot of nastiness, and no matter how sharp her tongue she gets the best man in the end, contradicting my mother, who claimed I'd never get married if I didn't stop making wisecracks. Although the heroine's great wit might seem to scare all men, it actually frightens off only the ones you wouldn't want"(12). But the truly comic heroine, it can be argued, is almost exclusively a product of the female writer. There are a number of examples of desirable witty women in books written by women. From Elizabeth Bennett to Jane Eyre to Scarlett O'Hara to Praxis Duveen, there is a tradition of the witty woman winning the day and, incidentally, winning the man, in texts by women. But where are the witty, sexually desirable, and enormously marriageable women in books by male authors?

All too often the male writer will create a female character who, if she has the gift of a quick tongue, will look like Captain Bly; if she is a beautiful woman, she often has the conversational flair of Bartelby the Scrivener. There are, of course, exceptions. Shaw gives us women with courage and a way with words, as does Congreve. George Gissing, George Meredith, and David Lodge all present comic heroines who win respect as well as desire. But the argument, admitting occasional impediments, I believe still works in most cases. When there is a witty woman in a man's novel, she is all too often a version of Becky Sharp: sexually manipulative, slyly nasty, and emotionally dishonest. Or she is the generic discount-hooker-with-a-heart-of-gold, just a phase a man goes through before he gets to the love of his life. In contrast to the wild and witty woman—one thinks of the endless and nameless barmaids populating both English and American novels—the hero inevitably chooses to marry the witless woman with whom he will settle down —and for whom he settles. The bad woman with the sense of humor is shut out of domesticity; she forfeits the right to a husband when she makes her first wisecrack. The witty woman does not fare well in conventional writings by men. Even Oscar Wilde suggested that "Nothing spoils a romance so much as a sense of humor in the woman—or the want of it in a man." A turn of the century American essayist, Minna Antrim, believed that "Man forgives woman anything, save the wit to outwit him." The witty woman in the man's novel is either sexually promiscuous (because making a joke is seen as making a pass), asexual, or married to someone else. The witty woman in the woman's novel is, in contrast, triumphant. Or to put it another way, in a woman's novel, the witty woman is in control.

Humor is about risk and privilege; for women and other groups exiled from the centers of power, it can signal the transformation of speechless outrage to persuasive, vocal and joyous audacity. Humor works by bending or breaking the rules; it always has. But at this moment in our culture we are uncertain which rules apply. This is one reason why the relationship of women to humor is at an important point of what can best be called "conflagration," of destruction and, literally, recreation. The "gags" directed at women in masculinist humor have for too long served exactly that purpose: to shut women up. It is time to remove the gag so that our humor and our laughter is heard.

Women's humor has not so much been ignored as it has been unrecognized, passed over, or misread as tragic. Because literary critics, analysts, novelists, and academics can all supply reasons why the creation of comedy by women is impossible, it does not follow that women have not created comedy. It is similar to the situation in which experts in physics and aeronautics have explained to their own satisfaction that the bumblebee cannot possibly fly given its weight and wingspan, even as they dash about hoping not to be stung. In other words, if you're not looking for it you are probably not going to find it. It does not mean that it's not there. "Universal negatives are seldom safe," explains Arabella from Lennox's *The Female Quixote*, "and are least to be allowed when the disputes are about the objects of sense; where one position cannot be inferred from another. That there is a castle, any man who has seen it may safely affirm. But you cannot, with equal reason, maintain that there is no castle because you have not seen it" (414).

Women may not even be able to recognize their own humor at first glance because they have, since infancy in most cases, been initiated into the world held tight by masculine humor. "Men have used humor against women for so long—we know implicitly whose butt is the butt of their jokes—

17

that we do not trust humor," explains Kate Clinton. Clinton asserts in her article "Making Light" that "Masculine humor is deflective. It allows denial of responsibility, the oh-I-was-just-kidding disclaimer. It is escapist, something to gloss over and get through the hard times, without ever having to do any of the hard work of change. Masculine humor is essentially not about change. It is about the maintenance of the status quo. There is nothing new under the sons; they are always dead serious" (39). Men and women, Judith Wilt claims, have different uses for comic constructs because women

> are only just beginning to realize that male humour has various functions, but none of them is intended to please or benefit them. It can be a bonding device, assisting male solidarity (and excluding women). It can be a smoke-screen, set up to dissipate an aura of good humour (distracting and deceiving women). Finally, it can be a form of assault, a teasing attack (putting women in that mythical region, their place). In any event it is used to avoid, to impede, or to deride the possibility of free equal relationships between men and women. (187)

Women's comedies may contain joyous celebration, but they do not rely, finally, on the idea of a perpetual celebration. They use comedy not as a safety valve but as an inflammatory device, seeking, ultimately, not to purge deire and frustration but to transform it into action.

Judith Wilt unhesitatingly confronts the relationship between women's comedy and anger. In "The Laughter of Maidens, the Cackle of Matriarchs," Wilt argues that there is, for women, a "boundary where comedy ceases to cheer and succor and becomes violent, destructive, murderous" (174). Emblematic of the growing awareness that the definitions of comedy define a masculine tradition and cannot account for patterns particular to women's writing, Wilt's argument raises important questions concerning the definition of comedy itself. If we look at the ways in which theoreticians have discussed comedy as a genre, we see that they are concerned with a number of central ideas all regarded as possible constituents in the proper definition of the term "comedy": comedy as celebration of fertility and rebirth; comedy as the vulgar and debased presentation of the familiar; comedy as catharsis of desire and frustration; comedy as social safety valve; comedy as carnival; comedy as unconscious, psychological reaction to personal and social instabilities; comedy as happy ending, joyous celebration, and reestablishment of order. We can see, then, that women's comedies have often been misread since they often do not adhere to these essentially conservative conventions of comedy. If comedy written by women is meant to include certain elements (reconciling gentility, soft admonitions for social lapses, sweet mirth) and if these elements are markedly absent, the work might be misread as non-comedic. This might occur despite the fact that the work contains aspects of fiction usually associated with "traditional" comedy: irony, hostility, aggression, the grotesque, explicit or implicit political agendas, for example. While providing at least some of the distinguishing signs of comedy—exaggerated characters, use of puns or wordplay, absurd situations—women writers still manage to undercut the conventions they employ by shifting the very framing devices used to give definition.

For women, therefore, there is a different set of endings, or non-endings, leading to pleasure. The traditional comedic plot insists that the boy gets the girl and creates a new social order with himself as its leader. Being the girl the boy "got" so that he can then found a nice little society around himself is not her happy ending. Instead, from a woman's "own anarchic point of view, it is pleasure in breaking apart; but from the other's point of view, it is suffering, because to break apart is to aggress. The suffering is not originally hers: it is the other's which is returned to her, by projection" (Cixous and Clement 34). Smiling through an experience is different from undergoing catharsis: the experience remains potent, dangerous and enraging despite the smile. The experience is put towards the impetus of destruction, not catharsis. It disables one from continuing as before, rather than enabling the continuation of the status quo. The pleasure derives not from the perpetuation of the familiar but from its destruction. This pleasure depends on surprises, disruptions, reversals, disunity and disharmony. The experience cannot be absorbed into the prefabricated cultural structures; it doubles on itself, not purged but strengthened.

It is not revolutionary to claim that comedy raises questions concerning authority. Indeed, this principle has been demonstrated in works from Juvenalian satire onwards. Comedy has often been linked to man's (*sic*) ability to transcend his oppression by laughing at his chains. Comedy has been seen as part of the natural cycle of regeneration and renewal. Renewal, however, implies the continuation of established patterns: new figures in unalterable positions. Regeneration has the same attendant sense of change-without-change, sons replacing fathers, daughters replacing mothers, but without any slippage in the power structure. Once the younger figures achieve their new and rightful positions in the power structure, the tensions are released and, presto, we have comedy. A seemingly straightforward affair—except when the texts are written by women.

When it *can* be seen, comedy written by women is perceived as trivial, silly and unworthy of serious attention. These reactions might appear understandable, given that women are writing outside the locus of power and authority; writing about women's activities appears to many critics to have less purpose than writing about men's activities. By writing comedy, in which the unofficial nature of the world is explored (to paraphrase Bakhtin), women are damned to insignificance twice over. As we have seen, traditional arguments posit the following: in women's comedy, as in women's gossip, the unimportant discuss the unofficial. Why, the argument runs, should it concern serious scholars of comedy?

Obviously, I want to argue that subjects of women's comedy are far from unimportant, however unofficial their designation within the dominant discourse. The prevailing attitude continues to maintain that comedy written by women must be gentle and conciliatory. The number of histories of comedy which classify women's comedy in these terms confirms what I believe is central in the misreading of women's texts: the belief that women are incapable of producing the challenging, angry and subversive comedy that they do in fact write.

For some critics, the fact that many women writers choose to write about the so-called details of life (birth, death, marriage, and sex) implies that women cannot master the universal (sports, finance, and academics). Virginia Woolf alerts women to this difference in *A Room of One's Own* when she explains that

> is it obvious that the values of women differ very often from the values which have been made by the other sex; naturally, this is so. Yet it is the masculine values that prevail. Speaking crudely, football and sport are "important"; the worship of fashion, the buying of clothes "trivial." And these values are inevitably transferred from life to fiction. This is an important book, the critic assumes, because it deals with war. This is an insignificant book because it deals with the feelings of women in a drawing-room. A scene in a battlefield is more important than a scene in a shop—everywhere and much more subtly the difference of value persists. (76)

Significantly, a discussion of women's comedy is necessary because, as Annette Kolodny has argued, "lacking familiarity with the woman's imaginative universe, that universe within which their acts are signs," men can neither read nor "comprehend the meanings of the women closest to them despite the apparent sharing of a common language" (256). The author, Kolodny continues, must be able to "depend on a fund of shared recognitions and potential inference. For their intended impact to take hold in the reader's imagination, the author simply must . . . be able to call upon a shared context with her audience. When she cannot, or dare not, she may revert to silence, to the imitation of male forms or . . . madness" (256). If women appear unlaughing at conventional, masculinist humor, this might in part be because the directive to find something amusing is as inappropriate, even impossible, as the inverted directive not to find something funny. The women-have-no-sense-of-humor cliche is applied by men to every threatening woman according to Mary Daly, and causes female energy to be directed "against the Self while remaining disguised" (19). Reflex action against this accusation—women laughing at something they do not find funny, or at a joke directed against their own values—can be characterized by Daly's phrase "smiling at the boss" (7). As Judy Little claims, the woman writer of comedy "realizes that she progresses not from rhetorical illusion to transcendent truth, but from one rhetorical illusion to another" ("(En)gendering Laughter," 190 18). It is the inability of the critical tradition to deal with comedy by women, rather than the inability of women to produce comedy, that accounts for the shortage of critical material on the subject.

Women's writing of comedy is characterized by its thinly disguised rage. The woman writer of comedy is often more careful to appear conciliatory than her male contemporaries, but clearly decorum disguises mutiny. Like a handgun hidden in a handbag, the woman writer often obscures her most dangerous implements by making use of her most feminine attributes. Often she will mask her satire by appearing to describe faithfully a series of events, a method to which the heroine in Lennox's *Female Quixote* is devoted: "When actions are a censure upon themselves, the reciter will always be considered a satirist" (315). By simply repeating the sometimes mild, sometimes grave, atrocities directed towards women in everyday life, the woman writer assumes the tasks of the satirist. Those in power, therefore, are often the objects of a particularly insurgent form of feminine humor which, perhaps because it is often unexpected, is often very powerful. In *Three Guineas*, Woolf tells us that "the dominator" in our culture is "peculiarly susceptible. . . either to ridicule or defiance on the part of the female sex" (181–82). Woolf slyly suggests that "Laughter as an antidote to dominance is perhaps indicated" (181–2). Interestingly, myriad sociological and anthropological studies show that all women tend to laugh at those above them in the hierarchy. Emily Toth has shown in her article "Female Wits" that women use "the humane humor rule." Women, declares Toth, do not typically ridicule what people cannot change, such as social handicaps or physical appearance. Toth notes that women rarely use the typical scapegoat figures in their humor. "Rather," she asserts, "women humorists attack—or subvert— the deliberate choices people make: hypocrisies, affectations, mindless following of social expectations" (783). (The humane humor rule is descriptive, not prescriptive; Toth is not saying what women should do, but instead records what she sees as a pattern in women's discourse). In contrast to masculine humor, women's comedy takes as its material the powerful rather than the pitiful.

Women are more likely to make fun of those in high and seemingly invulnerable positions than their male counterparts. Think about the way Austen deflates Henry Tilney's pretensions in *Northanger Abbey*, and twin that with the flagrantly dangerous laughter in Spark's *The Driver's Seat*. Consider the filigree of slightly mad mirth in Elizabeth Bowen's novels, and pair that with the all-encompassing insight and irony of George Eliot. Directing the comedic vision in all its forms—irony, puns, repartee, irreverence and sarcasm—towards those arrogantly occupying positions of power is a hallmark of women's humor. And it probably accounts for why women who publicly exhibit their mocking response have always been considered dangerous. Think of Bertha's laughter echoing down the hallways as she goes to burn down her husband's house in *Jane Eyre*, or the more subtle but no less subversive wry smiles of Ruth after she does the same thing in Fay Weldon's *The Life and Loves of a She-Devil*. Women's humor is often anarchic and apocalyptic; the unsolicited laughter of women spells trouble to those in power. If you ever tried to run a group or teach a class, you know that when your audience laughs at you, you've lost them; it is equally true that if you can get them to laugh with you, you have them. Look at any group of three or four women—at the airport, waiting in line at the bank, gathering for a lecture—and see how long it takes for at least one of them to start laughing once they have started speaking. My estimation is that it takes a few minutes at the most: women have always cultivated a fine sense of the absurd as a way to carve out a space for themselves in what can be a hostile world. And, importantly, this shared experience does not purge our distress at a kind of cultural captivity but instead it underscores a sense of injustice and incites us to further action.

This is not to say, however, that women speak in one voice when they create comedy. There are various rooms in the house of mirth, and they are occupied by a variety of styles, methods, and subjects. We will see that Charlotte Lennox's *The Female Quixote* is a comedy in a way that Charlotte Bronte's *Villette* is not, for example. Lennox's novel is broadly and conspicuously comedic, relying on exaggerated detail, slapstick situations (with the heroine attempting to ford the Thames), and offering the standard finale of a wedding. Nevertheless, a close examination of *The Female Quixote* will reveal the methods Lennox employs to undercut the conventional values and satisfactions apparently offered by her novel. Bronte's *Villette*, rarely read for its comedy, will yield surprisingly rich results when regarded in such a light. *Villette* must be included in a discussion of women's comedy because of the text's reliance on humor to break certain cultural frames. In *Villette*, Bronte employs slapstick situations: Lucy shoves Ginevra Fanshaw into a closet when she won't behave; Madame Beck gives her spying self away when she sneezes at an inopportune moment (in a chapter entitled "A Sneeze Out of Season" just to make sure we don't miss the point). Bronte's light-handed irony is indicated by the fact that she names a devilish trio of students Blanche, Virginie and Angelique. She also employs a comic subtext in counterpoint to the spoken word, so that Lucy says of one of the students: "'She does several things very well. ('Flirtation amongst the rest,' subjoined I, in thought)" (263).

Bronte is capable of writing in *Villette* the sort of shocking metatextual statement we usually associate with such contemporary writers as Fay Weldon when she interrupts her own text to instruct us: "Cancel the whole of that, if you please, reader—or rather let it stand, and draw thence a moral —an alternative, text-hand copy—"(*Villette* 118). The "text-hand" copy will draw much of our attention in all the works to be discussed. So will the idea of the "alternative" text.

Villette is a particularly intriguing example of a genre-defying novel, in fact, because of its consideration of alternatives. If Monsieur Paul returns to marry Lucy, for example, then does the book become a comedy? If he dies in the storm, does the book become a tragedy? By traditional definitions, whether the sailor comes home from the sea will determine whether the waiting woman's life is comic or tragic. Is it any wonder, then, that Bronte refuses to supply the scene that would determine Lucy's textual fate? Lucy has had, according to her own account, the best years of her life while he's been away. What, in fact, would be her happy ending?

What can be regarded as a nominal happy ending might, for example, include a number of elements usually regarded as tragic. The heroine of a Fay Weldon novel burns down her house (asphyxiating a gerbil in the process, thereby displaying a markedly unfeminine indifference to a house pet), abandons her children, destroys her husband's career and kills off her rival, but we still regard *She-Devil* as a comedy. It is women's comedy: "A comic turn, turned serious," as Ruth herself explains in the last line of the novel. What should we make of the ending of Weldon's *Heart of the Country*, for example, given that the narrator tells us at the end of the book that, for one particularly unhappy character, there "comes a proposal of marriage from a good man, who knows her every failing"? If we expect the usual applause for a union, we are disappointed because the narrator goes on to explain, matter-of-factly, that "She can't accept, of course. Happy endings are not so easy. No. She must get on with changing the world, rescuing the country. There is no time left for frivolity" (199). The union here is a union of a woman with the work of the world. Her happy ending does not lie with a man, not even with a "good man," however hard he might be to find.

The endings of comic works by women writers do not, ultimately, reproduce the expected hierarchies, or if they do there is often an attendant sense of dislocation even with the happiest ending. The narrator of Jane Austen's *Mansfield Park*, for example, refuses even to provide a substantial account of the courtship between Edmund and Fanny, the two protagonists. Edmund has been in love with a funny, bitchy Mary Crawford throughout the book, and he persists in the rather insensitive hobby of telling Fanny over and over that he cannot imagine any woman as his wife except Mary. Yet Edmund must fall in love with Fanny in order to provide the standard happy ending. Austen allows the reader only to impose a subjective fantasy on the process: entreating—rather like Mary Crawford—the reader to believe in her textual slight of hand, Austen writes in the last chapter: "I entreat everybody to believe that exactly at the time when it was quite natural that it should be so, and not a week earlier, Edmund did cease to care about Miss Crawford, and became as anxious to marry Fanny, as Fanny herself could desire" (470). In this way the unprepared-for happy ending can occur.

It must be seen that Austen refuses to provide the final satisfaction of a romance achieved through routes other than the path dictated by the textual necessity of a happy ending; there must be a Cinderella ending for poor Fanny, and so, with a wave of her inky magic wand, Austen provides it. She provides it, however, with the same sort of magical slight of hand associated more with fairy godmothers than novelists; there is no attempt to delineate a "realistic" progress from friendship to desire in the characters. The final chapter of *Mansfield Park* is filled with rhetorical questions about romance: whether a different kind of woman from Mary "might not do just as well"; "whether Fanny were growing as dear, as important to him in all her smiles, and all her ways, as Mary Crawford had ever been" (470). At best we have Fanny married to a man for whom she is "of course only too good." We hear that Edmund "must" be in the possession of a "delightful happiness" in the same way that "[i]t is a truth universally acknowledged, that a single man in possession of a good fortune, must be in want of a wife" (51). As Rachel Brownstein has described this opening sentence to *Pride and Prejudice*, "it is full of logical holes: a truth universally acknowledged is probably less than true; the truth at issue here is not really that single men want girls . . . but that poor girls need husbands. . . . We are encouraged to reflect that although this is not the case, it may be operatively true when people act as if it's true" (*Last Laughs* 64). Can a happy ending—any more than a stable beginning—be full of rhetorical questions, implicit or explicit?

No wonder women's comedy has gone unseen or misread; pain is projected onto the female character's pleasure, unhappiness onto her joy. The *refusal* to supply closure has been misread as an *inability* to do so, as a failure of imagination and talent on the part of the writer. Women's comedic writings depend on the process, not on the endings. For women writers of comedy, recognition replaces resolution. The resolution of tensions, like unity or integration, should not be considered a viable definition of comedy for women writers because it is too reductive to deal with the non-closed nature of women's writings. As Mary Ellman asserts, the woman writer cares less for what is resolved than for what is recognized in all its conceivable diversions into related or, for that matter, unrelated issues. Once rules are suspended, admirable and remarkable "exceptions are released," recognized and embraced (229). With the realization that rules can be suspended, that absolutes are only powerful when allotted power, when a unified, linear progression is given over to the recognition of multiplicity and diversion, all "else" becomes possible. Women writers of comedy can acknowledge, by the very form of their expression, that accepted authority is not authentically authoritative.

Comedy permits, and prepares women for, rebellion. Kate Clinton declares that women's questions and women's laughter

> have the potential of splitting the world apart. Light shines through the whys cracks we make and illuminates all aspects of our oppression. Consider feminist humor and consider the lichen. Growing low and lowly on enormous rocks, secreting tiny amounts of acid, year after year, eating into the rock. Making places for water to gather, to freeze and crack the rock a bit. Making soil, making way for grasses to grow. Making way for rosehips and sea oats, for aspen and cedar. It is the lichen which begins the splitting apart of the rocks, the changing of the shoreline, the shape of the earth. Feminist humor is serious, and it is about the changing of this world. (39)

Echoes of Clinton can be heard in both scholarly and non-scholarly writing on women's humor. In *GynEcology*, Mary Daly explores the difference between giggling along with the patriarchal laugh track and the "true" laughter of women. Daly explains that "*Webster's* defines 'titter' as follows: 'to give vent to laughter one is seeking to suppress: laugh lightly or in a subdued manner: laugh in a nervous, affected, or restrained manner, especially at a high pitch and with short catches of the voice' . . . Self-loathing ladies titter; Hags and Harpies roar" (17). Daly goes on to proclaim that "there is nothing like the sound of women really laughing. The roaring laughter of women is like the roaring of the eternal sea. Hags can cackle and roar at themselves, but more and more, one hears them roaring at the reversal that is patriarchy, that monstrous jock's joke . . . [and] this laughter is the one true hope, for as long as it is audible there is evidence that someone is seeing through the Dirty Joke" (17).

Since the 1983 publication of Judy Little's groundbreaking book, *Comedy and the Woman Writer*, there has been a growing critical interest in feminist perspectives on women and humor. Throughout *Untamed and Unabashed* I will refer with relief to the work of others who have arrived at similar questions and conclusions. Little's work on Virginia Woolf, Muriel Spark and other contemporary English authors has cleared a path for others to follow. In part, I have omitted Woolf from the selection of writers presented here because I believe that Little has already said what has needed saying about Woolf's humor. Nancy Walker has done powerful and significant recent work on women's humor, and has assembled the most important research in order to arrive at provocative and persuasive conclusions. Walker's *A Very Serious Thing: Women's Humor and American Culture* (1988), provides a thorough and provocative discussion of women's humor as it appears in both literature and popular culture, calling into question even those essentially arbitrary categories. Work by Sarah Blacher Cohen, editor of *Comic Relief: Humor in Contemporary American Fiction*, has opened doors to scholars such as June Sochen, editor of *Women's Comic Visions*, a collection of essays published in 1991. Essays by Judith Wilt, Carol Mitchell, Emily Toth and others have opened the field for further inquiry, raising issues and suggesting questions. Writers such as Joanna Russ and Mary Daly provide texts laced with delightfully venomous humor, employing the process even as they describe the method. I have had the good fortune to edit two collections of essays on the subject, *Last Laughs* (1988) and *New Perspectives on Women and Comedy* (1992). The thirty-nine contributors to these volumes have shaped *my* consideration of women's comedic writing, but they have also cleared the field for new scholars and critics as well.

It would be judicious, perhaps, to mention by way of preface to *all* recent criticism the seventeenth-century writer Aphra Behn, who was herself conspicuously concerned with the woman writer of comedy. Behn is perhaps best known now for her "historical" novel *Oroonoko*, but in her day she was applauded—and chastised—for plays such as *The Dutch Lover* and *The Forced Marriage*. Catherine Gallagher's discussion of Behn's embrace of the writer/whore mask and her creation of "overlapping discourses of commercial, sexual and linguistic exchange" in the critical essay "Who Was that Masked Woman? The Prostitute and the Playwright in the Comedies of Aphra Behn" allows us to see Behn not solely as someone who made writing more difficult for other women. Woolf argued in *A Room of One's Own* that once "Aphra Behn had done it, girls could go to their parents and say, You need not give me an allowance; I can make money by my pen. Of course the answer for many years to come was, Yes, by living the life of Aphra Behn! Death would be better! and the door was slammed faster than ever." Woolf continued: "All women together ought to let flowers fall upon the tomb of Aphra Behn which is, most scandalously but rather appropriately, in Westminster Abbey, for it was she who earned them the right to speak their minds. It is she—shady and amorous as she was—who makes it not quite fantastic for me to say to you tonight: Earn five hundred a year by your wits" (69). Gallagher argues that Behn was a woman "conscious of her historical role" and a playful challenge to "the very possibility of female self-representation" (41). It is in the prologues, epilogues and prefaces to her plays, however, that Behn treats most directly her position as woman writer. Behn realized that the judgment "That it was Bawdy" was the "least and most excusable fault in the men writers," yet for her own material she would be told "from a woman it was unnatural" (Cited in Goreau 215). If women are told that they cannot write, then obviously all that is written by women must, by definition, be criticized and dismissed as unnatural, monstrous, or aberrant in order for the theory to keep hold. However, as Behn writes in *The Town Fop*, "a monster is only so from its rarity."

Behn knew that she appeared as a woman playwright, not as "just" a playwright, to her critics, and that often her work "had no other misfortune but that of coming out for a woman's: had it been owned by a man, though the most dull, unthinkably rascally scribbler in town, it had been a most admirable play" (Cited in Goreau 215). Even as she argues the point, she seems to retreat from it in frustration: "but a devil on't—the woman damns the poet" (Cited in Goreau 219). Behn ridiculed the male playwrights who prided themselves on keeping to the three unities, who could only trace patterns rather than create their own:

> "Your way of writing's out of fashion grown.
> Method, and rule—you only understand;
> Pursue that way of fooling and be damned." (216)

(Nearly three hundred years later, Fay Weldon would write "I do pity contemporary male writers, who have wives to bring them coffee and answer the phone to the bank manager, and no excuse not to undertake, not to complete, not to get published, and who find themselves with nothing to say" [*Letters to Alice* 83]). Behn begins the "Epistle to the Reader" of *The Dutch* by addressing her audience member as "Good, Sweet, Honey, Sugar-Candied Reader," appearing to curtsy and flutter in his presence. The next line, however, splices the alternative, "text-hand" copy onto the coy invitation: "Which I think is more than anyone has called you yet . . . I presume you have not much to do and therefore are obliged to me for keeping you from worse employment, and if you have a better you may get you gone about your business." She describes a critic at one of her plays as

> a sorry animal that has nought else to shield it from the utter-
> most contempt of all mankind, but that respect we afford to rats
> and toads, which though we do not well allow to live, yet when
> considered as a part of God's creation, we make honorable men-
> tion of them. A thing, reader . . . this thing, I tell ye, opening that

27

> which serves it for a mouth, out issued such a noise as this to
> those who sat about it, that they were to expect a woeful play,
> God damn him, for it was a woman's. . . . [A]nd if comedy should
> be the picture of ridiculous mankind, I wonder anyone should
> think it such a sturdy task, whilst we are furnished with such
> precious originals as him. (Cited in Goreau 213)

That "it was a woman's" play, novel, poem, story has always been the first
definition of a text created by a woman, whether the author cared to seek
that appellation or seek to deny it. Ntozake Shange summed it up in a May
1989 interview with *The New York Times* as follows:

> Because whatever we may perceive of ourselves, we writers or
> anything else we want to be, when we go out of this building . . .
> any of these guys unloading trucks don't see playwrights. They
> see—they might not even see—a woman. They might see an (ex-
> pletive). . . . Because when we go outside, we can't write a sign
> that says 'I'm an intellectual woman, therefore don't speak to
> me that way.' That's not going to save you. (H2)

From Behn to Shange there exists a tradition of women's comedy informed by and speaking to the experience of being female in a world where
that experience is devalued. If the woman writer of comedy has been told
that she cannot possibly succeed in what she has set out to do, she has nevertheless persevered in her endeavor by ignoring the good advice of those who
counsel her against her inevitable failure. Jane Austen, that famous man of
letters, was given terribly good advice at one point when a gentleman suggested to her that she might write more profitably if she could only choose a
better subject, something like "an historical romance, founded on the House
of Saxe Cobourg." Austen replied that, although the gentleman might indeed be correct in his assumption, she "could no more write a romance than
an epic poem. I could not sit seriously down to write a serious romance under any other motive than to save my life; and if it were indispensable for me
to keep it up and never relax into laughing at myself or other people, I am
sure I should be hung before I had finished the first chapter" (Letters 458).
She thanks him, of course, and apologizes, explaining that "I must keep to
my own style and go on in my own way" (453). Apologizing to and thanking
her critics, Austen seems to anticipate Fay Weldon's advice, given to her
fictional, novel-writing niece in *Letters to Alice*, to "agree with your accu-
sers, loudly and clearly. They will shut up sooner" (107).

The apologies and thanks have for too long been misread as sincere
reflections of humble womanhood rather than as the social expedients they
are; the sooner writers are left to write, the sooner they can get back to
laughing at themselves and making jokes at the expense of others. As Elinor

in *Pride and Prejudice* has learned, some comments do not bear answering: "Elinor agreed to it all, for she did not think he deserved the compliment of rational opposition" (255). Although Jane Austen did not have to risk being hanged for writing comedy, her comment indicates her awareness of the dangers particular to the woman writer with a sense of humor. Her comments also hint at the outrage felt by the woman writer who is continually being offered suggestions by her male counterparts concerning the ways she might improve her work if only she heeded his advice.

This outrage is one reason why any argument concerning the relationship between anger and humor is powerful: clearly humor and anger are inextricably linked. Rachel Blau Du Plessis has already drawn our attention to the ways women "write beyond the ending" of the prescribed "script," and has changed our perspectives on women's use of closure. She provides the basis for an argument that posits a need for a redefinition of comedy along gender lines. How do women read other women's comedy? Applying once again Annette Kolodny's arguments from "A Map for Rereading," we see that her points apply with a vengeance to comedic writings. Kolodny writes that it is "gender-inflected interpretive strategies [which are] responsible for our mutual misreadings. . . . [This allows us to] appreciate the variety of women's literary expression, enabling us to take it into serious account for perhaps the first time, rather than, as we do now, writing it off as caprice or exceptions, the irregularity in an otherwise regular design" (259).

Much of women's comedy, like many of the larger meaningful aspects of women's writing—such as anger and rebellion—can only be viewed if one is prepared to deal with the covert narrative strategies employed by many women writers. For example, Gilbert and Gubar propose that Austen called into question the entire relationship of women to fiction, forcing her female readers to question the rules governing their own lives: women who were "living lives regulated by the rules provided by popular fiction," were shown by Austen characters just "how very bankrupt that fiction is" (*The Madwoman in the Attic* 115). There is a seductive element in comedy, as Patricia Spacks has noted in a discussion of the emblematic eighteenth-century heroine, since "as the creature of fantasy gets fleshed out, she becomes attractive, not just dangerous; the novel preaches subversive doctrine in the guise of supporting moral platitudes" (129). Significantly, Judy Little claims that it is the very "lack of closure, this lack of resolution, [which] characterizes the feminist comedy" (187). In the introduction to *Comedy and the Woman Writer*, Little states that the comedy of women writers "differs from rounded-off comic fiction in which the hero is ultimately reintegrated into society. The comedy [written by women] . . . mocks the deepest possible norms" (1). In addition to Little, Wilt claims that the woman writer "hesitates, laughing at the edge, withholding fertility, humility, community" (180)—in other words, withholding every elemental aspect of comedy traditionally associated with women. Wilt asserts that "No comedy is so obsessive, so hysterical, yet so pervasive, as that allotted to women. Not even comedy about women is so pervasive as comedy. . . by women" (177).

Perhaps the strongest argument for the importance of examining the complex relationship among women, comedy and subversion is initiated by Helene Cixous and Catherine Clement in *The Newly Born Woman* during their discussion of women's ability to undo socio-cultural constructs. Cixous and Clements' polemical statement, "all laughter is allied with the monstrous," could act as a banner for women and comedy. The last thing Cixous and Clement see as necessary for comedy is closure: "Laughter breaks up, breaks out, splashes over; Penthesileia could have laughed; instead, she killed and ate Achilles. It is the moment at which the woman crosses a dangerous line, the cultural demarcation beyond which she will find herself excluded" (33). In exploring laughter, women are exploring their own powers; they are refusing to accept social and cultural boundaries that mark the need or desire for closure as a "universal." Comedy is dangerous. Humor is a weapon. Laughter is refusal and triumph. Feminist comedy, according to Little, will say "truly dangerous things obliquely," using complex liminal imagery (178). Women's comedy is "dangerous" because it refuses to accept the givens and because it refuses to stop at the point where comedy loses its integrative function. This comedy by women is about de-centering, dislocating and de-stabilising the world. As Ellman puts it: "Laugh and choose evil" (216). In this, comedy again resembles anger: it is channeled through pathways not blocked by fear and authority and is therefore often misdirected. Often it turns directly against the self as the simplest target. Women's comedy is marginal, liminal, concerned with and defined by its very exclusion from convention, by its aspects of refusal and its alliance with subversive feminine symbols. The difference of women is viewed as a risk to culture.

Given that comedy has always been seen as a "marginal" form of literature (with another nod to Bakhtin), and given that women are considered creatures inhabiting the "liminal" world (with a nod to Little), anthropologists offer an interesting perspective on women's comedy. Mary Douglas explains in *Purity and Danger* that "all margins are dangerous. If they are pulled this way or that, the shape of fundamental experience is altered. Any structure of ideas is vulnerable at its margins" (121). She details the ways in which "in a chaos of shifting impressions" each of us "constructs a stable world in which objects have recognizable shapes, are located in depth and have permanence. In perceiving we are building. Taking some cues and rejecting others. The most acceptable cues are those which fit most easily into the pattern that is being built up. Ambiguous ones tend to be treated as if they harmonized with the rest of the pattern. Discordant ones tend to be rejected. If they are accepted the structure of assumptions has to be modified" (36). This, clearly, goes far in explaining why women's humor has remained virtually invisible within conventional criticism. It also explains the power of women's humor when it becomes impossible to overlook. Douglas writes that "each culture has its risks and its specific problems . . . the things that defile are always wrong one way or another, they are not in their place or else they have crossed a line they never should have crossed and from this shift a danger for someone results" (39). Women can defile, spoil, and ruin because they derive power from their exclusion. Simone deBeauvoir articulated this thought for the first time in *The Second Sex* when she asserted that a woman is

> not fully integrated into the world of men; as the other, she is
> opposed to them. It is natural for her to use the power she has.
> . . . Woman is the siren whose song lures sailors upon the rocks;
> she is Circe, who changes her lovers into beasts, the undine who
> draws fishermen into the depths of pools. The man captivated by
> her charms no longer has will-power, enterprise, future; he is no
> longer a citizen, but mere flesh enslaved to its desires, cut off
> from the community, bound to the moment, tossed passively
> back and forth between torture and pleasure. (196)

She is, therefore, unassimilable; she is, at best, an unreliable and dangerous observer. "She is servant and companion, but he expects her also to be his audience and critic and to confirm him in his sense of being; but she opposes him with her indifference, even with her mockery and laughter" deBeauvoir explains (229).

Mary Russo discusses the way in which using humor can be "dangerous" for a woman. Russo explains that "there is a phrase that still resonates from childhood. Who says it? The mother's voice—not my own mother perhaps, but the voice of an aunt, an older sister, or the mother of a friend. It is a harsh, matronizing phrase, and it is directed towards the behavior of other women." The phrase Russo refers to is "She [the other woman] is making a spectacle out of herself." Russo explains that "making a spectacle out of yourself" was a criticism applied only to women. "The danger," she writes, "was of an exposure. Men, I learned somewhat later in life, 'exposed themselves,' but that operation was quite deliberate" (213). For women, the very act of getting attention is regarded with suspicion. The women who got attention were the "possessors of large, aging, and dimpled thighs displayed at the public beach, of overly rouged cheeks, of a voice shrill in laughter" (213).

This leads us to the figure of the hysteric, the paradigmatic rebel

31

against reality-testing, a central figure for the discussion of women and comedy. The hysteric, the most marginal of marginal figures, is "caught in the contradiction between cultural restraint and sorceress repression." With her hidden "little implicit smile" she experiences "hell and pleasure at the same time" (Cixous and Clement 34). The hysteric refuses to acknowledge what others construct as reality. She has seen the boundaries created in order to delineate the real from the imaginary and she has concluded that they do not in fact exist. Smiling through heaven and hell at the same time, and experiencing them both as much the same, she is emblematic of the way women have been misread, and, by implication, the ways in which women's comedy has been misread. When pleasure is read as pain, and pain as pleasure, there is bound to be misunderstanding. The hysteric often laughs even as she howls. Juliet Mitchell writes in *Women: The Longest Revolution* that "The woman novelist must be an hysteric. Hysteria is the woman's simultaneous acceptance and refusal of the organization of sexuality under patriarchal capitalism" (101). Mitchell argues that the hysteric offers a particular set of permissions for other women, who will join her in saying:

> I, too, overflow; my desires have invented new desires, my body knows unheard-of songs. . . . And I, too, said nothing, showed nothing; I didn't open my mouth, I didn't repaint my half of the world. I was ashamed. I was afraid, and I swallowed my shame and my fear. I said to myself: You are mad! What's the meaning of these waves, these floods, these outbursts? Where is the ebullient, infinite woman who . . . hasn't accused herself of being a monster? Who, feeling a funny desire stirring inside her (to sing, to write, to dare to speak, in short, to bring out something new), hasn't thought she was sick? Well, her shameful sickness is that she resists death, that she makes trouble. (226)

Women's comedy is about making trouble. Agnes Repplier argues that "Humor distorts nothing, and only false gods are laughed off their earthly pedestals." In other words, an essentially sound target will not be damaged by humor since humor depends on the perceived righting of an injustice. This is one reason women's humor does deal with the most fundamental concepts in our culture. Women's humor has a particular interest in challenging the most formidable structures because they keep women from positions of power. Women's humor is about women speaking up: "speakin in our own tongue to whomever we goddam please," writes Ntozake Shange in *Nappy Edges.*

In comedies by women the straightjacket of conventional femininity is challenged, confronted, and, finally, thrown off. Certain forms of comedy can invert the world not only briefly but permanently; can strip away the dignity and complacency of powerful figures only to refuse to hand them back these attributes when the allotted time for "carnival" is finished. Comedy can effectively channel anger and rebellion by first making them appear to be acceptable and temporary phenomena, no doubt to be purged by laughter, and then by harnessing the released energies, rather than dispersing them. The world turned upside down can prove that the world has no rightful position at all. This kind of comedy terrifies those who hold order dear.

It should.

2

Dearly Loving a Good Laugh: Humor in Charlotte Lennox and Jane Austen

> **I** dearly love a laugh. . . . I hope I never ridicule what is wise
> or good. Follies and nonsense, whims and inconsistencies do
> divert me, I own, and I laugh at them whenever I can.
>
> Jane Austen, *Pride and Prejudice*

In novels by Charlotte Lennox and Jane Austen, books for women are regarded as a form of inoculation against action. A work of fiction is given
to a female character in the same spirit that a small dose of measles is
administered to a child: to prevent her from contracting the disease in a
more dangerous way, she is given a prescribed dosage under careful supervi-
sion. According to this theory, if women are permitted to exercise their spirit through reading romances or gothic novels, they then somehow exorcize
their spirit in the process. Give them a little of what they want, and perhaps
it will keep them quiet. How dangerous can a woman's book be, the blindly
self-satisfied argument runs, if it only deals with feminine matters?

Women in Lennox and Austen novels see themselves, as Rachel
Brownstein has cogently demonstrated in *Becoming a Heroine*, as heroines
in the making. They are instructed to overwrite and override their desire
for attention and action. In other words, they are taught to sit down and be
quiet. Laurie Langbauer, in her insightful work *Women and Romance: The
Consolations of Gender in the English Novel*, argues that "Romance's faults
—lack of restraint, irrationality, and silliness—are also [perceived as] wom-
en's faults" (78), and that women, like the form of the romance itself, must
learn control even at the expense of imagination and wit. "Inaugurated into
man's realm," claims Langbauer, taking Lennox's *The Female Quixote* as
her case in point, the heroine of such a tale inevitably "becomes indistin-
guishable from the men in it. She leaves romance by participating in the patriarchal discourse of moral law, and in that discussion loses her voice" (81).

And yet I believe the essential question remains unanswered: do the heroines of these tales ever learn their lessons? Do the narratives inevitably assert, as Langbauer claims is the case with Lennox, that although "those outside the influence of romance . . . are empty- headed, selfish, and ordinary," the "positive alignment of women and romance is wistful" because the author "recognizes how tenuous that position is" (89)? But in examining the narrative's response to these issues, we must still ask: Do the heroines in Lennox or the heroines in Austen finally and fully surrender? Or does the humor of their position, humor so deftly woven into the infrastructure of these novels that it is nearly impossible to isolate from the larger textual concerns, make both text and heroine unassimilable into the cultural/sexual curriculum?

"She could not help fancying herself the future heroine of some affecting tale, whose life would be varied with surprising vicissitudes of fortune," declares Charlotte Lennox's 1758 novel, *Henrietta* (Vol.II, 36). The remark sums up quite succinctly the basic plot for Lennox's earlier work, *The Female Quixote*. While it would seem that Lenox supports the notion that, for her character, "these reflections were succeeded by others more reasonable and which indeed afforded her a more solid satisfaction" (*Henrietta*, Vol.II, 36), Lennox gives us a character in *The Female Quixote* who avoids surrendering to these textually unsatisfying satisfactions. Published in 1752, *The Female Quixote* concerns the initiation of a young woman into society, focusing primarily on her obsession with Romantic novels, her imagination, and her expectations for the future. On one level, Lennox presents us with a straightforward bit of comedy, a satire. As Margaret Doody writes in the introduction to the 1970 Oxford edition of *The Female Quixote*, "Lennox laughs at the romances for the repetitive improbability of the events . . . their inflated diction and their jargon of superlatives" (xvi–xvii). But Lennox goes beyond both gentle mockery and didactic satire and by presenting us with young Arabella, puts *The Female Quixote* into a category of works demanding careful analysis. Most significantly, Lennox's use of comedy throughout the work makes it a template for dealing with feminine inscriptions of humor. Like Austen, Lennox's habitual irony "distances her from appearances and behavior in her society, but it unites her with her readers by drawing us into a conspiracy of intellect. Whoever does not perceive it becomes its target" (Polhemus 41).

The action of *The Female Quixote* is based on a single standing joke: Arabella's repeated attempts to act out and live by tales of Romance. Arabella takes seriously what everyone around her knows to be the stuff of fiction, of fairy tales, of novels written for women who, like Arabella's mother, had to "soften a Solitude" which they found "very disagreeable" (7). "Unlike the male Quixote," Patricia Meyer Spacks points out, "she cannot travel through the world" (130). But Arabella is not a simple woman, blindly seduced by gaudy stories, nor is she uneducated. Rather, she is *mis*educated:

> Her ideas, from the Manner of her Life and the Objects around her, had taken a romantic Turn, and, supposing Romances were real Pictures of Life, from them she drew all her Notions and Expectations. By them she was taught to believe, that Love was the ruling Principle of the World; that every other Passion was subordinate to this; and that it caused all the Happiness and Miseries of Life. (7)

By informing the reader early in the first chapter that Arabella believes Romances are real pictures of life, and that she has drawn all her ideas, manners and expectations from this type of literature, Lennox provides us with the key for decoding both Arabella's words and actions. Only we, as readers, understand why she thinks every man is in love with her, because Lennox gives us this coded information. By informing us of Arabella's faulty education, we can understand and therefore sympathize with her as she faces the blank wall of a world that seems unable to either accommodate or correct her views on life. Having derived a view of the world and developed a system of values based on a faulty premise ("supposing Romances were real Pictures of Life"), Arabella is doomed to be separated from the common discourse, the everyday idiom and expression, acceptable to her society. She often speaks a different language from the rest of the people around her, and Lennox constantly emphasizes Arabella's inability to make herself understood. Examples tread on one another's heels: "I don't understand one Word you say," says Mr. Hervey (20); Edward "who understood not a Word of this Discourse, stared upon her like one that had lost his Wits" (101); Lucy, who usually understands her mistress, at times may "listen attentively to [a] fine Harangue, without understanding what it meant" (174); even Mr. Glanville cannot decipher her meaning on occasion: "Speaking these Words, which were wholly unintelligible to her amazed Admirer, she left him" (171).

Lennox's novel is often read as a corrective tale for young ladies who fancy themselves heroines. Even contemporary critics, making use of sophisticated feminist arguments, focus on little beyond the richly embroidered surface. "Lennox's principal concern is to ridicule heroic romances in the same way Cervantes ridiculed chivalric romances," claims James Lynch, maintaining that the essential lesson of the text is that a young woman must be taught—by men—to read "correctly": "The conflicts in the novel are thus semantic confusions that are ultimately resolved when Arabella is able to 'read' properly" (53). Men, in other words, are seen as necessarily, soberly, kindly, re-writing the incorrect, naively corrupt, self-indulgent feminine script, dictating a curriculum in order to instruct ladies in the ways of the "real" world. Lynch identifies Arabella's passion for her texts as "riding her hobby-horse," and seems to applaud Glanville for his ability to see through Arabella's "extravagancies" to her "sentimental qualities" (57). Lynch sees the book as ending "true to romance and sentimental conventions" (61). As we saw earlier, Laurie Langbauer emphasizes that "[i]t's not just that Arabella is out of her senses, but that the irregularities and improbabilities of romance are ravings, 'senseless Fictions'" (72). Arabella is, in fact, taking language literally, and interpreting metaphor, hyperbole, and convention as "real." In one extreme instance of this, Arabella takes Mr. Glanville's exasperated "I'm going to hang myself" as a plan of action: "'Hang yourself,' repeated Arabella, 'sure you know not what you say?—You meant, I suppose, that you'll fall upon your sword'" (318). She is not as upset to think he plans suicide as she is to think he plans so *unromantic* a suicide. The "romantic nonsense" of "bad translations" forms the bedrock of her language, and therefore, for her perception of the world. All of Arabella's language is a bad translation in itself, not from the French, but from the contemporary English. Only by a major retrenchment, by a wrenching shift in the basis for the whole of her imagination, can Arabella's ideas be made to fit the "real" society of her time.

In contrast, Patricia Meyer Spacks, in *The Adolescent Idea*, argues that "beneath the surface of its conventional happy ending, [*The Female Quixote*] conveys a pessimistic view of the possibility of any girl's getting what she wants" (131). Spacks goes on to make a number of points far more convincing than the standard women-must-learn-to-read-better-books fare when she states that "the loose sequence, with little causal connection, little sense of necessity or even control, with endings occuring after an arbitrary number of pages and of happenings, suggests a perception of existential meaninglessness in the adolescent female condition" (135). She concludes that such narratives covertly undermine their "ostensible endorsement of conventional expectations about the growing up of girls," and that "like other novels of its period, *The Female Quixote* draws on energies more potent than it can acknowledge" (135).

Certainly Lennox writes—and Arabella reads—across the established curriculum. A number of feminist critics, Leland E. Warren as well as Laurie Langbauer, produce the compelling argument that in Langbauer's terms, Lennox must "mock romance in order to leave it behind. Educating Arabella out of romance becomes a symbol of Lennox's own struggle as a writer" (378). Warren argues that "the underlying pathos of this comic novel is that, driven to an ideal world by being denied actuality, its heroine must deny the self she has created in order to be allowed once more a place in actuality" (378). He raises the intriguing point that "perhaps the most quixotic thing our Female Quixote does is to refuse the role allotted to women and to insist on becoming an active participant in the discourse of truth usually reserved for men" (377). Warren reads Arabella's "initiation" into male discourse as convincing and powerful, since she yields only after forcing her mentor to understand the "power of her fantasy" (378). But does Arabella yield to the yoke of male discourse, a communicant at the altar of the masculine "real world" by the end of the book? I believe the answer is no.

Arabella's language, we can argue, seems divorced from the larger, objective vision. But what is envisioned by this larger, objective vision? To claim that Arabella is mistaken in her perception is to presuppose some non-mistaken or true account of the world. But the world in which Arabella has grown up is almost totally artificial. Arabella, who keeps being told by various men that she sees castles where there are none, demands heroism in a world devoid of heroes; she has indeed been brought up in a castle where "[t]he most laborious Endeavours of Art have been used to make it appear like the beautiful Product of a Wild, uncultivated Nature" (6). How, then, could Arabella be expected to recognize, let alone appreciate, the natural or "real" world, when all she had known of nature was created artificially, literally created by "Endeavours of Art"? Lennox seems to indicate that even the apparently natural has some degree of arbitrary artifice attached to it. Arabella seems ridiculous to some of her peers because of her attachment to the unreal world of romance. But what does the "real" world include, as Lennox presents it?

The novel opens with an account of the fall of "the first and most distinguished Favourite at Court" whose "Enemies" plotted against him, forcing him to quit society and choose, for his retreat, "a Castle he had in a very remote Province of the Kingdom" (5). This is the apparently true, objective history of Arabella's father, and yet, it seems, such an opening would be more than suitable for a "bad translation." This objective world includes castles, love at first sight, highwaymen and, finally, a duel over the heroine. (Glanville "cry'd out to Sir George to defend himself" as he pulled out his sword; Sir George, wounded, bleeding, tells Glanville, "If I can but live to clear your innocence to Lady Bella and free you from the Consequences of this Action, I shall die Satisfy'd" [358]). Indeed, Glanville tells his father that he would "rather die than leave Arabella" (366). Many of Arabella's perceptions and expectations seem reasonable in light of these so-called Romantic occurrences.[1]

Added to these are the events set up by those close to Arabella which underscore her romantic vision. Almost no one corrects Arabella: Glanville is afraid of incurring her displeasure so does not "endeavour to undeceive her"; his sister hopes Arabella will disgrace herself; the Marquis (who is the one character with the authority to shape Arabella's behavior early in her life) recognizes "a great deal of his own Haughtiness of Temper" in his daughter and "could not resolve to check her for a Disposition so like his own" (39). Sir George is perhaps most guilty of playing unfairly with Arabella's beliefs. Sir George gives his lengthy history in heroic style, adopts all the conventions peculiar to Romantic behavior, and finally, in a truly insidious act, supplies Arabella with an "[a]dventure more worthy indeed to be styl'd an Adventure than all our Fair Heroine had ever yet met with" (341), by enlisting the arts of an actress who impersonates the princess of Gaul. Arabella is, of course, taken in, and wishes only to reveal publicly that such adventures do happen and to dispel the myth that "there were no more wandering Princesses in the World" (347). Does Arabella really create a world so extraordinary when the world as she experiences it can supply such events?

In fact, are Arabella's perceptions of reality more foolish than those held by many of her contemporaries? We click our tongues to her that Arabella "discovers a strong Dislike" for her cousin almost immediately upon meeting him, but should we then complacently accept that "Glanville in a very few Days became passionately in love" with Arabella (30)? If Arabella had fallen passionately in love within a few days, we would have complained about her Romantic ideas. Lennox implies throughout *The Female Quixote* that Arabella, despite, or perhaps because of, her separation from society, is superior in most respects, to her peers.

The Countess is the only woman deserving unmitigated admiration in *The Female Quixote*. However, as the lack of a given name implies, "the Countess" is more of a disembodied, archetypal fairy-godmother figure than a developed character. It is significant to note that the Countess has a great deal in common with Arabella, and that she recognizes something of herself in the younger woman. She resolves to rescue Arabella from the "ill-natured Raillery of her Sex" because she would have been, "but for an early Acquaintance with the World . . . as much a Heroine as Lady Bella" (323). Because the Countess has not "forgot[ten] the Language of Romance," she can initiate Arabella's movement away from the world of novels. The Countess can simultaneously evidence her understanding of and rejection of the forms of Romantic discourse. It is the Countess who, in Glanville's terms, attempts to "convert" Arabella to the Christian view of the world. She introduces religion as a superstructure which should supersede any Romantic notion: "Judging (the heroes) as Christians, we shall find them impious and base and directly opposite our present notions of moral and relative duties" (329). In fact, until Arabella is fully initiated into appropriate discourse by the Doctor, she is "unsaved" in society's terms, just as an unbaptized person would be "unsaved" in religious terms. It is the Countess who helps teach Arabella the most fundamental lesson she will learn, that "[c]ustom . . . changes the very Nature of Things, and what was honourable a Thousand Years ago, may probably be look'd upon as infamous now" (328).

Apart from the Countess, whose "universally acknowledg'd Merit" is the currency behind her words, there are no admirable female characters for Arabella to emulate. Miss Glanville is jealous, petty and selfish; Miss Groves is both proud and pathetic, being what the English would call "thick"; the ladies at Bath and in London are hardly models for Arabella. The editorial statement Arabella makes to her guardian seems both sane and reasonable: "If the World . . . affords only these Kinds of Pleasures; I shall very soon regret the Solitude and Books I have quitted" (278). Arabella may be immature in expecting everything to be in *Kairos* or important time, but there is something absolutely undeniable, and something fundamentally feminist, in her assertion that "[p]eople who spend their [lives] in such trifling Amusements, must certainly live to very little purpose." She goes on to wonder at anyone "who consumes her Days in Dressing, Dancing, listening to Songs and ranging the Walks with People as thoughtless as herself," considering how "mean and contemptible a Figure must a Life spent in such idle Amusements make in History?" (279).

Arabella questions the commonplace, and by doing so questions the place of women in her society. Granted, she would have women be warriors and queens, but is that so illegitimate? For eighteenth-century England, and unfortunately for Arabella, the answer is yes. Yet it is to her credit that Arabella, as manifested in her reluctance to join the ranks of conventional society, is one of the few characters to show original thought; she is one of the only women to defend her beliefs. It may well be that Lennox is indicating one of "the ways in which gender collaborates with class to contain forms of political resistance within liberal discourse," to apply Nancy Armstrong's line of reasoning (26).

Arabella's touchstones are regarded as faulty, but her *method* for argument is certainly sound. Like a good eighteenth-century thinker, she refers to authority and to the ancients; she cites what she considers decorum ("the authority of Custom is sufficient to prove it" [44]); she argues from her belief in the timelessness of human nature; she is concerned with hierarchy and manners (she rebukes Miss Glanville for the impropriety of *her* language: "I must find Fault with the Coarseness of your Language! Courting, and Old Woman! What strange Terms!" [112]) and she aspires to dignity, to nobility, and, most ironically, to correct form and behavior. Her method is impeccable; once again, it is her original set of beliefs which causes her to veer so far from the norm on certain subjects.

On subjects apart from those to which she applies her so-called

"Romantic notions," Arabella impresses her listeners with her intelligence, insight and wit. Because of her fundamentally sound method of argument, she often appears to great advantage when placed in the company of her peers. "If she had been a Man," says Sir Charles, "she would have made a great Figure in Parliament, and Speeches might have come perhaps to be printed in time" (311). Arabella is, in her own way, asking the question women asked before and after her: "What if my words / Were meant for deeds?" (George Eliot, "The Spanish Gypsy" 240), and answering with a primitive attempt to actually translate the words of romance *into* deeds; since these are the only words she knows, these are the only deeds she can attempt to commit. We cannot risk idle speculation on what Arabella would have been like had she been exposed to the education given men in her day, but it is likely Sir Charles is correct in his estimate of her potential.

Lennox forces this question: is the ordinary, educated discourse of those around her superior to Arabella's in its logic and objectivity? The author does not appear to think so. Lennox presents one particularly clear example of the way each individual projects from his/her own possibly faulty set of beliefs, and shows us how members from the objective society draw conclusions and form a view of the world. Arabella wears her veil into the Pump-Room at Bath, and gives rise to a "Diversity of Opinions," a range of responses that indicate far more about those speaking than about the object of their attention: "Some of the Wiser Sort took her for a Foreigner; others of still more Sagacity, supposed her a Scots Lady, covered with her Plaid; and a third Sort, infinitely wiser than either, concluded she was a Spanish Nun, that had escaped from a Convent, and had not yet quitted her Veil" (263). If Arabella has "a most happy Facility in accomodating every Incident to her own Wishes and Conceptions" (25), then so does everyone else. This gives rise to the importance of Arabella's irregular use of language: by speaking the way she does, other people are forced to try to make sense of what Arabella says by involving their own peculiar set of expectations. She is the puzzle they must solve. Thus Glanville believes Arabella initially rejects him because of their difference in station; Miss Groves believes Arabella deliberately tries to shame her because she has done things for which she, Miss Groves, is ashamed; Miss Glanville believes Arabella's language "was designed to sneer at her Eagerness to make Conquests, and Liberties she allowed herself in, which has probably come to her attention" (89); Mr. Selvin is ashamed because he saw himself "posed by a Girl" (265), and several others react similarly. Each projects onto Arabella's words and actions his or her own insecurities, and makes more of her commentary than she herself intends. Arabella is a threat to their self-esteem and self-expression.

What Arabella believes is truth can be interpreted as true in light of the criteria of truth presented in her own personal culture and society: that of the romance novel. Other people interpret her words in light of their personal dogma, and, although the logical rules governing the public world may be purely matters of convention, it is necessary for Arabella to adopt these conventions, and be initiated into public discourse, if she is going to be permitted to live outside her father's estate. Armstrong argues that there is, at this point in the eighteenth century, a shift in "moral emphasis from the claims of the individual asserted through female desire to those of the community, which required such desire to submit to rational control . . . [so that the heroine is] outside a now-openly competitive system where she is 'different,' rather than on the inside where she might clamber up" (56). She cannot be permitted to undermine the rules as they stand. She must not jump in rivers, make ladies feel insecure about their dresses, or inspire duels among young men of good families. Women did not do such things. They did not do very much at all.

Arabella must be persuaded that such a stagnant fate is actually a desirable one. Only a "few and natural Incidents" can "compose the History of a Woman of Honour," instructs the Countess (327). The "material Passages of a woman's life" are, as the Countess explains, to "be born and christen'd," have a useful education, receive the addresses of a man chosen by her family, marry with "their Consent and [her] own Inclinations," and live in harmony (327). Why should Arabella be content with such a fate after hoping for battles, travel and Adventure? Can we blame her for hoping life would offer something more?

When she is about to jump into the Thames, Arabella makes a speech which seems heretical in light of the Countess's litany of passivity:

> The Action we have it in our Power to perform will immortalize our Fame, and raise us to a Pitch of Glory . . . We may expect Statues erected to our Honour . . . be propos'd as Patterns to Heroines in ensuing ages. . . . Once more, my fair Companions . . . if an immortal Glory be worth your seeking, follow the Example I shall set you. . . . (363)

Since no woman could be permitted to say such things, Arabella must be made to sound brave but seem foolish. The Doctor must save her and see to it that she conforms—for everyone's sake.

His argument finally convinces Arabella that "the Books which I have hitherto read as Copies of Life . . . are Empty Fictions" by telling her that:

> your Ladyship must suffer me to decide, in some Measure authoritatively, whether Life is truly described in those Books; the Likeness of a Picture can only be determined by a Knowledge of the Original. You have yet had little Opportunity of Knowing the Ways of Mankind. . . . I have lived long in a Public character. (379)

Having convinced Arabella that her "[w]riters have instituted a World of their own" (380), Arabella drops her eccentric cosmology, and no longer balances her romantic ideas "against Life" (381). Arabella now apparently shares the same concepts forming her society's view of the world, accepting their reference points and bowing to their authorities.

And yet the crucial part of the Doctor's argument rests on telling Arabella that the stuff of her fiction is simply impossible: "He cannot carry you to any of these dreadful Places because there is no such Castle, Desart [*sic*] . . ." (373). But Arabella's limited experience with the world includes, for example, the castle where she grew up. Arabella, it seems, must not only abandon the lifelong ideas she only imagined were true, she must also reconsider those she *knows* are true; she has to recreate her vision of the world in the pattern provided by masculine experience as "real" even though she knows that her experience has proven their vision invalid.

It is no wonder then that Arabella suffers "inconceivable Confusion" after speaking with the Doctor. We could read this section of the book as a blueprint for the endless queue of women who were placed in front of Freud's door in order to have their vision of the world "corrected" by that Doctor; women learn that when their stories cannot be easily spliced onto the dominant masculine text, they must be rewritten. Arabella emerges from a brief seclusion with a penitent, submissive, apologetic air, looking with "Tenderness and Modesty" towards Glanville. Driven away from the locus of her own power and vision, Arabella wil speak only in the language of the doctors, fathers, husbands and male (otherwise known as "good") writers. In her final speech, Arabella's language has radically altered, and she uses in one sentence phrases like "my remaining Imperfections," "making you a poor Present," "obligations," "your generous affection," "so happy to be desired for a Partner for Life by a Man of your Sense and Honour," and "make myself as worthy as I am able" (383). This last speech is reminiscent of, and as unsatisfying as, Kate's last speech in *The Taming of the Shrew*.

Lennox ends the novel, however, by stressing that a single act cannot necessarily be represented by a single word, implying that language and reality are not fixed in reality by a series of unalterable ratios. Sir George and Miss Glanville marry, as do Arabella and Mr. Glanville, and yet Lennox writes that:

> We chuse, Reader, to express this Circumstance, though the same, in different Words . . . as to intimate that the first mentioned Pair were indeed only married in the common Acceptation of the Word . . . while Mr. Glanville and Arabella were united in every Virtue and Laudable Affection of the Mind. (383)

Lennox indicates in this closing paragraph that the "common Acceptation of the Word" is not necessarily the desirable one. "Different words" indeed make all the difference. Arabella, with her Histories and her Adventures, as well as her preference for taking literally what was meant as figurative, hated above all else the "[i]ndifference which obliges some People to be pleas'd with All Things. . . . they neither love nor hate . . . are wholly influenc'd by Custom and are Sensible only of the Body, their Minds being in a Manner insensible" (310). Perhaps Lennox cannot happily abandon such a free-spirited, independently-minded young woman to "solid satisfaction" of the kind she seemed to despise. For whatever reason, Arabella's history ends abruptly with her marriage: presumably nothing else of interest happens to her. It is ironic that such oblivion is precisely what Arabella most feared, and surely Lennox was not unware of this irony.

Like Arabella, Austen's heroines are meant to subject themselves to the authorized editions of their own lives, with all the neccesary expurgations made and all footnoted explanations duly given. Yet written over the surface lesson, in "text-hand copy" and in a feminine hand, is a larger question concerning the authority behind the authorized edition. As Henry Tilney notes *Northanger Abbey*, the very idea of instruction makes women wary: "I use the verb 'to torment,' as I observed to be your own method, instead of 'to instruct,' supposing them to be now admitted as synonymous" (85). Learning a lesson by rote is easy enough; the narrative structure of the novels make clear, however, that these female pupils resist believing in what they are instructed to accept as the "truth." But, as Susan Morgan argues in a compelling understatement, "[t]he male urge to guide, to guard, and above all, to shape, along with, on the female side, a natural propensity to worship and be shaped, will not give us the parameters of an Austen love affair" (25).

An additional significant difference marking women's texts revolves around the condition traditionally regarded as a prerequisite for comedy: the assumption of a consensus opinion based on shared values. It is standard practice in comedies for the author and reader to share a system of values into which a main character must be initiated. The comedy of this plot arises when the main character's uninitiated behavior sets her apart from her peers: this would seem, then, to be the pattern for the plot of *The Female Quixote* as well as almost all of Austen's novels. But something else is at work in Lennox and Austen: the system of values shared by reader and author are not those of the didactic male teachers who appear in the novels, but rather the values espoused by the uninitiated female protagonists. The metanarrative of refusal is at the heart of the laughter in these books; the comedy works not against the renegade woman-reader-heroine, but against those who would confine her to the attic of "acceptable" behavior, who would write her out of her own text. Behind the humble curtsy to the teacher-lover, the narrative also presents a wink to readers, an encoded signal to those who understand that the heroine's apparent submission does not negate her instinctive rebellion. The values shared by reader and heroine remain in ascendancy; that is the final comic moment in these texts.

Austen struggles, according to Gilbert and Gubar, to "combine her implicitly rebellious vision with an explicitly decorous form" (155). Austen illustrates this double-talk by calling attention to, while at the same time denying the presence of, unacceptable behavior. The split lies between the articulation of rebellion and the denial of the desire, and is at the heart of much of women's humor; it doubles the irony of a woman's apparent submission to her assigned role even as she re-writes it from within. Comedy, therefore, rests on the reader's ability to detect the core of refusal wrapped within the layers of acceptance, rather like the princess sensing the pea under all those mattresses. Both Lennox and Austen illustrate the absurdities of a world which can only be effectively presented in a comic frame. Women's comedy functions along such lines because it underscores the way women's narratives often depend on the split between the "real" and the "imaginary," the incongruity between women's experience and so-called universal experience, the disparity between what women know to be true and what they are told is the truth.

We have already seen how this disparity between the real and the ideal is handled by Lennox, who illustrates the impossibility of accepting the masculine script except as the thinnest disguise for a text that mocks and parodies that script. The "real" is the masculine frame, which is no more valid or connected to a grid of "actual" values than the feminine "ideal" which is self-consciously a construct. Austen seems to label "history" as no less a matter of invention than "poetry and plays and things of that sort": "'The quarrels of popes and kings, with wars or pestilences, in every page; the men all so good for nothing, and hardly any women at all—it is very tiresome: and yet I often think it odd that it should be so dull, for a great deal of it must be invention. The speeches that are put into the heroes' mouths, their thoughts and designs—the chief of all this must be invention, and invention is what delights me in other books'" (*Northanger Abbey* 84). History, then, is invention with the good parts left out; it is creation without imagination, narration without delight.

In *Northanger Abbey*, for example, Austen takes up the same frame for women's experience—women's novels—as Lennox. Like Lennox, Austen is concerned with the female reader of female texts—books written by and for women, with plenty of women and hardly any popes at all. *Northanger Abbey* is concerned with women's scripts: women's texts being written, the scripts being "lived" within the larger text. Like Lennox, Austen looks carefully at the point where women's lives start to become too much like women's texts for the comfort of those who want the would-be heroines to be "simply" wives or daughters, to accept with pleasure their move from protagonist to bit-player, from individual to stock character. Women's scripts are supposed to be dictated by the father/husband; women are not supposed to inscribe themselves.

While Gilbert and Gubar argue that "the point of Austen's parody is precisely to illustrate the dangerous delusiveness of fiction" (*The Madwoman in the Attic* 115) which might encourage young women to become "addicts of feeling" (117), Austen underscores the centrality of the woman's text in what is perhaps the most vituperative defense of the art:

> I will not adopt that ungenerous and impolitic custom so common with novel writers, of degrading by their contemptuous censure the very performances, to the number of which they are themselves adding—joining with their greatest enemies in bestowing the harshest epithets on such works, and scarcely ever permitting them to be read by their own heroine, who, if she accidentally takes up a novel, is sure to turn over its insipid pages with disgust. Alas! if the heroine of one novel be not patronized by the heroine of another, from whom can she expect protection and regard? I cannot approve of it. . . . Let us not desert one another; we are an injured body. Although our productions have afforded more extensive and unaffected pleasure than those of any other literary corporation in the world, no species of composition has been so much decried. From pride, ignorance, or fashion, our foes are almost as many as our readers. (21)

It is true that Austen does not explicitly identify novel writers or readers as female, although in her cry not to "desert one another" she certainly fosters the idea of a closely-knit community of writers and readers very much like herself.

However, it is interesting to note that she does not hesitate to identify the abridger, collector, and dull essayist as male, and to contrast these mean accomplishments with the grossly undervalued triumphs of the novelist:

> And while the abilities of the nine-hundredth abridger of the *History of England*, or of the man who collects and publishes in a volume some dozen lines of Milton, Pope, and Prior, with a paper from the Spectator, and a chapter from Sterne, are eulogized by a thousand pens—there seems almost a general wish of decrying the capacity and undervaluing the labour of the novelist, and of slighting the performances which have only genius, wit, and taste to recommend them. (21)

In this brief treatise on the art of the novelist, delivered by the narrator of *Northanger Abbey* as a commentary on the novel-reading habits of her heroine, Austen denounces the misappropriation of value by the literary marketplace, those self-satisfied writers who hold the reins of power in one hand as they hold a pen in the other. By extension, she denounces the influence on the general reader of these "thousand pens" held by those who could not recognize "genius, wit or taste" if it danced before their eyes; the critics of the novel who can only function within the assigned machinery, she implies, can only see up to, and not beyond, the assigned standards.

As we have seen, *Northanger Abbey* resembles *The Female Quixote* most clearly in its refusal, ultimately, to condemn the texts outlawed by the authorities. Both Lennox and Austen address the concept of the woman-centered text, and while seeming to accept the masculine assessment of the romance and gothic novels, advance the concern of an essentially feminine discourse. Like *The Female Quixote, Northanger Abbey* is informed by an inherited and explicitly feminine tradition of narrative. Susan Morgan addresses this issue when she argues that Austen "explicitly mocks" traditional romances and "self-consciously transforms" the usual novelistic patterns (27).

Unlike most of women's writing, haunted by an anxiety of authorship rather than an anxiety of influence, *Northanger Abbey* offers a militant curtsey in the direction of its predecessors. Austen asks for the benediction of the writers whom Dale Spender would later call "the mothers of the novel": authors such as Fanny Burney, Ann Radcliffe and Maria Edgeworth. Austen's defense of the novel in general, and of the gothic novel in particular, takes shape as an offense against those who would malign a novelist's achievement by dismissing it as "full of nonsense and stuff" (31). For example, *Northanger Abbey* ridicules as ignorant and foolish a young man who attempts to assert the superior quality of his knowledge when he condescends to discuss women's novels with Catherine Morland. Catherine, heroine of Austen's novel (despite the narrator's coy protestations at the eccentricity of choosing such a heroine), sweetly suggests to John Thorpe that, despite his preference for *Tom Jones* and the like, he might enjoy "Udolpho, were you to read it; it is so very interesting." To this he replies, in the unhesitating voice of authority,

> "Not I, in faith! No, if I read any, it shall be Mrs. Radcliff's; her novels are amusing enough; they are worth reading; some fun and nature in them."
>
> "Udolpho was written by Mrs. Radcliff," said Catherine, with some hesitation, from the fear of mortifying him. (32)

As far from being mortified as Catherine is from being self-confident, Thorpe simply bluffs and blusters his way into a reply: " 'No sure; was it?

Aye, I remember, so it was; I was thinking of that other stupid book, written by that woman they made such a fuss about, who married the French emigrant" (32). By pretending to know something of which he is ignorant, by ignoring Catherine's expert knowledge, by saying he actually knew *Udolpho* was indeed written by Radcliffe and had only momentarily forgotten the information, by grouping all women writers under one heading and so rendering them "types" rather than individuals (don't all books by female authors have identical plots?), by calling them "stupid books," and by identifying Fanny Burney only by her marital status (not to mention his horror at the very thought of marrying a foreigner), Thorpe becomes the template for all readers who dismiss women's novels by "taking up the first volume" and "look[ing] it over," only to find quite "soon . . . it would not do" (*Northanger Abbey* 32).

Thorpe becomes an object of humor in this novel because of his ignorance of other novels; this self-reflexive impulse is present throughout *Northanger Abbey*. It elicits in the reader a sense of conspiracy with both the narrator and the main character; Austen's narrator addresses those of us enjoying *Northanger Abbey* as a group already comfortably initiated into the rites and codes of feminine discourse. Thorpe is made ridiculous by his foolish misreadings (or non-readings) of important literature; he would not read, in all likelihood, the very book in which he plays a major role. He is a fit object for Austen's humor, immune as he is from any self-reflection. The humor manufactured at his expense cannot harm him because he is typical of the man who cannot see—and therefore will himself remain unaffected by —the joke. We laugh at Thorpe because he is both pretentious and insipid, aggressively searching out the speck in his sister's book while ignoring the blanks in his own. The man who disparages books because they are written by women or the one who refuses to read books suggested to him by a female companion is equalled in his arrogance only by the man who draws up a reading list for his uninformed female friend (who may indeed have read a great deal more than he). Men who supply a reading list during courtship will only go on to hand out a syllabus when it comes time for marriage.

Significantly, Catherine's preference for women's novels does not reflect her earliest literary tastes. Catherine was weaned away from Pope, Gray, Thompson, and Shakespeare before starting on Radcliffe. Why didn't these esteemed gentlemen, offering their readers the best that is thought and felt in the world, set Catherine on a straight path to "great books?" Perhaps the answer lies in what Catherine learned. As one might expect, "from Shakespeare she gained a great store of information," yet even such a standard remark carries more than a trace of irony. What Catherine learned from Shakespeare—"amongst the rest"—is that:

—'Trifles light as air,
'Are, to the jealous, confirmation strong,
'As proofs of Holy Writ';

that

'The poor beetle, which we tread upon,
'In corporal sufferance feels a pang as great
'As when a giant dies';

and that a young woman in love always looks

—'like Patience on a monument
'Smiling at Grief.' (4)

Do these lessons reflect a vision closer to the "real" than those offered in texts of Edgeworth and Burney? A young woman in love does not always look like Patience smiling at Grief any more than she always gets locked up in a tower by a brutish father; one set of expectations can replace the other, but both are by-products of culture. Shakespeare's assignment for women is no less—or no more—"truthful" than Radcliffe's. Austen chooses these passages from Shakespeare to illustrate, humorously, the artificiality of their observations. Shakespeare and Pope equally construct rather than report reality; in this they are in the same position as their female colleagues. This realization embodies a brief moment of particularly feminine anarchic humor, akin to the humor of discovering that the emperor wears no clothes despite the fact that everyone has been commenting on his charmingly masculine and marvelously despotic apparel. But we knew that Catherine Morland was a character born to make trouble declares Claudia Johnson, "when we read in the opening pages of *Northanger Abbey* that as a child she was 'noisy and wild, hated confinement and cleanliness, and loved nothing so well in the world as rolling down the green slope at the back of the house. . . .' As if this were not bad enough, later in life, when her mysterious sweetheart fails to show up at a ball, Catherine returns home in her disappointment not to weep or toss sleeplessly in bed, but instead to 'appease' her 'extraordinary hunger,' and then to fall asleep early, for nine refreshing hours" (164). We must ask of Catherine the same question we asked of Arabella: is the discourse of those around her superior to hers in its logic and objectivity? Does Austen lead us, finally, to condemn Catherine's taste in books?

Widely regarded as the passage that will put paid to the doubts harbored by suspicious readers troubled by this question is the following: "it seemed as if the whole [of Catherine's worries] might be traced to the influence of that sort of reading which she had there indulged. Charming as were all Mrs. Radcliffe's works, and charming even as were the works of all her imitators, it was not in them perhaps that human nature, at least in the midland counties of England, was to be looked for" (*Northanger Abbey* 160). In the same paragraph, we read that "in the central part of England there was surely some security for the existence even of a wife not beloved, in the laws of the land, in the manners of the age" (161). Ignoring for the moment that *Jane Eyre* will present in Bertha Mason-Rochester a portrait of what happens to a wife not beloved in the central part of England, the phrase Austen uses to reassure us has an echo of that ambigious-because-falsely-authoritative opening to *Pride and Prejudice*. We have learned to doubt any phrase that includes the words "surely," "certainly" or "without a doubt."

Gilbert and Gubar suggest that the story of the young woman needing to be "taught" correct values is "especially flattering to male readers because it describes the taming not just of any woman but specifically of a rebellious, imaginative girl who is amorously mastered by a sensible man" (*The Madwoman in the Attic* 154). Seeming to uphold their argument that male readers enjoy seeing a woman tamed is a critic such as Patrick Bizzaro, who argues that Henry Tilney of *Northanger Abbey* is, "in short, a great teacher for Catherine of those values we can assume by the novel's outcome to be Jane's values as well" (87), and who says of Austen's heroine "what an idiot she is, at first, made out to be" (85). It appears, however, that recent feminist critics are more able to read in Austen textual patterns that make sense of her humor without reducing it to the presentation of young women as objects of ridicule.

Indeed, Gilbert and Gubar render explicit in *The Madwoman in the Attic* what Austen left implicit in her text: "*Northanger Abbey* is, finally, a gothic story as frightening as any told by Mrs. Radcliffe, for the evil it describes is the horror . . ., the terror, the self-loathing that results when a woman is made to disregard her personal sense of danger, to accept as real what contradicts her perception of her own situation" (143). Catherine listens to conversations only to find out that "it seemed as if a good view were no longer to be taken from the top of an high hill, and that a clear blue sky was no longer proof of a fine day" (86). Catherine is being taught to doubt the validity of her own experience.

In much the same way as Lennox ultimately refuses to submit her vision to the authorized edition of reality, Kate Fullbrook argues convincingly, in an article entitled "Jane Austen and the Comic Negative," that Catherine's view of the world is as valid as any other:

> What Catherine needs to learn is that the world is full of "artrocities"—General Tilney is in fact a cruel and conniving man who neglected his wife and who throws Catherine out of his house. . . . This is horror enough, and Jane Austen makes it clear that the Gothic romances are not wrong in their portraits of the mechanics of the human heart. . . . The final joke in *Nor-*

thanger Abbey is not on Catherine . . . but on those who are so unimaginative as to think Catherine completely misguided in the horrors she fancies lurking within the Abbey walls. . . . In many ways, Catherine, even in her delusions, is more correct in her view of the world than Henry. (48)

Henry's view of the world is sanctioned by the most powerful structures of society, and so he must appear to prevail. In the event that Fullbrook's argument should seem so persuasive that it appears self-evident, we should contrast it with a more traditional vision of the novel. Patrick Bizzaro, for example, regards Henry as "a wise teacher of human nature because he presents himself as a teacher, assured in his knowledge and ability to affect others. . . . Henry's certainty in all matters pertaining to his observations is a uniquely endearing quality both for the reader and for Catherine" (87). This comment is economic in conflating under the aegis of "assumed values," nearly every point regarded by recent feminist criticism as misguided. Henry's certainty in his own correctness is neither unique (every male protagonist in these novels believes in his own correctness) nor endearing. That he should be taken seriously as a "wise teacher" because he sets himself up that way underscores, if anything, the totally arbitrary nature of authority. When Catherine admits to Henry that she does not understand him, his response is: "Then we are on very unequal terms, for I understand you perfectly well" (103). Henry firmly believes he knows everything. Catherine is uncertain about what constitutes truth. Who is wiser? If the Henrys do not prevail immediately, they prevail eventually. When women insist on the validity of their experience, they are at best left unmarried and alone, at worst, institutionalized as mad—as if their own persistent belief, that women are indeed locked away, causes it to happen to them.

The ending of *Northanger Abbey* echoes the ending of *The Female Quixote* in its hurried conclusion—the textual equivalent of a shot-gun wedding where the fewer questions asked, the better. As in *Mansfield Park*, the narrator refuses to supply the details of the "true romance" of the main characters, relying on her reader's experience of books to supply the necessary information: "The anxiety, which in this state of attachment must be the portion of Henry and Catherine, and of all who loved either, as to its final event, can hardly extend, I fear, to the bosom of my readers, who will see in the tell-tale compression of the pages before them, that we are all hastening together to perfect felicity" (203). Elinor's husband is dismissed without any identifying signs apart from his rank and that he is "to a precision the most charming young man in the world." Austen explains that "any further definition of his merits must be unnecessary" because her readers will do the rest: "the most charming young man in the world is instantly before the imagination of us all" (204). She cannot give more details, in any event, because she is "aware that the rules of composition forbid" the introduction of character not directly "connected with my fable" (204). In providing the "perfect felicity" required by the "rules of composition," Austen nevertheless manages to undermine the rules by her wish to leave "it to be settled by whomsoever it may concern" in order to decipher the "tendency of this work" (205) in the last sentence of the novel. Morgan's comments concerning the way Austen ends *Emma* are equally useful when applied to *Northanger Abbey*: "Yet surely we can see that replacing a love scene that has become so established as to be considered di rigueur in domestic fiction with a joke about its predictability is a beautifully simple way to make the point that such a scene is merely a convention. Honoring such a convention would violate the values of this novel" (37).

In *Mansfield Park* we are not given the story we expect; we are, in fact, actively denied that story. The reader expects details concerning the love affair between Fanny and Edmund. We are given instead several hundred pages of the love affair between Edmund and Mary Crawford. Mary Crawford has irritated and delighted critics by her bad behavior. As Fay Weldon confesses, Mary is "certainly the one character in the book with whom one would gladly spend a week on an off-shore island" (*Letters to Alice* 134). She has been seen as Austen's alter-ego, as the paradigm of the anti-heroine, as a nasty little piece of work generally. But there is something compelling about Mary—her sense of humor. For example, Mary can parody a parody; she knows by heart "Hawkins Browne's 'Address to Tobacco,' in imitation of Pope," and she can render her own satiric verse on the local families based on this: "Blest Knight! whose dictatorial looks dispense / To Children affluence, to Rushworth sense" (131). Mary makes jokes about the clergy, the aristocracy and society in general, joking even about the possibly fatal illness of her beloved's elder and—therefore inheriting—brother: "upon my honor, I never bribed a physician in my life" (353).

Mary is in direct comparison to Fanny, about whom the narrator exclaims "Fanny in a state of actual felicity" (331) as if it were as unlikely an occasion as Fanny being on fire. Where Fanny can be "doubly silenced" (330), Mary can rarely be silenced at all. It is interesting to note where Mary does leave gaps. Her style is in direct opposition to Edmund's. In his letter to Fanny, Edmund comments, "I shall be able to write much that I could not say," whereas Mary could say much more than she cares to write. In her own letter to Fanny, Mary states that since "it is impossible to put an hundredth part of my great mind on paper, so I will abstain altogether, and leave you to guess what you like. . . . suffice it, that every thing was just as it ought to be" (337). Mary ends her letter "But-but-but" (338) and that triple, unsigned qualification reflects once again on her creator's endings. We can do worse than read Austen's happy endings as written with "But-but-but" after the final paragraph. Letting other pens dwell on guilt and misery, Austen's impatience to detach Mary from Edmund so that he can be attached to Fanny results in a comic ending. The comedy of *Mansfield Park* relies on the improbability of our accepting it as a love story.

At the end of the book we are given only a set of those unnervingly unanswerable, apparently rhetorical questions: "With such regard for [Fanny], indeed, as his had long been, a regard founded on the most endearing claims of innocence and helplessness, and completed by every recommendation of growing worth, what could be more natural than change?" and "Even in the midst of his late infatuation, he had acknowledged Fanny's mental superiority. What must be his sense of it now, therefore?" (384). Creating a remark that once again must remind us of what Brownstein called laughing at "authoritative sentence-making," the first line of the penultimate paragraph of *Mansfield Park* claims "With so much true merit and true love, and no want of fortune or friends, the happiness of the married cousins must appear as secure as earthly happiness can be" (386). And men with money must be in search of wives—these equations are not supported, they are asserted. They are, ultimately, comic in their stubborn refusal to supply what is called for; they are funny in their refusal to meet expectations.

What is also humorous is that these passages are often read as failed rather than funny. Her refusal to meet reader expectations does not make Austen a bad writer; it is not, as some critics have argued, that Austen cannot write an ending. It seems more consistent to see refusal rather than inability at work. Such passages should make Austen's readers examine closely the fissures she exposes in presenting us with badly wrapped, prepackaged endings. In *Mansfield Park*, where marriage has been described in enormously disparaging terms, is it any wonder that the author chooses not to reproduce the scene as a happy ending: "It was a very proper wedding. The bride was elegantly dressed—the two bridesmaids were duly inferior— her father gave her away—her mother stood by with salts in her hand, expected to be agitated—her aunt tried to cry" (163).

The same sort of apparently rhetorical questions finish off Marianne's story in *Sense and Sensibility*. Perhaps not quite as problematic as Mary Crawford since she is plagued by bouts of desire rather than flights of wit, Marianne nevertheless resembles Mary in her refusal to be silenced—until her illness. Marianne is another novel-reading woman. She is headstrong, opinionated and passionate. For the marriage-plot to reproduce itself properly, she must be taught a lesson; like Arabella and Catherine, she must be wrenched away from the ideas she holds most firmly in order for her to be acceptable to society. Marianne must not be wed to the man for whom she literally falls: dangerous Willoughby is introduced into the text as "a gentleman carrying a gun," emblematic of all of the violence and sexuality he carries with him and Marianne takes a "false step" which brings her "suddenly to the ground" when she sees him (74). Instead she must marry Colonel Brandon. Brandon is made known to the reader as someone "neither very young nor very gay" (66) and "silent and grave" (67). Marianne points out that "he is old enough to be *my* father" and her wise sister Elinor comments that "Perhaps . . . thirty-five and seventeen had better not have anything to do with matrimony together" (70). When her mother tells Elinor in chapter 45 that Colonel Brandon can make Marianne happy, "Elionor was half inclined to ask her reason for thinking so, because satisfied that none founded on an impartial consideration of their age, characters, or feelings, could be given" (328). However, by chapter 50 (forty or so pages later), the final episode presents us with the following:

> Marianne Dashwood was born to an extraordinary fate. She was born to discover the falsehood of her own opinions, and to counteract, by her conduct, her most favourite maxims . . . [W]ith no sentiment superior to strong esteem and lively friendship, voluntarily to give her hand to [a man] . . . she had considered too old to be married,—and who still sought the constitutional safeguard of a flannel waistcoat!
>
> But so it was. Instead of falling a sacrifice to an irresistible passion, as once she had fondly flattered herself with expecting . . . she found herself at nineteen, submitting to new attachments, entering on new duties, placed in a new home, a wife, the mistress of a family, and the patroness of a village. . . . Marianne could never love by halves; and her whole heart became, in time, as much devoted to her husband, as it had once been to Willoughby. (367)

For over three hundred and fifty pages we have heard about Marianne's love for Willoughby. In two lines on one of the final pages we have the entire story of Marianne's love affair with Brandon. Their romance follows the same pattern of argument Austen has taught us to distrust: because this must happen, it happened. Because Marianne is passionate by nature, she became as passionate about Brandon and his flannels as she was about Willoughby and his gun. The equation once again shatters; Austen delivers the ending with the same challenge to the reader's credulity as in *Northanger Abbey* and *Mansfield Park*.[2] Austen does essentially the same thing Charlotte Bronte will do in *Villette*: tells the reader that if she or he wishes to construct a happy ending, the possibility is there, but the author will refrain from the imposition of the "rules of composition" on this point. The comedy of the plotting is ultimately meta-textual rather than textual: it lies in the refusal of the author to meet our expectations and our own desire to write those wrongs presented by the ending.

That Austen refuses to construct an ending that supports unhesitatingly the perpetuation of the marriage-plot, should not be taken to mean that Jane Austen fails. Laurence Lerner says that "by not remaining a comedy *Sense and Sensibility* fails in its professed aim: it does not succeed in winning us to the side of Sense" (164). Lerner sees it as a "great flawed novel" but obviously cannot reconcile a great novel with Austen's particular form of comedy. But in regarding the book in this light, these critics appear to be like Lady Middleton who cannot like the Dashwood sisters because they do not support her vision of the world: "Because they neither flattered herself nor her children, she could not believe them good-natured; and because they were fond of reading, she fancied them satirical; perhaps without knowing exactly what it was to be satirical; but that did not signify. It was a censure in common use and easily given" (250).

Indeed, according to the satirical plotting—and wording—of Austen's conclusion, everybody has a happy ending: "and setting aside the jealousies and ill-will continually subsisting between Fanny and Lucy, in which their husbands of course took a part, as well as the frequent domestic disagreements between Robert and Lucy themselves, nothing could exceed the harmony in which they all lived together" (366). Even Willoughby manages to receive a fair allotment of satisfaction in his life, thus proving that happy endings are widely available:

> But that he was for ever inconsolable, that he fled from society, or contracted an habitual gloom of temper, or died of a broken heart, must not be depended on—for he did neither. He lived to exert, and frequently to enjoy himself. His wife was not always out of humour, nor his home always uncomfortable; and in his breed of horses and dogs, and in sporting of every kind, he found no inconsiderable degree of domestic felicity. (367)

Pride and Prejudice subverts the idea of consensus from its first sentence onwards: "It is a truth universally acknowledged, that a single man in possession of a good fortune, must be in want of a wife" (51). The sentence undermines its own authority by asserting it so unequivocally, and thus we are on shaky ground right from the beginning. If, from the opening line, we equate the idea of the universal with the false, we are on the grounds of women's comedy. Elizabeth's wit is sharp and, to a certain extent, uncontrolled; she is described as "almost wild" (81) on several occasions, and her mother tells her not to "run on in the wild manner you are suffered to do at home" (88). Unlike Emma Woodhouse, Elizabeth's wit does not undergo intellectual surgery to remove the center of impropriety. Elizabeth maintains her signature sense of humor throughout the book. She resists the notion that there are some things she must not laugh at—Mr. Darcy, among them.

"Mr Darcy is not to be laughed at!" protests Elizabeth, apparently for her own sake as much as anyone else's. "That is an uncommon advantage, and uncommon I hope it will continue, for it would be a great loss to me to have many such acquaintance. I dearly love a laugh. . . . I hope I never ridicule what is wise or good. Follies and nonsense, whims and inconsistencies do divert me, I own, and I laugh at them whenever I can.—But these, I suppose, are precisely what you are without" (102). In fact, Elizabeth recognizes in Darcy what Austen seems to have recognized in her readers: the desire for wit, wickedness, and, in some measure, something wild. Austen understood the need not to fulfill expectations but to challenge them, in much the same way as Elizabeth tells Darcy that: "you were sick of civility, of deference, of officious attention. You were disgusted with women who were always speaking and looking, and thinking for your approbation alone. I roused, and interested you, because I was so unlike them" (388).

Interestingly, Elizabeth realizes that Darcy could have hated her for the very reasons he loves her. Indeed, his earlier emotions for Elizabeth bordered on dislike, as she herself notes. And although Georgiana listens with "astonishment bordering on alarm" to her sister-in-law's "lively, sportive manner" of talking to Darcy (395) after they are married, we had but recently learned that Elizabeth, earlier protestations notwithstanding, needed to "check herself. She remembered that he [Darcy] had yet to learn to be laughed at, and it was rather too early to begin" (380). Brownstein argues that in the passage of two chapters, Darcy had contracted the capacity to laugh at himself, but the passage remains problematic. Brownstein sees Georgiana's attention to Elizabeth as undercutting the conventional marriage-plot ending: "just as the marriage plot comes to triumphant closure it is neatly undercut: female bonding and women's laughter are elements of this novel's happy end. . . . This subtle subversion of the conventional romantic plot accords with the novel's attitude toward verbal tissues that appear to wrap things up once and for all" (*Last Laughs* 67). But it can also be argued that Elizabeth's check on herself indicates a hesitation and caution that will confine her once she is married; like Gwendolyn Harleth in *Daniel Deronda*, the text indicates that the witty woman will stop laughing when she meets the man who will exert power over her. Elizabeth "had a lively, playful disposition, which delighted in anything ridiculous," we are told at the inception of *Pride and Prejudice* (58). Austen does not make it clear whether Elizabeth keeps this prize possession after her marriage.

Granted, it is risky to say that perhaps Lydia has a last laugh, even though her story comes in the center of *Pride and Prejudice*. Little sister Lydia plays the marriage game the way a gambler plays roulette: willing to take a risk, Lydia chances all on Wickam. She is the sister who laughs after her wedding and although we have dark hints about a possible future, Austen seems no more willing to write Lydia out of a possible happy ending than she was willing to write off Willoughby. Lydia remains "untamed, unabashed, wild, noisy and fearless" as she "demands" congratulations from each of her sisters (328). She ignores the ban on her pleasure her father and sisters attempt to impose. Bowing and smiling "like anything" Lydia rolls down the carriage window to show off her wedding ring to the neighbors. Of this scene Margaret Drabble—not usually a great fan of what she refers to as Austen's "desperate wit"—has written: "my heart goes out to the vulgarity of . . . Lydia at fifteen gaily flashing her wedding ring through the carriage window" (65). Lydia's "ease and good spirits increased" as those around her became more embarrassed. Lydia is all subtext: she is the husband-hunter without the decorous surface. She is desire and ambition unmediated; Lydia is not a great reader. She doesn't know she had to learn to be ashamed of herself and so she isn't. She is a Marianne who attained Willoughby instead of Brandon; is hers an unhappy ending? Martha Satz regards Lydia as "morally reprehensible. . . . For her, the interchangeability of officers is as without consequence as that of bonnets. One strikes her notice, and therefore it is hers. . . . Her total lack of discrimination, her total failure to see events within any sort of hierarchy of value, and her complete absence of priorities reflect themselves in the humorous letter she leaves before she runs off with Wickham" (180). But it is exactly that "failure" to see events in a hierarchy of values that sets Lydia in a tradition of later heroines who can insist that what the world reads as their failure is a denunciation of values whose power they have withstood rather than ignored.

What of Emma? What of a heroine who, like Elizabeth, prides herself on her sense of humor? Emma, who must warn the supposedly impeccable Mr. Knightly in the third to last chapter that he must do everything for "poor little Anna Weston," that he "do as much for her as you have done for me, except falling in love with her when she is thirteen" (445)? Mr. Knightly has loved in Emma what he saw in her from her childhood—not what he sees in her as a woman. Although Knightly is probably not another Ruskin or Dodgson, it is still unnerving to know that Knightly liked her "saucy looks" when she was a young girl and that even after their declarations to one another, Emma insists: "I can never call you anything but 'Mr Knightly'" (445). Once again, Margaret Drabble takes a provocative stand on Austen concerning this point: "Emma got what she deserved, in marrying Mr. Knightly. What can it have been like, in bed with Mr Knightly? Sorrow awaited that woman; she would have done better to steal Frank Churchill, if she could" (65). The tenderest moment between George Knightly and Emma Woodhouse occurs when Emma can finally follow the script, when the script replaces her own language: "What did she say?—Just what she ought, of course. A lady always does" (418). Emma becomes "a lady" and so has her lines prescribed; we are back to the idea of the generic formula.

However, as Gilbert and Gubar have rightly observed, Emma, like Austen's other heroines, uses "passivity to gain power(;) . . . the heroines seem to submit as they get what they both want and need" (163). In his introduction to the Penguin edition of *Emma*, Ronald Blythe declares that "All the women in *Emma* are described with unusual psychological insight and most of them betray degrees of feminine neurosis. But Emma herself is a masterpiece of feminine understanding" (14). Blythe no more explains what he means by "feminine neurosis" than he explains "feminine understanding," and the thought that these terms are agreed upon by all intelligent, well-informed readers of Austen shows just how far we are from a consensus that will permit a "universal" reaction to Austen's comedy. Austen explains that "seldom can it happen that something is not a little disguised, or a little mistaken" (*Emma* 419) and to read her works without taking the disguise into account is to misread refusal as inability, irony as sentiment, considerable contempt as pleasant affection, and women's comedy for men's.

Rachel Blau Du Plessis argues in *Writing Beyond the Ending* that female authors often "reinsert discontent" even at the moment they construct the requisite happy ending. The cry for the happy ending is often—by the author herself—"castigated as reader banality" and as "reductive" (12). Austen short-cuts through even the most reductive drive for closure by leaving the creation of the happy ending to the reader, having recognized that the imaginative powers of the author are no longer required. Anybody can create a happy ending; it is as generic as a snap-on spare part, widely available and easy to assemble. Karen Newman rightly points out that "by reading an Austen novel as a unity with romantic marriage as its final statement, we impose a resolution on her work that makes it conform to the very expectations that it undermines" (694). She further comments that "if we turn to the endings themselves, we find an ironic self-consciousness that emphasizes the contradiction between the sentimentality of Austen's comic conclusions and her real view of marriage and the woman's plight" (704). Austen's comic endings depend, once again, on a consensus of values held between reader and narrator in contrast to the values held by the society portrayed within the novel. In *Comic Faith*, Robert Polhemus suggests that Austen's "willingness to question social surface and conventional assumptions" italicizes her concern with the "tentative nature of perception" (54), clearly a concern taken up by Lennox. Polhemus argues that Austen "mocks the presumptions and pretensions of others by accepting them at face value in order to make clear their foolishness. It protects by performing a nearly miraculous psychological reversal, turning incongruous misfunctioning and the inconsistencies of the world into a positive source of delight for the mind. This verbal irony liberates by suggesting different options in assessing life and different strategies for coping with it" (54). Suggesting that Austen illustrates certain conventions only in order to undercut their authority clearly places her within a tradition of women's comedy.

H. W. Garrod takes an interstingly gender-specific offense at the focus of Austen's books, complaining in 1928 that "[i]t is has been observed that nowhere in any of her books does one man talk to another. Clearly Miss Austen did not know how young men do talk to one another; and it is an essential condition of her talent that she never strays outside the range of her knowledge and experience" (29). Given that, as Virginia Woolf has pointed out, there are virtually no female friendships in novels written by male authors, it is worth remarking that this male reader takes extreme umbrage at the idea that the conversation of young men is simply not of interest to Jane Austen. His declaration is the perfect example of a critic naming in a female writer "inability" where there is instead refusal. Such critics are like Mr. Collins in *Pride and Prejudice* who cannot see refusal when it is writ large; Austen seems to be in the position of Elizabeth when she declares, in frustration, that "I know not how to express my refusal in such a way as may convince you of its being one" (149). If a writer is going to take on the truly important task of creating male characters, Garrod desperately needs to believe, then certainly they must be central. If they are not central, then the novelist has placed things incorrectly. But men, as Fay Weldon remarked in a context different but suitable, are often "simply decorative" in books written by women. (Weldon defends herself by using what we can call the Arabella Defense: I'm not satirizing, sir, I'm only reporting. Weldon notes that "The complaint is that my men characters are just plain horrible. I don't think they're any worse than the women!" [Barreca, *Belles Lettres*]). Jane Austen's men are of little consequence apart from how they function in the lives of the female characters, so that, in fact, the only important things about men are their marital status, income, rank, and looks. When they insist on explaining their ideas, one must often turn away in embarrassment or chagrin. Men, in Jane Austen, are at their best when they are out of the room: "When Mr Collins could be forgotten, there was really a great air of comfort throughout, and by Charlotte's evident enjoyment of it, Elizabeth supposed he must be often forgotten" (*Pride and Prejudice* 192).

What does Austen do to deflect the expected attack on her works? Brownstein writes in "Jane Austen: Irony and Authority" that Austen's narrative voice raises "highly subversive questions about the seriousness of all definitive statements and sentences, in what is after all a tissue of words, a series of sentences" (66). She raises to the forefront of her discussion the multiple-frames of Austen's works by pointing out that Austen "mimes so as subtly to mock the certainties of authoritative discourse" (65). Karen Newman puts it another way: "In Austen's novels, our conventional expectations are often met but at the same time undermined by self-consciousness and parody" (704). Newman, in an article delightfully titled "Can This Marriage Be Saved: Jane Austen Makes Sense of an Ending," suggests that readers of Austen "recogni[ze] common [writing] strategies among women and men who are, and for whatever reason, excluded or alienated from traditional patriarchal power structures. In Austen's case, irony and parody are subversive strategies that undermine the male hegemony her novels portray and reveal the romantic and materialistic contradictions of which her plots and characters are made" (707–8).

In *Madwoman in the Attic*, Gilbert and Gubar find Austen's parodic strategies effective in disguising her dissent; they argue that by using forms that "had been legitimized by the most conservative writers of her time," her books "therefore were then (and remain now) radically ambiguous" (120). They argue that she exploits the "very conventions she exposes as inadequate" (121) and is fascinated by "conversations that imply the opposite of what they intend, narrative statements that can only confuse, and descriptions that are linguistically sound, but indecipherable or tautological" (127). Kate Fullbrook is succinct in her deciphering of Austen's apparently paradoxical position: "she speaks precisely in the voice of the culture she mocks—hers is one of the most civilised voices in English fiction, and one of the most subversive" (41). Fullbrook goes on to identify what she sees as the power behind Austen's narrative strategies, drawing on Freud's theories of humor: "Comedy, which imaginatively takes to pieces the order which it ostensibly allows to persist, has been and is one of the most significant weapons in the imaginative armory of those excluded from privilege or alienated from power" (42).

The recognition that order is arbitrarily imposed rather than divinely awarded leads to the sort of double-voiced endings provided by Lennox and Austen. The plot seems to lead to the conclusion that the rules broken by the heroine are indeed right, and so she must learn to live by these rules: this is the acceptable and accepted comic plot. However, that comic plot is replaced by a more subversive one in which the rules appear only to show themselves arbitrary and subjective. The comedy in Lennox and Austen springs from their eagerness to write across and over the established curriculum.

3

"I'm No Angel": Humor and Mutiny in *Jane Eyre* and *Villette*

> **I** like you more than I can say; but I'll not sink into a bathos
> of sentiment: and with this needle of repartee I'll keep you
> from the edge of the gulf, too; and, moreover, maintain by its
> pungent aid that distance between you and myself most con-
> ducive to our real mutual advantage.
>
> Charlotte Bronte, *Jane Eyre*

Both *Jane Eyre* and *Villette* by Charlotte Bronte are laced with unsettling and powerful uses of humor. Charlotte Bronte's heroines discover that intelligence and oppression forge for them a signature sense of
irony. Jane Eyre and Lucy Snowe use their wit in a combination of self-
defense and mutiny, as a way of negotiating with a world they often dislike
and always distrust. Armed with their wit, these women must protect themselves against a world that values neither their inherent nor their acquired
talents. Unmothered, unmonied, and unmarried, they must confront without mediation the harshest experiences of life. Their wit evolves into an essential strategy for survival.

Because she originates from a position handicapped by poverty and
neglect, Jane Eyre learns to feed off an instinctive and unbridled intelligence. Not for Jane is the passionless, the opinionless or the neutral perspective; not for Jane the tepid smiles of agreement when there is conflict in the
heart; not for Jane silence when there could be speech, or compromise when
there could be victory. She learns early that her power proceeds from a refusal to be frightened: "if you dread them, they'll dislike you" (71). It follows
then that if you refuse to dread them they might dislike you less—and occasionally they might admire you. One thing is certain: it is Jane's defiant wit
which captivates Rochester's admiration.

Competitive humor forms the basis for much of Jane's relationship with Rochester. Theirs is a romance formed and maintained by repartee, refusal and perpetual renegotiation. Jane understands the inequity of their positions from the very establishment of their relationship, even if it is something Rochester would rather forget. "Leaving superiority out of the question, then, you must still agree to receive my orders now and then, without being piqued or hurt by the tone of command. Will you?" demands Rochester, to which Jane, smiling, silently replies, "Mr Rochester *is* peculiar—he seems to forget that he pays me thirty pounds per annum for receiving his orders" (165).

Jane matches Rochester in pride and outstrips him in insight. Their intelligence is also equally well-matched. Their conversations are exchanges between equal parties, resembling a fencing match more than a waltz: "'Do you doubt me Jane?' 'Entirely.' 'You have no faith in me?' 'Not a whit'" (283). Their dialogue is fueled by intelligence and wit, not flattery and deception. Of Rochester, Jane cannot be sure "whether he is in jest or earnest, whether he is pleased or the contrary" (136). Of Jane, Rochester insists that "any other woman would have melted to marrow at hearing such stanzas crooned in her praise," but he is corrected by the recipient of these praises: "I assured him I was naturally hard—very flinty, and that he would often find me so" (301). Her wit is a fence against encroachment; it will guarantee distance and thereby permit perspective on the relationship: "I like you more than I can say; but I'll not sink into a bathos of sentiment: and with this needle of repartee I'll keep you from the edge of the gulf, too; and, moreover, maintain by its pungent aid that distance between you and myself most conducive to our real mutual advantage" (301). "I laughed in my sleeve at his menaces," explains Jane, correctly locating her ability to do just that as a source of her power: "I can keep you in reasonable check now ... and I don't doubt being able to do it hereafter" (302). At one point she mockingly threatens to create a revolution among a harem of women which Rochester mockingly threatens to buy:

> "And what will you do, Janet, while I am bargaining for so many tons of flesh and such an assortment of black eyes?"
>
> "I'll be preparing myself to go out as a missionary to preach liberty to them that are enslaved—your harem inmates amongst the rest. I'll get admitted there, and I'll stir up mutiny; and you, three-tailed bashaw as you are, sir, shall in a trice find yourself fettered amongst our hands: nor will I, for one, consent to cut your bonds till you have signed a charter, the most liberal that despot ever yet conferred." (298)

The larger irony looming over these passages is, of course, the figure of Bertha, the one "inmate" whose "black eyes" already looked at England after being shipped from her own exotic homeland to be bound to Rochester.

It is due to this reliance on wit as a lattice for the healthy growth of their romantic exchanges that Rochester's lapses into earnestness are signals of approaching danger, of his inability to put Jane *as she is* in the forefront of his thoughts. Jane attempts to read Rochester's cliched remarks concerning her beauty as ironic, and thereby nearer to her own frame of reference, rather than interpret them as an attempt to fold her character into a prefabricated tale:

> "I will make the world acknowledge you a beauty, too," [Rochester] went on, while I really became uneasy at the strain he had adopted, because I felt he was either deluding himself or trying to delude me. "I will attire my Jane in satin and lace, and she shall have roses in her hair; and I will cover the head I love best with a priceless veil."
> "And then you won't know me, sir; and I shall not be your Jane Eyre any longer, but an ape in a harlequins' jacket—a jay in borrowed plumes. I would as soon see you, Mr. Rochester, tricked out in stage-trappings, as myself clad in a court-lady's robe; and I don't call you handsome, sir, though I love you most dearly; far too dearly to flatter you. Don't flatter me."
> He pursued his theme, however, without noticing my deprecation. (288)

Jane's humor in this passage expresses her extreme discomfort at Rochester's "veiling" of her singular personality. She compares herself to a bird, to an ape, nearly calls him a "trickster" and finally risks insulting him in order to make her point. However, even her witty deprecation of his charms remains unheeded; he insists on type-casting her as a bride. That Rochester cannot be teased out of his determination to dress Jane as he might dress Adele—or any other female of the species—is a signal that grave matters are at hand. Rochester values Jane's wit; that he is impervious to it at this moment, and that she persists in her teasing, indicates the distance between his script for their marriage and her plans for their future.

Rochester sells a counterfeit future to Jane, trading goods already sold: himself. The submerged figure of Bertha has received so much feminist attention, has become such an icon for feminist theory, that there is little need to underscore her position as focus for much of the text's energy. But it is interesting to note that the metonymic device associated with Bertha is laughter. Bertha's laughter echoes the halls and haunts the bedrooms of Thornfield. Her laugh is "tragic" and "preternatural" (138). It is the sound Jane least expects to hear as she explores the mansion: "It was a curious laugh—distinct, formal, mirthless. I stopped. The sound ceased, only for an instant. It began again, louder—for at first, though very distinct, it was very low. It passed off in a clamorous peal that seemed to echo in every lonely chamber, though it originated but in one, and I could have pointed out the door whence the accents issued" (138). Bertha's laugh is both ubiquitous and specific, ranging throughout the house even as it is confined. The "clamorous peal" of her laughter is indicative of Bertha's uncontrolled and uncontrollable presence in the text. It is indicative of the danger she represents to the very systems that try to silence her. Perhaps Catherine Clement offers the best discussion of the madwoman's apocalyptic laughter: "All laughter is allied with the monstrous. . . . Laughter breaks up, breaks out, splashes over. . . . It is the moment at which the woman crosses a dangerous line—the cultural demarcation beyond which she will find herself excluded" (33).

It is reductive to say that the split between Jane's dryly ironic humor and Bertha's thickly loud laughter is simply the split between the signified and the sign, or an unbridgeable gap between a woman who can only manufacture the cause and one who can only offer the effect. Yet however reductive these observations appear, they raise crucial points concerning the relationship between women and laughter in Bronte's text. Jane is capable of describing the day of her aborted wedding in the following terms: "The morning had been a quiet morning enough—all except the brief scene with the lunatic" (323). She writes a sentence nearly itself mad with irony. Jane makes the joke and Bertha laughs; the territory surrounded by the forces of these two women is the household belonging to both—and to neither—of them.

Jane is in no hurry to inhabit a celestial sphere. Religious experience is framed by "barely repressed" sarcasm from the moment we meet Jane's earliest religious instructors, those adults who wish to terrorize her into obedience, who use heaven as a carrot and hell as a whip. Jane Eyre refuses to give the expected answer to the moral, religious and emotional bullies who control her world. She supplies instead an alternate, "copy-hand text" of her own—acting on the assumption that "unheard-of combinations of circumstances demand unheard-of rules," and that "the human and the fallible should not arrogate a power with which the divine and perfect alone can be safely entrusted . . . [t]hat of saying of any strange, unsanctioned line of action, 'Let it be right'" (169).

Brocklehurst, for example, quizzes Jane to make sure she knows that the good go to heaven while the wicked go to hell. Jane, however, re-invents the plot, refusing to reproduce the scripted ending and coming up with an "objectionable" but nevertheless unanswerable solution of her own:

> "No sight so sad as that of a naughty child," he began, "especially a naughty little girl. Do you know where the wicked go after death?"

"They go to hell," was my ready and orthodox answer.

"And what is hell? Can you tell me that?"

"A pit full of fire."

"And should you like to fall into that pit, and to be burning there for ever?"

"No, sir."

"What must you do to avoid it?"

I deliberated a moment: my answer, when it did come, was objectionable: "I must keep in good health, and not die." (64)

Jane's lateral thinking does not impress Brocklehurst. He cannot see the humor in such a reply, although the reader surely can. Brocklehurst is a figure to be satirized, and yet he possesses the power to bludgeon Jane with what appears to be the weight of righteousness.

But he is as dangerous as he is ridiculous. Brocklehurst attempts to impose his text on the young women under his authority, and he controls the methods of reward as well as punishment. When Jane candidly admits that she is not fond of the psalms, Brocklehurst offers the following paradigm of goodness upon which he counsels Jane to meditate: "I have a little boy, younger than you, who knows six Psalms by heart: and when you ask him which he would rather have, a ginger-bread-nut to eat, or a verse of a Psalm to learn, he says: 'Oh! the verse of a Psalm! Angels sing Psalms,' says he; 'I wish to be a little angel here below.' He then gets two nuts in recompense for his infant piety" (65). His "infant piety" will get the tiny hypocrite a few good nuts, but Jane's honest answers will get her nothing but the lash of disapproval. The hypocrite who can parrot the accepted text is blindly rewarded, even though it is quite obvious that he gives the correct answer not because of his saintliness but in order to get the reward. The system anticipates Skinner more than it reflects God.

Jane wields her words like weapons, especially towards religious men. In contrast to Rochester, St. John Rivers threatens to flood her with unwanted, if not unexpected, moral invectives. For Rivers she is able to prepare an effectively humorous antidote to his ecclesiastical prescription for her: "'Oh! I will give my heart to God,' I said. 'You do not want it.' I will not swear, Reader, that there was not something of repressed sarcasm both in the tone in which I uttered this sentence, and in the feeling that accompanied it" (431). Rivers cannot interpret Jane's remarks fully because he cannot allow himself to believe she would joke at such a time: "He was silent after I had uttered the last sentence, and I presently risked an upward glance at his countenance. His eye, bent on me, expressed at once stern surprise and keen inquiry. 'Is she sarcastic, and sarcastic to me!' it seemed to say. 'What does this signify? Do not let us forget that this is a solemn matter,' he said ere long; 'one of which we may neither think nor talk lightly without sin'" (432). This time the woman's joke explicitly borders on the heretical, not just the disturbing. Like the pastor in Lockwood's dream, Rivers seems to have a "private manner" of interpreting sin and he is ready to condemn Jane's wit as sinful. Women's wit has always been transgressive, but the wit in *Jane Eyre* transgresses even the most sacred territories.

Indeed, contemporary critics of *Jane Eyre* saw in Bronte's book a fearful portrait of radical behavior. According to the *Quarterly Review* in 1848: "We do not hesitate to say that the tone of mind and thought which has overthrown authority and violated every code human and divine abroad, and fostered Chartism and rebellion at home, is the same which has also written *Jane Eyre*." No wonder the reviewers worried: Bronte's book appeared to question, and by extension, threaten everything from table manners ("Thanks having been returned for what we had not got . . ." [78]) to the romance-plot itself ("'What tale do you like best to hear?' 'Oh, I have not much choice! They generally run on the same theme—courtship; and promise to end in the same catastrophe—marriage'" [228]). The sharp irony informing much of the narration heightens the subversive power of the text. The fact that the ironical frame is constructed by a poor, unattractive governess gives it an added measure of strength by allowing the codes of accepted behavior to be satirized by one who by rights should be envious, not contemptuous, of them. Particularly stinging is Jane's joking refusal to accept the pedestal built for the feminine idol; she does not take seriously the role scripted for a generic romantic heroine any more than she took seriously the earlier role scripted for a dutiful child. For example, Rochester wants to revise his story with Jane along to provide an appendix to his original, sordid tale: "all the ground I have wandered over shall be retrodden by you. . . . I shall revisit it healed and cleansed, with my angel as my comforter," he insists. Jane responds as follows: "I laughed at him as he said this. 'I am not an angel,' I asserted; 'and I will not be one till I die: I will be myself. Mr Rochester, you must neither expect nor exact anything celestial of me—for you will not get it, any more than I shall get it of you: which I do not at all anticipate'" (288). As Jane will refuse to be St. John's ministering angel, so does she refuse to play such a role for Rochester. If heaven in *Wuthering Heights* was described as a place as dull as the stereotypical heroine's happy ending—"an ecstasy of peace . . . only half alive," where Cathy believes she would "fall asleep" (280)—heaven in *Jane Eyre* seems equally objectionable. Certainly the pastorally-named representatives of heaven, the institution of Lowood (in contrast to Lockwood?) or the person of Rivers, point to a path trodden by only the embittered or the hypocritical.

Jane does not parrot back answers and seems destined to revise every script placed before her. Jane breaks both familial and feminine codes which depend on the duplicitous exchange of silences: exposing secrets by naming

them, Jane realizes that the power of speech can shatter the power of silence. She threatens to expose her aunt's duplicity by refusing to be duplicitous herself, destroys her aunt's "feminine" guise of caretaker by refusing to
act "feminine" herself. Originality of thought is not prized; it is considered a
fault. In an unheeded defense of her honesty, a very young Jane cries that
"Deceit is not my fault" (69) but such a cry belies her ignorance of a system
that does not value honesty in women or children. Both must learn to curb
their tongues and their passions—assuming a virtue when they have none.
But Jane learns early the paradoxical power that resides in truth-telling: although she cannot win her aunt's affection by being honest, she can frighten
her aunt by threatening to tell the "true" story of how she has been treated:
"I will tell anyone who asks me questions this exact tale. People think you a
good woman, but you are bad, hard-hearted. *You* are deceitful" (69). At the
moment of this revelation, this epiphany of speech, Jane experiences "the
strangest sense of freedom, of triumph. . . . [I]t seemed as if an invisible bond
had burst, and that I had struggled into unhoped-for liberty" (69).

Her honesty is one the most profoundly threatening aspects of
Bronte's heroine. Charlotte Bronte does not rely on a subtext which, like a
brass rubbing, requires further art for the central figures to be brought into
relief. Her heroines do not rely on double-talk to assure themselves a respectable position in the social order; they are already exiled from that order
because of their poverty. At several points in the narrative, for example,
Jane questions whether she has "too rashly overleaped conventionalities"
which would permit someone to find "impropriety in my inconsiderateness"
(460); she understands that her lack of duplicity is usually powerful and often unacceptable. That Jane asks these questions shows more of an interest
in the delineation of her emerging identity than it shows a willingness to
amend her ways. She tests the reactions of those around her in order to
gauge rather than to change the effect she has on them.

She has learned that the pretty ways taught to privileged little girls
will not work for her. Learning "partly from experience and partly from instinct," Jane comes to the conclusion that apologies, for example, will only
elicit "double scorn" and thereby "re-excite" every "turbulent impulse" of
her nature (70). She learns to be "venturesome and hardy" (71) and to challenge rather than observe or submit to the world around her. When Helen
Burns counsels Jane to love her enemies and bless those who curse her, Jane
earnestly explains that "then I should love Mrs. Reed, which I cannot do: I
should bless her son John, which is impossible" (90). Jane makes explicit her
position on turning the other cheek: "When we are struck at without a
reason, we should strike back again very hard . . . so hard as to teach the person who struck us never to do it again" (90). She explains without apology to
her meek friend Helen that "I must dislike those who, whatever I do to

please them, persist in disliking me; I must resist those who punish me unjustly" (90). These are defiant words, with a nascent sense of self-awareness which will develop into a profound sense of irony as Jane matures.

Jane makes explicit her refusal to write in order to "flatter . . . egotism, to echo cant, or prop up humbug" (140)—asserting this in such a way as to make obvious the point that she assumes most writing can be placed into one of these three categories. Having anticipated the opposition's argument, she can then promise "merely" to tell the truth (140). Her "truth" will shatter the convenient containers prescribed for narrative truths, however, because she intends to "open my inward ear to a tale that was never ended—a tale my imagination created, and narrated continuously; quickened with all of incident, life, fire, feeling that I desired and had not in my actual existence" (141).

Like Jane Eyre, Lucy Snowe of *Villette* is divided from her own responses; while it seems at times that Bertha's laugh is drawn as much from Jane's depths as from her own, it seems that Lucy relies on others to manifest her reactions: "I wished *she* would utter some hysterical cry," laments Lucy while observing another woman, "so that *I* might get relief and be at ease" (71, italics mine). Lucy's wry observations, satiric perspectives and humorous insights amuse the reader while she appears to remain unlaughing. But it is significant to note that Lucy does indeed laugh during those moments when, as she asserts, it becomes "impossible to do otherwise" (148). What drives Lucy to laughter at this moment is the assurance by a Roman Catholic friend that she will burn forever in hell and that "pour assurer votre salut la-haut, on ferit bien de vous bruler toute vive ici-bas ("to ensure your salvation up above, they would do well to burn you alive down here"). In the same way that Jane refused to deal "properly" with the guardians of religion and money, so does Lucy refuse to respond with fear or humility to the authority of the church, the arts or the academy.

At one point, after describing her sea voyage in a series of widely-accepted, wildly-misrepresentative, wholly standardized phrases, Lucy suddenly addresses the audience directly: "Cancel the whole of that, if you please, reader—or rather let it stand, and draw thence a moral—an alternative, text-hand copy." Among the phrases she wishes to cancel are the following: "divine the delight I drew from the heaving channel-waves," "the quiet, yet beclouded sky," "In my reverie, methought I saw the continent of Europe, like a wide dream-land, far away," and "tiniest tracery of clustered town and snow-gleaming tower" (117). Towards the end of this elaborately detailed paragraph, she calls attention to her mocking voice by referring to the process of creating rather than describing a scene: "*For background*," Lucy indicates, one should "spread a sky . . . grand with imperial promise, soft with tints of enchantment . . . from north to south a God-sent bow, an arch of hope" (117).

But, finally, it is such writing she wishes to mock, to cancel, to replace with something more unsettling, unconventional and amusing because it destroys a sense of particularly "feminine" decorum: instead of manufacturing a scene full of heaving waves and rainbows, she presents the following: "Becoming excessively sick, I faltered down into the cabin" (118). So much for the voyage out. So much for the standardized version of the rite of passage. After repeating—even in order to mock—all that bad writing, being sick seems the only appropriate gesture.

Lucy does indeed laugh, but she tells of hiding her laughter even as she records it: "Indeed, I confess, for my part, I did laugh till I was warm; but then I bent my head, and made my handkerchief and a lowered veil the sole confidants of my mirth" (396). No doubt Lucy is responding to the maxim that the laughter of women is naturally suspect. For example, Lucy watches a young and beautiful bride onboard ship whose groom is "the oldest, greasiest, broadest" man in the group, as she smiles "a smile of which the levity puzzled and startled" her, and of whom Lucy declares: "Her laughter . . . must be the mere frenzy of despair" (113). As in the case of Bertha Rochester, the laughter of this mis-married wife is a discharge of emotion rather than a sign of pleasure.

Paradoxically, Lucy Snowe appears to be more amusing while less easily amused than Jane Eyre. Yet Lucy is in many respects similar to Jane: she is the teller of her own tale, which is marked by irony; she is involved in a romantic relationship characterized by wit and repartee; alone and unmonied (in *The Madwoman in the Attic* Gilbert and Gubar call the novel "the most moving and terrifying account of female deprivation ever written" [400]), she uses her intelligence as a weapon, wielding words as her only means of self-defense. Her description of her employer, Madame Beck, easily seems a projection of herself, the qualities she ascribes to the older woman being ones Lucy herself possesses: "watchful and inscrutable; astute and insensate—withal perfectly decorous—what more could be desired?" (137).

The humor of *Villette* manages to be both watchful and astute while, for the most part, remaining perfectly decorous. Bronte does, however, create scenes of nearly slapstick comedy. When Lucy confronts her first classroom of adolescents, the girls are ruthless in their misbehavior. The trio of particular offenders, tellingly named "Mesdesmoiselles Blanche, Virginie, and Angelique" (143), believe that Miss Snowe will be "an easy victory." Lucy is doubly frustrated by her situation because she cannot use her wit to empower herself: "Could I but have spoken in my own tongue, I felt as if I might have gained a hearing; for . . . nature had given me a voice that could make itself heard. . . . I could, in English, have rolled out readily phrases stigmatizing their proceedings as such proceedings deserved to be stigmatized; and then with some sarcasm, flavoured with contemptuous bitterness, for the ringleaders, and relieved with easy banter for the weaker" (143). Because she cannot carry out this precise plan for using her wit as a weapon, Lucy resorts to another "unfeminine" form of persuasion, and the resulting scene is a rare instance of sheer physical comedy:

> I noted that she sat close by a little door, which door, I was well aware, opened into a small closet where books were kept. She was standing up for the purpose of conducting her clamour with freer energies. I measured her stature and calculated her strength. She seemed both tall and wiry; but, so the conflict were brief and the attack unexpected, I thought I might manager her.
>
> Advancing up the room, looking as cool and careless as I possibly could, in short, *ayant L'air de rien*, I slightly pushed the door and found it was ajar. In an instant, and with sharpness, I had turned on her. In another instant she occupied the closet, the door was shut, and the key in my pocket. (144)

Another example cut from a similar pattern of physical comedy has a chapter of its own: "A Sneeze Out of Season"—chapter 13. Madame Beck has already made it apparent that she sees surveillance as part of her duties as headmistress of a school; she is as equally determined to investigate Lucy's private life as she is to survey the life of the most unruly pupil. But Madame Beck cannot keep up her secretive, unflappable guard: "Here the latch of Madame Beck's chamber-door (opening into the nursery) gave a sudden click, as if the hand holding it had been slightly convulsed; there was the suppressed explosion of an irrepressible sneeze. These little accidents will happen to the best of us. Madame—excellent woman!—was then on duty" (193). The little explosion gives the excellent woman away; like Lucy's sea-sickness, physical demands will inevitably undermine the plausibility of any script.

Although Lucy Snowe's satiric commentary on those around her occasionally remains unspoken, it is rarely uncensured. If Jane Eyre is renegade, to use Judy Little's term, in her use of humor and her relentless honesty, then Lucy is her more subtle and therefore more insidious sister. Lucy does not threaten the structure at the risk of being absorbed into it; she remains essentially an outsider. She evidences an ironic acceptance of conditions or events imposed against her volition but without her refusal—such as acting "a disagreeable part,—a man's—an empty-headed fop's" (203) role in the school play, or wearing a pink dress when she "would almost as soon clothe myself in the costume of a Chinese lady of rank" (283). She accepts both sets of garments, even as she says "that is not for me" (283), and in so doing enters a less fixed position than any of her predecessors. Lucy's unspoken but carefully reasoned scrutiny of her relationship to the dominant order often reveals itself in her satiric or sarcastic response to an "ordinary" situation. When, for example, Graham makes the fairly innocent comment "Your friend is spending her vacation in travelling, I hear?" concerning Ginevra, Lucy cannot refrain from allowing her humor some play: "'Friend, forsooth!' thought I to myself: but it would not do to contradict; he must have his own way; I must own the soft impeachment; friend let it be. Still, by way of experiment, I could not help asking whom he meant?" (263). When Graham asks Lucy the slightly more dangerous question—"'You, who know her, could you name a point in which she is deficient?'"—the reader is privy to the subtext of Lucy's remark: "'She does several things very well.' ('Flirtation amongst the rest,' subjoined I, in thought)" (263). The quick-witted reply is the hallmark of Lucy's unspoken commentary. Although her immediate company is denied the pleasure of these remarks, she offers the reader these verbal treats without apology.

Often her wit serves to deflate what she considers to be pretentious or disingenuous. When, for example, M. Emanuel is instructing the actors, Lucy's rejoinder to his recommendation that "each . . . penetrate herself well with a sense of her personal significance" is: "God knows, I thought this advice superfluous for some of us" (209). Perhaps the most carefully constructed deflation of pretentions occurs when Lucy chances, at the museum, to observe a painting applauded for its luxurious heroine. Lucy has little patience for the gentleman viewer's ritual appreciation of the museum's holdings: "How daintily he held a glass to one of his optics! With what admiration he gazed upon the Cleopatra! . . . Oh, the man of sense! Oh, the refined gentleman of superior taste and tact! I observed him for about ten minutes, and perceived that he was exceedingly taken with this dusk and portly Venus of the Nile" (281). Lucy, however, remains unimpressed, and her carefully chosen words slice away at the figurative frame of presuppositions upon which the picture's assessment of excellence rests:

> [T]his picture, I say, seemed to consider itself the queen of the collection.
>
> It represented a woman, considerably larger, I thought, than life. I calculated that this lady, put into a scale of magnitude suitable for the reception of a commodity of bulk, would infallibly turn from fourteen to sixteen stone. She was, indeed, extremely well fed: very much butcher's meat—to say nothing of bread, vegetables, and liquids—must she have consumed to attain that breadth and height, that wealth of muscle, that affluence of flesh. She lay half-reclined on a couch: why, it would be difficult to say; broad daylight blazed round her; she appeared in hearty health, strong enough to do the work of two plain

cooks; . . . Pots and pans—perhaps I ought to say vases and gob-
lets—were rolled here and there on the foreground; a perfect
rubbish of flowers was mixed amongst them, and an absurd and
disorderly mass of curtain upholstery smothered the couch and
cumbered the floor. On referring to the catalogue, I found that
this notable production bore the name 'Cleopatra.' (275)

Obviously Lucy is less than impressed with the standard depiction of
female beauty, but it is her refusal to allow for the grand scale of things that
operates in this scene; she reduces the queen to a fattish woman who, instead of performing the work of which she is clearly capable, lounges about
in poorly constructed clothing. Once again, she refuses to adopt the language of convention; she applies her domestic and sarcastic grammar to the
work of art and debases the currency of the image. It is very much a case of
the empress's new clothes—or lack thereof, to be more precise. In contrast
to Lucy's scrutiny, the gentleman museum-goer responds according to the
script and Lucy's satiric vision encompasses his response as well as her own.
Tellingly, however, the other images of women in the room—the more acceptable and domestic ones—please Lucy as little as the voluptuous mon-
arch. She regards the four versions of women's existence as "four 'Anges'"
who are as "grim and gray as burglars, and cold and vapid as ghosts. What
women to live with! Insincere, ill-humoured, bloodless, brainless nonenti-
ties! As bad in their way as the indolent gipsy-giantess, the Cleopatra, in
hers" (278). The artist's version of "La vie d'une femme" is an object of derision to Lucy, and she delineates most carefully in this scene her indictment
of convention, posing as mimesis, which can only offer the "rather remarkable style" of presenting what is "flat, dead, pale and formal" as if it were
real (278).

In this passage, we have the subtextual rendition of the procession of
feminine types and most notable in Lucy's discussion of them is her distrust
of the decorous surface all four present:

The first represented a 'Jeune Fille,' coming out of a church-
door, a missal in her hand, her dress very prim, her eyes cast
down, her mouth pursed up—the image of a most villanous little
precocious she-hypocrite. The second, a 'Mariee' with a long
white veil, kneeling at a prie-dieu in her chamber, holding her
hands plastered together, finger to finger, and showing the
whites of her eyes in a most exasperating manner. The third, a
'Jeune Mere,' hanging disconsolate over a clayey and puffy baby
with a face like an unwholesome full moon. The fourth, a
'Veuve,' being a black woman, holding by the hand a black little
girl and the twain studiously surveying an elegant French monument, set up in a corner of some Pere la Chaise. (277)

The artists' representations of women merely offer Lucy an opportunity to exercise her wit; they do not offer her examples to follow, raise her spirits or elevate her thoughts. M. Emanuel would have her contemplate the pre-scribed 'vie d'une femme' but she declines: "Excuse me, M. Paul; they are too hideous: but if you admire them, allow me to vacate my seat and leave you to their contemplation" (280). Lucy has little time for the perfect flowers of femininity, however they are presented; "these 'rose et blanches' specimens of humanity" hold little attraction for a woman who has a precise understanding of their limitations: "In English, they had been under my own charge, and hard work it was to get them to translate rationally a page of *The Vicar of Wakefield*" (291). If M. Emanuel wishes to accept the stand-ard version of a woman's life, then he may; Lucy will neither interrupt or attempt to alter his gaze. Yet, the implication is that her remark might per-haps serve as a filter.

In contrast to her refusal to elevate art to whispered, spiritual heights is her elevation of hairdressing to precisely that level; she describes the cere-monial aspects of coiffure in terms decidedly religious:

> Sacrilegious to state (the hairdresser) fixed his head-quarters in the oratory, and there, in presence of beniter, candle, and crucifix, solemnized the mysteries of his art. Each girl was sum-moned in turn to pass through his hands; emerging from them with head as smooth as a shell, intersected by faultless white lines, and wreathed about with Grecian plaits that shone as if lacquered. I took my turn with the rest. . . . the lavish garlandry of woven brown hair amazed me—I feared it was not all my own, and it required several convincing pulls to give assurance to the contrary. (199)

The passage itself is fairly sacrilegious. Described in the flinty, distanced, self-deprecating style which is the signature of Lucy Snowe, she manages to braid the vain with the venerable until they can hardly be distinguished— the implication then being that they are indeed closer than usually acknowl-edged. Lucy does not challenge any aspect of this scene: she observes and records it, giving equal weight to sacrilege and to style.

The danger Lucy poses to the system is not so much the danger of chal-lenge, but that of disinterest. Unlike the combative strategies employed by Jane, Lucy chooses "not to" as her encoding of defiance. When, for example, a boatman demands what she knows to be too high a price for the voyage, Lucy nevertheless pays the full amount despite her knowledge of being cheated: "'You ask too much,' I said. . . . A young man, the steward as I found afterwards, was looking over the ship's side; he grinned a smile in anticipa-tion of the coming contest; to disappoint him, I paid the money" (111). Lucy

73

complies in order to disappoint—rather than to affirm—the expectations of
the system. To refuse to be disappointed at a loss is to rob the thief of his
most poignant pleasure. In her acquiescence, Lucy in fact defies the system.
She treats the arbitrary rules and customs under which she must function as
a perpetual foreigner handles the currency of other countries: understanding
that there is a value carefully allotted to every document without really believing in the validity of the exchange. Lucy's relationship to the customs of
the countries she inhabits is more ceremonial than spontaneous. In other
words, she undertakes the gestures demanded of her because she is determined to remain removed from—not because she believes in—prevailing
conventions.

In part because of this ceremonial relationship to life, Lucy's perspective is characterized by distance. This renders her irony particularly
effective. She maintains a studied distance from herself, significantly
enough, which enables her to describe her own behavior—as well as the behavior of the two men she loves—in the same sardonic voice as she treats
lesser characters. Lucy treats Graham, the man for whom she forms her first
romantic attachment, with affection that often borders on contempt.
Graham is seduced by the charms of Ginevra Fanshawe, an attractive,
wholly unapologetic flirt whom he views with the blinkered vision of the in-
fatuated lover. He believes that because Ginevra is young and lovely, she is
good and unspoiled. He mistakenly attributes to Ginevra every cliche-rid-
den romantic characteristic imaginable, and expects Lucy to do the same.

Using his words against him, however, Lucy repeats his litany nearly
word for word—except for the fact that she applies it to the young man who
is a rival for Ginevra's affections. When Graham asks Lucy whether she is
"not a little severe" on Ginevra, she replies: "I am excessively severe—more
severe than I choose to show you. You should hear the strictures with which
I favour my 'beautiful young friend,' only that you would be unutterably
shocked at my want of tender considerateness for her delicate nature." Graham continues to push his point:

> "She is so lovely, one cannot but be loving towards her. You
> —every woman older than herself, must feel for such a simple,
> innocent, girlish fairy, a sort of motherly or elder-sisterly fond-
> ness. Graceful angel! Does not your heart yearn towards her
> when she pours into your ear her pure, child-like confidences?
> How you are privileged!" And he sighed.
>
> "I cut short these confidences somewhat abruptly now and
> then," said I. "But excuse me, Graham, may I change the theme
> for one instant? What a god-like person is that de Hamal! What
> a nose on his face—perfect! Model one in putty or clay, you
> could not make a better, or straighter, or neater; and then, such
> classic lips and chin—and his bearing—sublime."

"De Hamal is an unutterable puppy, besides being a very white-livered hero."

"You, Graham, and every man of a less refined mould than he, must feel for him a sort of admiring affection, such as Mars and the coarser deities may be supposed to have borne the young, graceful Apollo."

"An unprincipled, gambling, little jackanapes!" said Graham curtly, "whom, with one hand, I could lift up by the waistband any day, and lay low in the kennel, if I liked."

"Sweet seraph!" said I. "What a cruel idea? Are you not a little severe, Graham?" (222)

By employing his own words against him, Lucy illustrates perfectly the humorous, mocking voice that characterizes the woman writer, in much the same way as she ridiculed the stock phrases used to describe the sea voyage at the opening of the book. Graham does not even realize what she is doing; he cannot hear her joke because he is so self-absorbed. He ignores the repetition of his own words, hearing only that Lucy praises his rival. Her elaborate ridicule of the stock romantic phrases employed by Graham at this moment of his deepest emotion is an indictment of both his particular romantic folly as well as an indictment of the standard, scripted text for romance. Lucy's reading of the exaggerated and superficial text adopted by Graham to praise Ginevra, and her reversal of it, point by point, illustrates the gender-specific nature of his remarks: they become "ridiculous" when applied to men. That Graham, as an older man, should be delighted by his role as "a sort of admiring affection, such as Mars and the coarser deities may be supposed to have born the young, graceful Apollo" is, of course, absurd. But to examine that point is also to reach the conclusion that for Lucy to adore hearing the "pure, child-like confidences" of Ginevra is equally absurd.

That Lucy does indeed preserve a wry affection for the antics of her spoiled, flirtatious student does not negate the absurdity of Graham's claim that as an "older woman" Lucy "must feel . . . a sort of motherly or elder-sisterly fondness" for her. Where, in the romantic cosmology purchased by Graham, Ginevra is child-like, innocent and angelic in her youth and unformed nature, her counterpart, de Hamal is an "unutterable puppy" who can be lifted up with one hand. The insubstantial nature of the woman in her youth makes her angelic, according to the masculine script, while a young man is rendered animalistic by that same condition. In the end, Lucy drives home her conscious mimicking of Graham by questioning whether he is not too severe, echoing in the finale the opening statement made to her; she has cross-dressed the script by adopting masculine values for a moment in much the same way as she adopted masculine attire to act the fop in the school play.

75

But even so, Lucy herself wonders whether she has not gone too far in mimicking him: "I was going beyond myself . . . speaking in an unpremeditated, impulsive strain" (222). Repeating Graham's phrases with a difference, Lucy here underscores the way women change even what they appear to echo, reinventing even when they seem to repeat. This stress on the importance of the miming voice underscores the importance of Bronte's repetition-with-difference, even though the particular strategy employed by Bronte is only a shard broken off from the larger issues. When Bronte writes a scene exposing the difference in the employment of the same words and concepts by men and women, she illustrates the gendered nature of language itself. That she treats this difference playfully is an indication of the importance of humor in the text: it allows the introduction of monumental ideas without distracting the reader into theory and away from the narrative. That Lucy can laugh while pointing out the absurdity of romantic conventions shows her ability to remain elsewhere even as she employs the same strategies as her male counterpart. The scene with Graham is equally significant, however, in drawing attention to *his* inability to escape the confines of convention.

M. Emanuel, for all his admiration of Lucy, is locked into patriarchal culture; he is far more representative of that tradition than, for example, Rochester. He has very definite ideas concerning the "Woman of intellect." Not surprising for a male academic; Lucy sighs that "here he was at home." Lucy records his theories about intelligent women, and the transcription of such ideas by a woman obviously both object and subject of this tirade places them within a frame that renders them the object of her derision:

> A "woman of intellect," it appeared, was a sort of "*lusus naturae*," a luckless accident, a thing for which there was neither place nor use in creation, wanted neither as wife nor worker. Beauty anticipated her in the first office. He believed in his soul that lovely, placid, and passive feminine mediocrity was the only pillow on which manly thought and sense could find rest for its aching temples; and as to work, male mind alone could work to any good practical result—hein? (443).

The final "hein?" indicates both her exact transcription of his voice as well as pointing to M. Emanuel's anticipation of agreement from his audience. She makes it clear, however, that these remarks are more worthy of ridicule than respect.

M. Paul will not permit Lucy unmediated access to those materials he considers dangerous to her as a woman. Her gender defines what she may and may not read, for example. In a passage particularly satisfying because of its explicitly satiric treatment of the male-constructed curriculum, M.

Emanuel will not give his younger colleague the gift of a book without first whipping out his penknife and editing the text:

> After looking over the two volumes he had brought and cutting away some pages with his penknife (he generally pruned before lending his books, especially if they were novels, and sometimes was a little provoked at the severity of his censorship, the retrenchments interrupting the narrative), he rose.... (435)

In his desire to control Lucy's reading, he resembles the male characters created by Lennox and Austen. But the most significant aspect of M. Emanuel's desire to control Lucy's reading is his well-articulated and unmistakable fear of what he defines as the "contraband appetite for unfeminine knowledge." Lucy is perplexed, like many female students before and after her, by her mentor's withdrawal of approval at the exact moment when she felt herself to be achieving her goals:

> But, strange grief! . . . when I voluntarily doubled, trebled, quadrupled the tasks he set, to please him as I thought, his kindness became sternness; the light changed in his eyes from a beam to a spark; he fretted, he opposed, he curbed me imperiously; the more I did, the harder I worked, the less he seemed content. Sarcasms of which the severity amazed and puzzled me, harassed my ears; then flowed out the bitterest inuendoes against the "pride of intellect." I was vaguely threatened with, I know not what doom, if I ever trespassed the limits proper to my sex, and conceived a contraband appetite for unfeminine knowledge. (440)

M. Emanuel's unwillingness to allow Lucy free reign in her studies, his desire to control the process and progress of her learning, is reminiscent of those lover/teacher characters we have already encountered, and who continue to present themselves in women's writings until the present day. The teacher/lover is an attractive figure for many reasons, but it is interesting to note the ways in which these characters have their pretensions deflated by the humor of their female student/lovers. Only wit could effectively undercut the power of these figures. Their representation in literature by women is significantly different from the way they are inscribed in works by male authors, and one of the most apparent differences is the female writer's refusal to allow for the high seriousness demanded by the gentleman scholar. Eliot will, of course, take this figure to his most dangerous extreme in Casaubon, but M. Emanuel is certainly a version of this character. As such, he is open to Bronte's deft satire; his comments on the education of women sound more like a fool's than a hero's.

But M. Emanuel is the romantic center of the text; he does procure Lucy a schoolroom of her own, after all. She can and does speak intimately to him, refusing to censure herself, unwilling to cut passages from her own tale even if her words must sound "literal, ardent, bitter" (591). Finally, Lucy realizes that she prefers him "before all humanity" (592), and agrees to be his wife. They then immediately part: "he gave me his pledge, and then his farewell" (592). A narrative tangle, surely? Lovers can meet, pledge and then be driven apart by outside forces working against their will, but it is disruptive to the traditional marriage plot to have them decide to go on to other things besides the cultivation of their relationship. Bronte, who has already presented the reader with several important passages undercutting the supremacy of both textual and social convention, must be understood to be demonstrating the same refusal to adhere to the "script" at the end of her novel.

Bronte indicates her refusal to adhere to convention in a number of ways, not the least of which is the final comic piercing of the gothic cloud that hangs over the novel. When Ginevra explains the mystery of the ghostly nun, we realize along with Lucy that this subplot has been falsely wrought all along. Relief at the discovery that de Hamal was dressing up as a nun so as to spend time in Ginevra's company is compounded with disappointment that the tale should have deceived us, but it is also laced with laughter at the willingness of the viewer/reader to adapt experience to meet the "plot"—in this case, the gothic plot. Lucy Snowe discovers the error of her interpretation only to find the intricacies of her own life to be far more baroque than gothic. Like one of Austen's creations, Ginevra elopes, waves her hand out the carriage window at her friends in hopes of getting their attention, and remains perfectly unapologetic. In light of the expected narrative response to such illicit activity—the death and/or dishonor of the provoking character—Bronte's response to Ginevra is telling: "In winding up Mistress Fanshawe's memoirs, the reader will no doubt expect to hear that she came finally to bitter expiation of her youthful levities. Of course, a large share of suffering lies in reserve for her future" (575). Of course, such a phrase itself encodes Bronte's refusal to do exactly that—provide the prescribed sentence for such crimes.

Ginevra seems essentially unchanged by marriage. One of the things Lucy describes, interestingly enough, is Ginevra's continued appreciation of her wit: "my dry gibes pleased her well enough, and the more impassable and prosaic my mien, the more merrily she laughed" (576). Ginevra, it turns out, does not seem to receive much of a share of suffering at all: "she was pretty sure to obtain her will, and so she got on—fighting the battle of life by proxy, and, on the whole, suffering as little as any human being I have ever known" (577).

Lucy states the terms of her own finale as explicitly as possible. In the third paragraph of the final chapter Lucy states that "M. Emanuel was away three years. Reader, they were the three happiest years of my life. Do you scout the paradox?" (593). She describes working hard at her profession, receiving a small inheritance, and buying more property. Certainly the three years contained in these few last paragraphs show Lucy in control of her circumstances through financial and intellectual independence. What, then, would be her happy ending? The return of the teacher/lover?

Not only does Bronte refuse to supply closure, Lucy herself will not tell us the ending of her own story; it is not a metatextual refusal to supply a suitable ending, but a textual refusal to supply any *one* ending at all. She offers "alternative" texts at the finish of the story as she suggested she might at the beginning—the "cancel the whole of that, if you please, reader" at the ending of the text appears in the following words:

> Here pause: pause at once. There is enough said. Trouble no
> quiet, kind heart; leave sunny imaginations hope. Let it be theirs
> to conceive the delight of joy born again fresh out of great ter-
> ror, the rapture of rescue from peril, the wondrous reprieve from
> dread, the fruition of return. Let them picture union and a hap-
> py succeeding life. (596)

Bronte refuses to give even sketchy outlines concerning the fate of the two major characters in the book. If the reader wants a happy ending, Lucy will not stand in the way of one being contrived.

But it is finally the very idea of contrivance itself that stands prominent at the end of *Villette*; it is the emphasis on text, created not by fiat but by will, manufactured art not reflected nature, that is the copy-hand signature of this novel as well as *Jane Eyre*. Wit is used by these characters to protect themselves as much from sweetly suffocating sentimentality as from stern condemnation; their humor is as effective against that which would threaten their autonomy as it is against that which would threaten their virtue. When St. John Rivers tells Jane that there are matters "of which we may neither think nor talk lightly without sin" (432), she is not silenced. Like her counterpart Lucy Snowe, she records with mirth and a sense of delight in her own heretical humor her bravely comic response.

4

Laughter as Reproof, Refutation, and Revenge in *The Mill on the Floss* and *Middlemarch*

Maggie looked bewildered for a moment, and Tom enjoyed that moment keenly; but in the next, she laughed, clapped her hands together and said, "O Tom, you've made yourself like Bluebeard at the show."

It was clear she had not been struck with the presence of the sword—it was not unsheathed. Her frivolous mind required a more direct appeal to its sense of the terrible, and Tom prepared for his masterstroke. Frowning with a double amount of intention . . . he drew the sword from its sheath and pointed it at Maggie.

. . . . (t)he sword swung downwards, and Maggie gave a loud shriek. The sword had fallen, with its edge on Tom's foot, and, in a moment after, he had fallen too.

George Eliot, *The Mill on the Floss*

Maggie's difficulty in controlling both her laughter and her anger is emblematic of the nineteenth-century heroine's relationship to what Charlotte Bronte referred to as the "copy-hand text" of irrepressible self-expression. Maggie's laughter, like her anger, is evidence of both her conscious and unconscious, as well as spoken and unspoken, refusal to abide by the rules. While a number of critics have offered excellent discussions of the way rage becomes a shaping principle of *The Mill on the Floss*,[1] few have addressed the subtle but nevertheless significant way in which Eliot uses humor to structure her novels.

Eliot acknowledges that laughter is not without its penalties, as we can see from the passage concerning Maggie, Tom, and Tom's unsheathed sword. Clearly, Tom Tulliver is frustrated by his sister's laughter and so draws his sword in order to impress upon her the serious nature of his masculinity. Maggie's laughter is taboo because it violates the ceremonial aspects of Tom's ritual dressing up. It is all too easy for the object of laughter to trace a path to its cause, however, and Tom's displeasure at Maggie's delight is swift and certain. Tom's "masterstroke," however, harms himself not his sister: he is temporarily disabled by the cut he inadvertently administers to his foot.

Women are not meant to laugh at weapons, but are instead meant to cower before them in a form of homage fed by fear. Maggie did not know she was supposed to quail at the flimsy props of power brandished by her brother. In other words, she misread the script he had prepared for her. She laughed in the wrong place—something female characters do with astonishing frequency in literature written by women. (In *Daniel Deronda*, satirical Gwendolyn muses that "Being acquainted with authors must give a peculiar understanding of their books: one would be able to tell then which parts were funny and which serious. I am sure I often laugh in the wrong place" [76].) Maggie does not understand that Tom, having costumed himself in the paraphernalia of an adult male, feels he is no longer simply her brother or a boy she loves. He now considers himself initiated into the ranks of the powerful, inaccessible and venerated.

Maggie's laughter is the response of a woman to a masculine insistence upon the singular correctness of is own vision. Maggie offers her own reading of the material by comparing Tom to a pantomime figure and in doing so shows a vision not too vague or muddled, but instead too *clear*. Tom, we suspect, would prefer to be feared as a genuine Bluebeard than laughed at as a panto character. He wants her to fear the image of power, not discover its unimpressive source. Maggie's choice of comparison, in fact, undoes her because she betrays her own intelligence in the making of it; in comparing her brother to a clownish, artificial figure, she shows both delight and disrespect. This combination marks her as the heroine. Lamentably, it also marks her as the woman who will die.

Eliot situates her narrative humor within a larger, complex, ultimately non-comedic structure. The distinction between comedy and humor is perhaps made most effectively by Umberto Eco in his essay "Frames of Comic Freedom" in which he explains that humor does not pretend "to lead us beyond our own limits. It gives us the feeling, or better, the picture of the structure of our own limits. It is never off limits, it undermines limits from inside. . . . In doing so it undermines the law. It makes us feel the uneasiness of living under a law—any law" (8). Maggie from *The Mill on the Floss* and Dorothea from *Middlemarch* are women who feel the uneasiness of living under the law, particularly when the "law" is implicit, unwritten or derived from simple consensus. Maggie resents the law whereby the blond heroine inevitably triumphs, and Dorothea resents the law that assumes she will be the foundress of nothing. Maggie is aggressive in her own use of humor, especially as a child. In *Middlemarch*, the humor derives to a great extent from the narrator's coolly disruptive voice. Yet in both novels, the presence of humor has a decidedly emancipatory effect because of its challenge to the very idea of moral, religious, and social orthodoxy.

Whether Eliot's humor takes shape as the irony lacing the narrative or slapstick scenes in a nursery, one thing is clear: Mary Douglas's definition of humor as a "juxtaposition of control against that which is controlled . . . such that the latter triumphs" is shared and illustrated by Eliot's novels. The insipid subversion implied by the mocking voice of the woman writer gives Eliot what Judy Little would identify as the "contraband" (*Last Laughs* 180) or "renegade" (*Comedy and the Woman Writer* 1) nature of her humor. Little applies her argument most directly to modern women writers, but her comments seem equally relevant to earlier female authors. Little considers women's humorous writing renegade because "it mocks the deepest possible norms . . . norms which have been considered stable values for millenia" (*Comedy and the Woman Writer* 1–2). Certainly George Eliot breaks through the prohibitions of her culture by seizing on such sanctified subjects as religion, marriage, education, politics, and money as subjects of humor. Perhaps most significantly, Eliot does not offer a splendid alternative as a replacement for the satirized system. Her humor resists functioning as a corrective, as many of her more severe critics have noted with alacrity.

Virginia Woolf's important and influential essay on Eliot rather unnervingly addresses what Woolf regards as Eliot's native inability to create any form of humor beyond a simple, if not actually simple-minded, commentary on the rustic. "Her humour has shown itself broad enough to cover a wide range of fools and failures, mothers and children, dogs and flourishing midland fields, farmers, sagacious or fuddled over their ale, horse-dealers, inn-keepers, curates, and carpenters," offers Woolf, ungenerously reducing Eliot's accomplishment to a list of stock-figures and buffoons ("George Eliot" 156). Woolf categorically dismisses the possibility of charm or wit in Dorothea, for example, by complaining that "Mrs. Casaubon would have talked for an hour, and we should have looked out of the window" (159). While Woolf believes that Eliot's "sympathies are with the everyday lot, and play most happily in dwelling upon the homespun of ordinary joys and sorrows," she argues that Eliot "has none of that romantic intensity which is connected with a sense of one's own individuality. . . . [T]he flood of memory and humour which she pours so spontaneously into one figure, one scene after another, until the whole fabric of ancient rural England is revived, has so much in common with a natural process that it leaves us with little consciousness that there is anything to criticize" (155).

Examining this passage, we see that Woolf can be accused of acting out what Gilbert and Gubar regard as a masculinist reflex, in *The Madwoman in the Attic*: the need to "condemn" certain women writers "as natural," and as unconscious artists who write almost in spite of [themselves]" (110). Most damningly, Woolf asserts that Eliot "is no satirist. The movement of her mind was too slow and cumbersome to lend itself to comedy" ("George Eliot" 155). Taking particular offense at a passage where Eliot is "out of her element, as her clumsy satire of what she calls 'good society' proves," Woolf attacks the following section from *The Mill on the Floss*: "Good society has its claret and its velvet carpets, its dinner engagements six weeks deep, its opera, and its faery ball rooms . . . gets its science done by Faraday and its religion by the superior clergy who are to be met in the best houses; how should it have need of belief and emphasis?" (158). Woolf concludes that "There is no trace of humour or insight there, but only the vindictiveness of a grudge which we feel to be personal in its origin" (158). We, however, might well feel *Woolf's* comment to be personal, given her selection of a passage so effective in capturing the singular smugness of good society. Eliot's satire hits rather close to home, perhaps, and in this case seems to put her otherwise unusually insightful reader at the mercy of a pronouncement which can be summed up by saying "You're not to laugh at this because I declare that it is not funny." Despite such a declaration, Eliot remains an admirable satirist. Indeed, Eliot's passage combines both insight and humor, and blends them both with ample vindictiveness and the hint of a grudge. This gives a particular flavor to her fiction which is clearly not to every taste. Given that the marriage between humor and vindictiveness is representative of Eliot's prose, she is often read as an author divided against herself. Like Will Ladislaw from *Middlemarch*, Eliot appears to be "divided between the impulse to laugh aloud and the equally unseasonable impulse to burst into scornful invective" (237). Unlike Will, however, Eliot manages to combine laughter and invective effectively.

The Spectator's 1872 review of *Middlemarch*, for example, finds what it calls Eliot's "harsh, caustic tone" disturbing. It cites as its example a paragraph in which Eliot drives home a point about the social organization of a small branch of society by describing the subtext to a scene from the bible:

> When the animals entered the Ark in pairs, one may imagine
> that allied species made much private remark of each other, and
> were tempted to think that so many forms feeding on the same
> store of fodder were eminently superfluous, as tending to diminish the rations. (I fear the part played by the vultures on that occasion would be too painful for art to represent, those birds

being disadvantageously naked about the gullet, and apparently without rites and ceremonies). (Eliot, 365)

Eliot anthropomorphizes the Ark's inhabitants in such a way that they do not symbolize a community bound by hope and promised salvation but instead represent a petty, Hobbesian crowd, made bitter by fear and presided over by birds of prey. The picture is humorous, but not pretty. The commentary is ungenerous, but then so is the object of the narrator's humor. The vultures, like the creators of humor, show disrespect for rites and ceremonies, yet in essence act on the whispered desires and fears of the rest of the group.

In response, *The Spectator* rails that "[s]entences such as these give an occasional impression that George Eliot really likes jeering at human evil, which it is most painful to imagine in one who has so noble and so high a conception of good" (Carroll, 82). "Jeering" is a reductive but not inappropriate label for much of Eliot's sarcastic wit, and it is certainly applicable to this passage in particular.

Like Austen's Darcy, Eliot's gentlemen wish to reserve the right to be treated with a solemnity befitting their superior position. But even in an illumination of that superior position, George Eliot's sacrilegious humor cannot be disregarded. We must read satire into such remarks: "A man's mind —what there is of it—has always the advantage of being masculine—as the smallest birch-tree is of a higher kind than the most soaring palm—and even his ignorance is of a sounder quality . . . [A] kind Providence furnishes the limpest personality with a little gum or starch in the form of tradition" (*Middlemarch*, 44). Although Tom would have thrust his sword at such a remark (even at the risk of slicing up his other foot), Eliot unhesitatingly asserts the folly of a system which automatically rates the masculine more highly than it rates the feminine. For example, Maggie learns early that while girls possess a "great deal of superficial cleverness," they are unable to "go far into anything. They're quick and shallow" (*Mill on the Floss* 220). When Tom's schoolmaster reassures him that despite her obvious abilities, Maggie is necessarily inferior to her brother, Maggie is suitably mortified. Eliot tells us that "She had been so proud to be called 'quick' all her little life, and now it appeared that this quickness was the brand of inferiority" (220). In other words, Maggie learns that authority works against her.

We can see, then, that when Maggie laughs at Tom, she laughs at his wish to appear "genuinely" authoritative—her laughter shrinks the base of power upon which he attempts to stand. Whether or not this is what Maggie intended, it is certainly the effect. Tom's furious response is called out by his instinctive understanding of her reaction—he knows, even if she does not, that she is laughing at the sacred objects of male culture. It is as if Maggie embodies the dangerous position later outlined by Helene Cixous and

Catherine Clement in *The Newly Born Woman*. By threatening "the stability of the masculine structure," which passes itself off as "eternal-natural," by "conjuring up from femininity the reflections and hypotheses that are necessarily ruinous for the stronghold still in possession of authority" (65), Eliot apparently chooses chaos over culture (if these are the only two positions open).[2]

Finally, in light of Tom's injury, Maggie wishes she had supressed her laughter. She feels guilty, but then guilt is nothing new to her. Maggie, as a number of critics have noted, is expert in guilt because indeed she is expert at transgression. She is caught in an emotional snare with Tom, bound by hate and competition as well as by love and need, and her rage manifests itself through a number of impulsive actions which no doubt loom particularly large in the landscape of childhood. For example, Maggie starved her beloved brother's rabbits to death, licked the paint off his lozenge-box, let the boat drag his fish line down, and pushed her head through his kite "all for nothing" (88). Her guilt on these occasions does not, however, prevent them from recurring, and so it is clear to the reader that they are not "all for nothing." Repetition of these distressing events underscores their meaning; the "all for nothing" itself becomes comic because it is clearly inaccurate. Maggie's apparently inadvertent destruction of all those things her brother holds dear is no more her "fault" than her sense of the ridiculous is her "fault." If she is to be blamed for her rage, she is also to be blamed for her laughter. They are equally unmanning to Tom. Tom punishes Maggie for these sins but since Tom is as rule-bound as Maggie is unruly, neither can expect to live happily. Indeed, the lack of situational ethics or judgments is at the heart of much of Eliot's humor since she stresses that any rigidly rule-bound position reflects not natural justice, but rather the blinkered vision of the believer. Eliot systematically undercuts authority by mocking its very voice.

It should be noted that both Mary Jacobus and Margaret Homans give persuasive and profoundly important readings of Maggie's defiant relationship to authority. Jacobus, in "The Question of Language: Men of Maxims and *The Mill on the Floss*," constructs an argument for reading Eliot through the lens of Irigaray's testimony to sexual difference in language. Jacobus quotes Irigaray at length concerning the "playful repetition" (40) available to the woman writer who, in order to be able to represent herself, must assume a "stance of dissociation and resistance" to the prevailing order and so remain "outside" the order. How, then, can she speak at all? Jacobus cites Irigaray: "To play with mimesis, is, therefore, for a woman, to attempt to recover the place of her exploitation by discourse, without letting herself be simply reduced to it. . . . [If] women mime so well, they do not simply reabsorb themselves in this function. *They also remain elsewhere*" (author's italics, *Question* 40). Even when the woman appears to repeat or mime, she

85

inevitably mimics and mocks. "Error . . . must creep in where there's a story to tell," Jacobus writes, "especially a woman's story" (48). Homans, in her article "Eliot, Wordsworth and the Scene of the Sisters' Instruction," explores most specifically Eliot's literalization of Wordsworthian themes in *The Mill on the Floss,* but her ideas are useful in terms of their emphasis on Eliot's fascination with repetition which, she argues, is part of a larger gendered response to authority and language. "The temptation to silence or rote repetition is an especially feminine one, a temptation to docility and self-supression" (70), writes Homans. Homans also argues that the more literal the repetition by a woman, the further language moves from masculine authoritative discourse (71). The most literal repetition, then, is still a form of challenge in the mouth of a woman.

And repetition of the language of the powerful by the powerless is a staple for much humor, particularly satire. For example, to have an angry, starving worker repeat, *verbatim,* the speech made by a fat businessman is to produce a form of satire without changing a word of text. Universal maxims throughout Eliot are regarded in the unwavering light of satire; the authoritative voice is relentlessly mocked. In *Middlemarch,* a mob of people ridicule a poorly prepared speech by merely repeating the speaker's words until they lose their meaning. The gesture of imitation is not flattering but viciously challenging: "The most innocent echo has an impish mockery in it when it follows a gravely persistent speaker, and this echo was not at all innocent; if it did not follow with the precision of a natural echo, it had a wicked choice of the words it overtook" (548). In just such a way does the woman writer parody and, by extension, challenge authority. Eliot's heroines use humor to combat the restrictions of their roles. Their defiance often cloaks itself in wit and their anger appears cross-dressed as laughter. Eliot uses humor to underscore her refusal to create that particularly confusing oxymoron: the mimetic novel. As Penny Boumelha rightly notes concerning Eliot, the novels are forced to the point where "realism must yield to something else" (26), where the very form of the novel is "hard up against the limits of its own realism" (29), and where the "dammed-up energy created by the frustrated ambitions and desires, intellectual and sexual, of the [central female characters] is so powerful that it cannot be contained within the forms of mimesis" (30).

Eliot's repeated concern with the ways that women smash against the walls of their emotional and sexual containment echoes Boumelha's remark. Eliot's concern is enhanced, I believe, by her treatment of the issue with deft and defiant wit. Humor shapes her metaphors and delineates her central concerns. The confinement of her female characters might take the shape of the newlywed who discovers that "having once embarked on your marital voyage, it is impossible not to be aware that you make no way and that the sea is not within sight—that in fact, you are exploring an enclosed basin" (*Mill on the Floss* 228); or take the shape of Mrs. Tulliver who

> had lived thirteen years with her husband, yet . . . retained in all the freshness of her early married life a facility of saying things which drove him in the opposite direction to the one she desired. Some minds are wonderful for keeping their bloom in this way, as a patriarchal goldfish apparently retains to the last its youthful illusion that it can swim in a straight line beyond the encircling glass. Mrs. Tulliver was an amiable fish of this kind, and after running her head against the same resisting medium for thirteen years would go at it again to-day with undulled alacrity. (*Mill on the Floss* 134)

The passage dealing with Mrs. Tulliver's remarkable gift is worth noting in full for a number of reasons. The image of the goldfish repeatedly pushing against the glass of its artificial container echoes the image of marriage as an enclosed basin where, we presume, the newlywed suddenly pushes up against the walls of containment instead of heading out towards a limitless journey. In addition, it is clear that both images evoke a sense of water as a primitive force which seeks to burst any barrier, as does any primitive force, including passion. It is also crucial to note the characteristic pattern of Eliot's humor in this passage. She sets up this section by invoking the spirit of the conventionally domestic narrative when she writes that Mrs. Tulliver "had lived thirteen years with her husband, yet she retained in all the freshness of her early married life a facility of saying things . . ." so that it is only when we get to the jarring words "which drove him in the opposite direction to the one she desired" that we see Eliot undercut both the conventional and the domestic in one stroke. Words like "retain," "freshness," "early married life," and "facility" suggest that we might expect a happy ending to the sentence. This expectation is undone by the actual details of the Tullivers' relationship. To compare Mrs. Tulliver to a goldfish (women are compared to fishes in a number of unflattering ways in several of Eliot's novels), and to say that she would keep hitting her head against a glass wall with "undulled alacrity" is to position her humorously but nevertheless immutably, as one whose authority will collapse under its own weight. She is a character controlled by habit, one whose mechanical movements prevent her from adapting to the world. She is, therefore, a fit object for humor because she refuses to admit the possibility of change. Eliot is italicizing the nature of unexamined and inefficient habit rather than poking fun at the nature of a pathetic creature. Mrs. Tulliver's so-called "natural" behavior is learned; this is where she parts company with the patriarchal goldfish. Given that she has learned to act a certain way, clearly she can alter her behavior. We are, therefore, permitted by the author to be amused by Mrs. Tulliver's lack of self-knowledge.

Under the guise of "natural" behavior, Mrs. Tulliver conceals a complicated emotional life built on stubbornness, narrow ideas and distressing compulsions. But we are warned against judging *too* quickly. Even nature itself, Eliot argues in *The Mill on the Floss*, "has the deep cobbing which hides itself under the appearance of openness, so that simple people think they can see through her quite well, and all the while she is secretly preparing a refutation of their confident prophecies" (85). As we have seen, the repeated refutation of their confident prophecies is the structuring principle of Eliot's novels. Her ironic narrative stance, is one of Eliot's most effective weapons against the blockade of public or so-called natural authority. Even nature is presented as an intricate text, with multiple and possibly deceptive encodings which need to be deciphered carefully. Indeed, nature seems "unnatural" in its inherent inaccessibility, identified by Eliot as a locus of conflict instead of a common meeting ground. By examining the concept of nature in such detail, Eliot redefines what we mean by the very term. Her humor articulates the tension in what presents itself as "natural" although it is, in fact, nothing less than a formal framework for consensus opinion.

Eliot repeatedly alerts the reader to the shifting and subjective basis for all received wisdom. As the narrator of *The Mill on the Floss* summarizes, "if you deliver an opinion at all, it is mere stupidity not to do it with an air of conviction and well-founded knowledge. You make it your own in uttering it, and naturally you get fond of it" (76). In this aphorism, Eliot illustrates the manner in which authority is assumed. In addition, she illustrates the way that confidence in the rightness of a particular vision depends more on the self-confidence of the individual uttering it than it depends on any objective truth. Mary Jacobus's argument once again proves useful in unpacking this complex narrative mechanism. She claims that Eliot's central narrative formula in the novel serves to uncover "the divide between language or maxims of the dominant culture and the language itself which undoes them" (43). Jacobus adds that Eliot "drastically undermines the realist illusion of her fictional world, revealing it to be no more than a blank page inscribed with a succession of arbitrary metaphoric substitutions" (43). In other words, when Eliot draws attention to the very rhetoric she employs to enforce an air of verisimilitude, she destroys that verisimilitude.

This is especially true in scenes where Eliot discusses language as the mechanism which creates our vision of the universe. In this often-quoted passage, Eliot renders explicit her concern with the thought that all language is, ultimately, figurative, while calling our attention to the "different result one gets by changing the metaphor":

It was doubtless an ingenious idea to call the camel the ship of the desert, but it would hardly lead one far in training that useful beast. O Aristotle! if you had had the advantage of being "the freshest modern" instead of the greatest ancient, would you not have mingled your praise of metaphorical speech as a sign of high intelligence, with a lamentation that intelligence so rarely shows itself in speech without metaphor, —that we can so seldom declare what a thing is, except by saying it is something else? (209)

Jacobus comments that "an eye for resemblances . . . is also here a satiric eye," as well as noting that "the price one pays for such freedom is the recognition that language, thus viewed, is endlessly duplicitous rather than single-minded" (48). As Boumelha reflects in her article "George Eliot and the End of Realism," these moments, when Eliot "pauses a little to allow a consideration of the kind of writing in which the novel is engaged," serve to "undermine any pretensions the work may have to that 'illusionism' held to be typical of realism" by "interspersing a narrative with a discussion of the principles on which it is constructed and organized" (20). The humor in Eliot's fiction also serves to highlight this disparity between (to use Boumelha's phrase) the "neutral transcription of a pre-existing reality" (21) and the forging of a text that is, in its questioning of the inherited script, inexorably self-reflexive and self-conscious. The narrative repeatedly returns to examine itself, intensifying the reader's awareness that what is being explored is explicitly a construction, not a reflection, of a necessarily limited reality. In other words, in fiction as in marriage—as we have already seen—one is "exploring an enclosed basin." In her refusal to create a fictional world that holds a mirror up to nature (even if she occasionally asserts that such a goal is desirable), Eliot instead underscores the novel's own textuality and she exaggerates certain plot elements at the expense of others. For example, the ending of *The Mill on the Floss* has been berated time and again, by critics contemporary to Eliot and ones contemporary to ourselves, for its "unrealistic" flourish. But there is in Eliot an identifiably feminine concern with closure, whether in a narrative or in a more obvious construction: "Tom could build perfect pyramids of houses; but Maggie's would never bear the laying-on of the roof: —it was always so with the things that Maggie made, and Tom had deduced the conclusion that no girls could ever make anything" (146). In a similar fashion, Maggie does not finish certain books she begins to read. *Corinne* she dismisses because she anticipates an ending of which she cannot approve, and of *The Pirate* she says: "I went on with it in my own head, and I made several endings; but they were all unhappy. I could never make a happy ending out of that beginning" (401).

Yet Eliot's satire is based more on reduction than exaggeration; she grapples with the minutiae of experience in order to cast a satiric light on the largest issues. The "enclosed basin" of the text offers no outlet to the sea, but nevertheless in it one can see framed issues of great significance. We have already seen that Maggie's laughter at Tom's weaponry contains the essential elements of feminine refusal and masculine demand. Eliot's ability to reduce the play of dynamics between characters to their essential qualities is a hallmark of her insurgent humor. She provides the background to a character's thoughts or words and in doing so proclaims them objects to be debased rather than valued. For example, Tom might appear most noble in being "very fond of his sister," and meaning "always to take care of her," except for the succeeding information that looking after his sister means that he intends to "make her his housekeeper, and punish her when she did wrong" (92). The same pattern recurs throughout *The Mill on the Floss*, a subtle but ubiquitous threat to the propagation of appearances. We find that Mrs. Tulliver applauds Lucy Deane as "such a good child" only to find that "such a good child" translates into the following: "you may set her on a stool, and there she'll sit for an hour together and never offer to get off" (96). The aegis under which the comment is made may seem grand, but its practical aspect is comic in its pettiness, in the smallness of its application.

Tom's teacher, Mr. Stelling, is one of the chief representatives of patriarchal authority. He is chosen to usher young Tulliver into the confines of a suitable education, but Stelling's own view of the universe is less than imaginative, original or valid. Stelling reproduces unhesitatingly the litany of received wisdom, since he remains "very far from being led astray by enthusiasm, either religious or intellectual." Stelling maintains all the correct assumptions, believing that "religion was a very excellent thing, and Aristotle a great authority, and deaneries and prebends useful institutions, and Great Britain the providential bulwark of Protestantism, and faith in the unseen a great support to afflicted minds," in other words, upholding every virtue of the system. But once again Eliot renders comic and undercuts the authority of the initial description by supplying the following punch-line: "he believed in all these things as a Swiss hotel keeper believes in the beauty of the scenery around him, and in the pleasure it gives to artistic visitors" (207). This ultimate judgment of Stelling makes his opinions appear self-serving and second-hand rather than dispassionate and intellectually objective. What appears at first to be firm belief founded on scholarship and spiritual study turns out to be a cultural package-deal, marketed widely and geared toward the indiscriminate consumer: "All gentlemen learn the same things" (236). (The "same things that all gentlemen learn" are illuminated in *Middlemarch* by the statement: "A liberal education had of course left him free to read the indecent passages in the school classics" [173].) Tom wants to know only the authorized version of things; he disparages his sis-

ter's imaginative outpourings by defining them as "girls' stories": "My sister
Maggie is always wanting to tell me stories but they're stupid stories. Girls'
stories always are" (237). Eliot's humor in these passages is a reminder of the
need to examine, rather than purchase wholesale, such commodified, conventional wisdom.

The power behind conventional wisdom relies, Eliot suggests, on its
mindless appropriation by individuals for their own purposes. Stelling
doesn't have to think about what he teaches, for example. "How should Mr.
Stelling be expected to know that an education was a delicate and difficult
business?" inquires the narrator, apparently giving Stelling the benefit of
the doubt in his limited abilities. But again the punch-line deflates the apparent generosity of the initial remark: "any more than an animal endowed
with a power of boring a hole through a rock should be expected to have
wide views of excavation" (241).

In a similar manner, Maggie's uncle Mr. Glegg spends a great deal of
time with the bible, but in the volume he can only scout for answers to his
own particular problems: the "subject of meditation was the 'contrariness'
of the female mind, as typically exhibited in Mrs Glegg" (187). He ponders
the concept of creation as a process leading unswervingly to his wife: "That
a creature made—in a genealogical sense—out of a man's rib, and in this
particular case maintained in the highest respectability without any trouble
of her own, should be normally in a state of contradiction to the blandest
propositions and even to the most accommodating concessions, was a mystery in the scheme of things to which he had often in vain sought a clue in
the early chapters of Genesis" (187). In Glegg's hands the bible becomes a
marriage manual.

Eliot's humorous treatment of her characters' appropriation of texts
braids together various strands of the narrative. For example, Tom's hated
Latin grammar becomes, in Maggie's hands, a delightful toy; he hates it because it is imposed on him, and he is depressed by the weight of its authority.
She adores it because she can both play with its language and refuse to acknowledge its weight. Maggie has an almost clandestine relationship with
the sacred texts of male learning and her acquaintance with Latin is placed
in a humorous frame. In creating this provocative scene of intelligent-girl-
meets-supposedly-inaccessible-masculine-text, Eliot can indicate the ambiguity inherent in such a meeting. In a moment prefiguring the criticism that
will be aimed at feminist scholars in generations to come, Maggie feels no
remorse in taking information "out of context," thereby showing her disregard for the cultural apparatus set up to protect the sacred word from such
scavengers as herself. "The fragmentary examples were her favorites,"
offers Eliot, who reveals that Maggie has no qualms about being preoccupied with:

> [T]hese mysterious sentences snatched from an unknown context, —like strange horns of beasts and leaves of unknown plants, brought from some far-off region, gave boundless scope to her imagination, and were all the more fascinating because they were in a peculiar tongue of their own, which she could learn to interpret. It was really very interesting—the Latin Grammar that Tom had said no girls could learn: and she was proud because she found it interesting. (217)

But then Maggie has grown up stealing the language, raiding books the way Eve raided the orchard, taking what is not properly her own in order to appropriate the parts she finds fascinating or useful. In one of the novel's earliest revelations of Maggie's character, we are given her interpretation of a text deemed "not quite the right book for a little girl" (67), Defoe's *History of the Devil.* Maggie is drawn to Defoe—"I can't help looking at it"—because she is puzzled by the premise by which the "old woman in the water" is judged. As Maggie knowledgeably explains, to the chagrin of her father's friend, "they've put her in, to find out whether she's a witch or no, and if she swims she's a witch, and if she's drowned—and killed, you know,—she's innocent, and not a witch, but only a poor silly old woman." But, in a line whose irony becomes apparent only in retrospect, Maggie asks the simple but crucial question "what good would it do her then, you know, when she was drowned?" She goes on to explain that the figure with "his arms akimbo, laughing" is "'the devil really' (here Maggie's voice became louder and more emphatic)" in the guise he must assume to be accepted in society because "if people saw he was the devil, and he roared at 'em, they'd run away, and he couldn't make 'em do what he pleased" (67). The devil must assume a pleasing shape in the same way that nature must present an apparently simple canvas, or a woman must assume a conventional pose—in order to hide the secret preparations progressing beneath the surface which, when they appear, will first refute and then reinvent the confident prophecies of the dominant discourse.

Like Jane Austen's Elizabeth Bennett or Charlotte Bronte's Jane Eyre, Maggie Tulliver grows up relying on her humor. She can get away with refusing to do her patchwork and dragging her bonnet on the floor, much to her mother's displeasure, because she can get her father to "laugh audibly" despite her mother's protests at his response: "'I wonder at you, as you'll laugh at her, Mr Tulliver,' said the mother, with lymphatic fretfulness in her tone. 'You encourage her i' naughtness'" (61). But the laughter Maggie provokes by her defiance is not always supportive. When she begs Tom to cut her mass of dark, unruly hair, she thinks only of her "deliverance from her teasing hair and teasing remarks about it," as well as about "the triumph she should have over her mother and her aunts by this very decided course of action" (121). But when Tom, who is delighted to cut her hair and equally delighted by the mess he makes of the job, laughs at her and says that she resembles "the idiot we throw our nutshells to at school," Maggie has a "bitter sense of the irrevocable" (121). She tells Tom not to laugh at her, but he refuses to stop, despite her protests. She cannot, as Tom does in the equivalent situation, draw a sword to prove her seriousness; she absorbs his laughter and translates it into her pain.

Maggie's refusal to comply with the ceremonies of femininity and her desire to triumph through her cleverness provide several scenes that are both comic and indicative of the ways in which intelligent women are regarded by their peers. These passages illustrate that although "the only great pleasure" certain restrictions allow is "the pleasure of breaking [them]" (162), such pleasure is not without consequence. Maggie wishes to be "a clever woman," but Tom slices through her ambition with the remark that reduces "clever woman" to "a nasty, conceited thing. Everybody'll hate you" (216). Maggie faces the additional problem associated solely with women: the problem that Wakem explains in no uncertain terms to Philip: "We don't ask what a woman does, we ask whom she belongs to" (543). Such a narrowly reasoned, widely accepted "wisdom" will not allow for the accomplishments of women, and will judge them solely by "ownership." Any gesture of self-assertion or self-congratulation, even when the gesture is made in order to help another, is denigrated. When, for example, Maggie suggests that she might be able to help Tom learn his lessons, she must go back on her words with the excuse so often used by women after they have made a remark rebuked by their listener: "'I was only joking,' said Maggie, putting her cheek against his coat sleeve" (319). (As Fay Weldon will make clear a hundred years later, the line "I was only joking" should be followed by "but of course she wasn't" [*Down Among the Women* 88].) As a child, Maggie laughs and provokes laughter. As an adult, her responses are far more guarded.

Maggie's passionate childhood-self permits her to be described as "a small Medusa with her snakes cropped" (161), reminding us of Cixous's comments about the figure of the Medusa whose laughter transfigures her world so that "you have only to look at the Medusa straight on to see her. And she's not deadly. She's beautiful and she's laughing" (255). Nina Auerbach argues that Maggie's "turbulent hair that is her bane as a child is an emblem of the destructive powers she is only half aware of and unable to control. . . . The traditionally demonic connotations of unruly hair are reinforced by Maggie's life" (47). Passionate Maggie chooses to run away to the gypsies only to find that "any thing was better than going with one of the dreadful men alone: it would be more cheerful to be murdered by a larger party" (178). But Maggie's adult-self is, in the words of Philip Wakem, hidden under a veil of "dull quiescence" (428). Philip once believed that Maggie would grow up to be "a brilliant woman—all wit and bright imagination" (428) but discovers instead a woman desperately trying to suppress her wit and imagination along with her desire and sexuality. Maggie tries to make herself into one of the "happiest women" who, "like the happiest nations, have no history" (494). But, as the narrator points out, there is more to the creation of character than character itself. In a passage of sharp humor and grave irreverence, Eliot suggests that:

> For the tragedy of our lives is not created entirely from within. "Character"—says Novalis, in one of his questionable aphorisms—"character is destiny." But not the whole of our destiny. Hamlet, Prince of Denmark, was speculative and irresolute, and we have a great tragedy in consequence. But if his father had lived to a good old age, and his uncle had died an early death, we can conceive Hamlet's having married Ophelia and got through life with a reputation of sanity notwithstanding many soliloquies, and some moody sarcasms towards the fair daughter of Polonius, to say nothing of the frankest incivility to his father-in-law. (514)

As we can see from this passage, the narrator gradually absorbs the responsibility for the creation of humor in the text. As a child, Maggie cultivates and thrives on her defiance and wit. As an adult, she learns to suppress these qualities, although she cannot forego them altogether. Where initially we would laugh at Maggie's antics or smile in surprise at her outspokenness (when young Maggie, for example, "subsequently pumped [sauce] on the bonnet with its green ribbons so as to give it a general resemblance to a sage cheese garnished with withered lettuces. I must urge in excuse for Maggie that Tom had laughed at her in the bonnet" [115] or when she asks Stelling whether all astronomers hate women), in the later volumes we rely on the narrator's subtle but nevertheless humorous commentary to explore the territory of defiance where Maggie once led us.

As the novel progresses, there is less laughing at Maggie's instigation or expense, and more wry amusement at the larger issues being raised by the text: questions of morality, character and the function of literature itself. We are told by the narrator that the local "religion was of a simple, semi-pagan kind, but there was no heresy in it, if heresy properly means choice, for they didn't know there was any other religion, except that of chapel-goers, which appeared to run in families, like asthma. . . . The vicar of their pleasant rural parish was not a controversialist, but a good hand at whist, and one who had a joke always ready for a blooming female parishioner" (364). The humor in this passage derives from Eliot's use of a discourse that owes more to the anthropologist than the literary critic, a tactic Eliot frequently employs. When the narrator informs the reader that "a female Dodson, when in 'strange houses,' always ate dry bread with her tea," or that "it is remarkable that while no individual Dodson was satisfied with any other individual Dodson, each was satisfied, not only with him or herself, but with the Dodsons collectively" (*The Mill on the Floss* 97), it sounds as if what is being recorded is fieldwork on some sort of primitive tribe. No doubt this is precisely the effect Eliot seeks: positioning the "Dodsons" as a tribe with strange ceremonial customs and dietary taboos dismantles the familiar domestic framework and thereby renders the Dodson an exotic and eccentric creature. While Eliot stops short of actual ridicule, the Dodsons are certainly moving targets for Eliot's wit. Nina Auerbach comments that "As for the Dodsons, occasional pious commentary about their honest virtues does not obscure the narrator's glee at the overwhelming ridiculousness of Aunt Pullet and Aunt Glegg and their muttering husbands" (45).

Eliot often transposes human behavior and animal behavior. If the Dodson is a rare "creature," actual creatures are often imbued with human frailties and concerns: "spiders were especially a subject of speculation with her: she wondered if they had any relations outside the mill, for in that case there must be a painful difficulty in their family intercourse: a fat and floury spider, accustomed to take his fly well dusted with meal, must suffer a little at a cousin's table where the fly was *au natural*, and the lady spiders must be mutually shocked at each other's appearance" (80). Eliot's humor also depends on the narrator's or characters' ability to alter perspectives radically as well as on the juxtaposition of dissonant images. Mr. Pullet, for example, is said to bear "about the same relation to his tall, good-looking wife, with her balloon sleeves, abundant mantle and large be-feathered and be-ribboned bonnet, as a small fishing-smack bears to a brig with all its sails spread" (111). In the same spirit, Bob's wife is described as "a tiny woman, with the general physiognomy of a Dutch doll, looking, in comparison with Bob's mother who filled up the passage in the rear, very much like one of those human figures which the artist finds conveniently standing near a colossal statue to show the proportions" (499). Eliot plays with reader expectations in her choice of analogies, but the center of her humor remains focused on perspective and the very notion of subjective perception.

During Maggie's commentary on *Corinne*, for example, we laugh at her *reductio ad absurdam* vision of dark-haired versus light-haired women. She makes herself out to be a "prejudiced reader" who is unable to accept the plot which dicates, in this instance, the triumph of the fair-haired lady. She is being deliberately humorous in her remarks, but the underlying issues of sexual attraction and romantic triumph are deadly serious, given her subsequent involvement with Stephen Guest. When Philip Wakem begins their discussion of *Corinne* by asking Maggie if she would like to be a tenth muse, Maggie offers humor in reply rather than the anticipated feminine sequence of modest blush, denial and acceptance of a compliment: "'Not at all,' said Maggie, laughing. 'The Muses were uncomfortable goddesses, I think—obliged always to carry rolls and musical instruments about with them. If I carried a harp in this climate, you know, I must have a green baize cover for it—and I should be sure to leave it behind me by mistake.'" She admits to Philip that she could not finish the book he had so eagerly lent her because "'[A]s soon as I came to the blond-haired young lady reading in the park, I shut it up and determined to read no further." She continues her explanation as follows:

> "I foresaw that that light complexioned girl would win away all the love from Corinne and make her miserable. I'm determined to read no more books where the blond haired women carry away all the happiness. I should begin to have a prejudice against them—If you could give me some story, now, where the dark woman triumphs, it would restore the balance—I want to avenge Rebecca and Flora Mad-Ivor, and Minna and all the rest of the dark unhappy ones. Since you are my tutor you ought to preserve my mind from prejudices, you are always arguing against prejudices."
>
> "Well, perhaps you will avenge the dark women in your own person: —carry away all the love from your cousin Lucy. She is sure to have some handsome young man of St. Ogg's at her feet now—and you have only to shine upon him—your fair little cousin will be quite quenched in your beams." (433)

Maggie, usually so alert to a witty remark and able to respond accordingly, has all the humor driven out of her by Philip's remark. In the manner of a number of female characters who will respond with more or less the same sentiments, Maggie understands that beneath the masculine joke is a rebuke:

> "Maggie," said Philip, with surprise, "it is not like you to take playfulness literally. You must have been in St. Ogg's this morning, and brought away a slight infection of dullness."
>
> "Well," said Maggie, smiling, "if you meant that for a joke, it was a poor one; but I thought it was a very good reproof." (433)

She responds to the reproof rather than to the humor in Philip's remark. In doing so, she privileges the subtext over the text in the same way that the novel's narrator uses humor to veil her own concerns, or the way nature hides its complex structure under a guise of simplicity.

A parallel can be drawn to the way in which critics have dealt with their frustrations at the finale of *The Mill on the Floss*, where Maggie and Tom are reunited only to perish in a sudden flood. In the same way that many readers balked at Austen's endings, arriving at the conclusion, like Tom Tulliver, "that no girls could ever make anything" (146), many critics have read only the surface text and shaken their heads at yet another woman's inability to come to a reasonable, believable conclusion. Yet, of course, Eliot has prepared us for the conclusion from the first lines of the novel, as a number of critics also note.[3] For example, we might well have been amused at her expense when Mrs. Tulliver moaned and whined "aloud, without reflecting that there was no one to hear her" in all her maternal foolishness that " '[t]hey're such children for the water, mine are. . . . They'll be brought in dead and drowned some day" (166), yet clearly Eliot both encourages us first to laugh and then to rethink our laughter by the end of the novel. Indeed, the narrative structure itself for Eliot seems to offer the very sort of restrictions to demand the insurrections of satire, irony and wit. Gillian Beer makes a similar point in her article " 'The Dark Woman Triumphs': Passion in *The Mill on the Floss*." Beer claims that "[d]esire in this society cannot be satisfied. Maggie gives expression to desires which cannot be contained in any of the social forms available: " 'I was never satisfied with a little of anything,' she says to Philip, in renouncing him" (134). By drawing our attention to Maggie's irrepressible drive for what the world considers excess—which is only what Maggie considers needful—Beer offers a way to bring Maggie's obstinate appetites into line with all her transgressive energies. And these appetites and energies, finally, mock the limitations of narrative structure itself. Interestingly Woolf, too, focuses on Maggie's appetites and transgressive energies without acknowledging Eliot's crafting of a character who cannot be contained. Woolf declares that "humor controls [Maggie] and keeps her lovable so long as she is small and can be satisfied by eloping with the gipsies or hammering nails into her doll; but she develops; and before George Eliot knows what has happened she has a full-grown woman on her hands demanding what neither gipsies, nor dolls, nor St. Ogg's itself is capable of giving her" ("George Eliot" 158).

Middlemarch resembles *The Mill on the Floss* in several ways, not the least of which is the creation of a rhetorical stance which repeatedly and often wittily demonstrates the limitations of narrative structure. The question of fate is translated into a textual matter, with Destiny as the rather ungenerous and untrustworthy narrator and author: "Destiny stands by sarcastic with our *dramatis personae* folded in her hand" (*Middlemarch* 122). If all of destiny is sarcastic, then we can certainly frame much of *Middlemarch* as satiric without offering excessive apologies.

It is once again useful to turn to what Woolf has to say about Eliot, this time in relation to *Middlemarch*. There is a particularly significant section in *A Room of One's Own* in which Woolf counsels women writers to "learn to laugh, without bitterness, at the vanities—say rather at the peculiarities, for it is a less offensive word—of the other sex" (94). She goes on to discuss the need for the unique perspective offered by humor, since "there is a spot the size of a shilling at the back of the head which one can never see for oneself. It is one of the good offices that sex can discharge for sex—to describe that spot the size of a shilling at the back of the head . . . that dark place at the back of the head!" (94). Woolf believes that if a woman writer were "very brave and very honest, she would go behind the other sex and tell us what she found there. A true picture of man as a whole can never be painted until a woman has described that spot the size of a shilling," and she then offers Mr. Casaubon as a primary example of a spot "of that size and nature" (94). Woolf makes it clear that she considers mere scorn and ridicule of men futile, but instead implores women to "Be truthful . . . and the result is bound to be amazingly interesting. Comedy is bound to be enriched. New facts are bound to be discovered" (94–95). I want to argue that Eliot does an exemplary job of detailing the "spot" known as Casaubon, and in fact offers precisely the sort of "true picture" available only through wit, not only of Casaubon but of *Middlemarch* society as a whole.

Lydgate's philosophies concerning science may be more sophisticated than Casaubon's, for example, but the primitive state of his thoughts on women bonds the two men in a brotherhood of ignorance. Summarized by the narrator as a belief in "the psychological difference between what for the sake of variety I will call goose and gander," Lydgate's psuedo-scientific "psychological differences" are transposed onto the cliched "goose and gander" (*Middlemarch* 391). The narrator's comment—"what *for the sake of variety I will call* goose and gander"—draws attention to the highly unoriginal nature of Lydgate's ideas (italics mine). The sentence ends with the narrator's explanation that Dr. Lydgate's philosophy arrives at the unsurprising belief that there exists an "innate submissiveness of the goose . . . beautifully corresponding to the strength of the gander" (391). Reduced to the cliche, "what's good for the goose is *not* good for the gander," Lydgate's modern view on the psychological differences between the sexes in fact comes down to the following formula: men should rule and women should serve. So much for modern psychology. (Eliot makes a point of telling us that Lydgate is even less sympathetic to women he does not consider decorative: "Plain women he regarded as he did the other severe facts of life, to be faced with philosophy and investigated by science" [121].) In *Middlemarch*, as in *The Mill on the Floss*, Eliot's satire is based more on reduction than exaggeration. The way men diminish women by sorting them into groups and types, as we have just witnessed in Lydgate's case, is only one of Eliot's targets. The narrator's humor functions, as the auctioneer says of a pack of riddles, as "an amusement to sharpen the intellect; it has a sting" (*Middlemarch* 653).

Under the guise of creating an apparently realistic novel, Eliot once again subverts the narrative expectations. She uses humor to displace and defy convention, all the while veiling her defiance in much the same way that Mary Garth shields herself from anticipated masculine criticism. Mary, an intelligent and quick (in the best sense of the word) young woman, is driven to offer "playfulness" as a cover for what is more precisely her insight and clear vision. Explaining to an older friend (with the comforting name of Mr. Farebrother) why she cannot marry her beau Fred if he joins the clergy, she confesses that Fred would seem a "caricature" to her if he began "preaching and exhorting and pronouncing blessings" since to do so would be "a piece of professional affectation" (560). Mary has to provide an acceptable disguise for her honesty, however, and offers as a caveat the following: "What you say is most generous and kind; I don't mean for a moment to correct your judgement. It is only that I have my girlish, mocking way of looking at things" (560). Eliot, too, offers a "mocking way of looking at things" throughout *Middlemarch*.

The novel opens with the same sort of misleading "truth generally acknowledged" that ushers in *Pride and Prejudice*. *Middlemarch* begins: "Who that cares much to know the history of man . . . has not dwelt, at least briefly, on the life of Saint Theresa, has not smiled with some gentleness at the thought of the little girl walking forth one morning hand-in-hand with her still smaller brother, to go and seek martyrdom in the country of the Moors?" (25). One could easily answer the apparently rhetorical question by saying that no doubt many persons considering the history of man have not thought of *any* little girl. The sweeping statement is deliberately misleading. The prelude to *Middlemarch* goes on to deal explicitly with the limitations of literary convention because, as Eliot indicates with only measured playfulness, misleading conventions cannot accommodate the "indefiniteness with which the Supreme Power has fashioned the natures of women" (26).

Eliot's irony becomes more pointed as the narrator then proceeds to instruct the reader about the mysteries of the female sex. With mock patience, and with disingenuous wide-eyed earnestness, the narrator explains that the "limits of variation are really much wider than anyone would imagine from the sameness of women's coiffure and the favorite love-stories in prose and verse" (26). In doing so, she defines and satirizes the masculinist tradition which groups women according to their "level of feminine incompetence" (26). Men who assume women's lives are made up only of hairstyles and cheap romance are the object of the narrator's scorn. Rather than damning women, the narrator damns the men who imprison women in the straightjacket of conventional femininity. The narrator of *Middlemarch* often seems to speak "objectively" and in what many critics have therefore considered a masculine voice; yet it is clear upon close examination that, using irony like a saw, she cuts away at the base of patriarchal culture. Often-quoted aphoristic comments such as "A woman dictates before marriage in order that she may have an appetite for submission afterwards" (98), seem, when taken out of context, to support the view that Eliot was a woman who regarded members of her own sex with disdain. But this line must be read in light of the novel's clear refusal to support any such notion. There are no women in *Middlemarch* who choose to dictate in order to earn the right to submit; not even Rosamond fills this empty outline. To repeat this line out of context is the same as repeating Polonius's advice to Horatio without factoring in the overriding parodic sense that shapes the original scene.

At the novel's center is Dorothea. Presenting her as a naive young woman at best, one who is "enamoured of intensity and greatness, and rash in embracing whatever seemed to her to have those aspects; likely to seek martyrdom, to make retractions" (30), the initial description of this heroine might seem daunting, until we recognize the narrator's lack of ceremony when describing her spiritual longings. Dorothea appears as interested in the process of renunciation as Maggie Tulliver but without Maggie's obvious passions or desire for affection. It is not that Dorothea lacks a passionate or sensual nature, but that she believes herself to be beyond all but a few self-indulgences: "Riding was an indulgence which she allowed herself in spite of conscientious qualms; she felt that she enjoyed it in a pagan sensuous way, and always looked forward to renouncing it" (320). In contrast to Maggie's pranks and impulsiveness, we are shown Dorothea's resolution to live out her minutely-calculated emotional agenda. She knows exactly what sort of man she wants to marry, since she imagines that "the really delightful sort of marriage must be that where your husband was a sort of father, and could teach you Hebrew if you wished it" (32). The reader is made to feel, of course, that such a marriage could hardly be described as "really delightful." The phrase exposes as folly the heroine's matrimonial ambitions. Dorothea sets her cap on one of those "great men whose odd habits it would have been a glorious piety to endure" (32), reassuring herself that "she would have accepted the judicious Hooker, if she had been born in time to save him from that wretched mistake he made in matrimony; or John Milton when his blindness had come on" (32). Unlike Jane Eyre, Dorothea seeks not a man who becomes disabled by the end of the story, but one whose disability makes him desirable from the outset. We are told that Dorothea is short-sighted (she nearly steps on her sister's pet dog) and shown that, at least as far as men are concerned, her vision is as narrow as it is shallow.

Since she "could not reconcile the anxieties of a spiritual life involving eternal consequences, with a keen interest in guimpe and artificial protrusions of drapery" (30), Dorothea falls between the established categories of acceptable feminine behavior. Her wishes for moral and spiritual greatness at such an early age at least keep her from the ordinary course of events since "such elements in the character of a marriageable girl tended to interfere with her lot, and hinder it from being decided according to custom, by good looks, vanity and merely canine affection" (30). If custom, looks, vanity and "merely canine affection" are what control the destiny of most women, then at least Dorothea has saved herself in some manner from a dreadful fate that would not even have the dignity of being of her own choosing. Dorothea is "open, ardent, and not in the least self-admiring" (32). She is not preoccupied with the cultivation of suitors or flirtatious liaisons. It is in this that she diverges most significantly from the prescribed script, which would have an heiress seeking attentions from all the young squires in the province. Like Maggie, she hungers for the greatness but without notions of feminine rebellion to feed her imagination.

Eliot takes the enthusiastic, spiritually ambitious, emotionally charged, attractive and powerful young woman through the steps made familiar by earlier writers, and then presents us with what has been regarded as the appropriately happy ending: the heroine meets and marries a man some years her senior who will shape her ambitions to fit acceptable conventions and teach her to harness her energies for use as his helpmate. But there is a catch in *Middlemarch*. In the same way that *Othello* can be read as a comedy (overcoming parental objections, true love wins against all odds) until the moment that Othello admits the possibility of Desdemona's infidelity, the narrative of *Middlemarch* can been seen to follow the outlines of the plot which dictates the yoking of the independent woman into wifedom for the good of all—until the moment Dorothea admits the possibility that she has mistaken a dull old man for a wise leader. In overturning the romantic possibilities for such a pair, Eliot simultaneously overturns Casaubon's right to respect and homage. That is part of what leads Gilbert and Gubar to refer to Casaubon as "Eliot's extremely subversive portrait of male authority" (*The Madwoman in the Attic* 502). The limitations of Casaubon's abilities are legion: he fails in direct proportion to his pretensions.

Dorothea has attempted to forge for herself a heroic pantomime, where Casaubon is cast as Locke, Pascal, Aquinas, and other bulky historical figures. When Celia challenges Dorothea on the authenticity of her affections for the aging scholar, Dorothea is adamant in her refusal to be swayed from the hero she has created in Casaubon. When Celia cannot help but remark " 'How very ugly Mr Casaubon is,' " Dorothea defends him by claiming that "He is one of the most distinguished-looking men I ever saw."

Such a defense appears admirable until, in the pattern we saw recur throughout *The Mill on the Floss*, Eliot renders comic and undercuts the authority of the initial description by having Dorothea explain what she means: "He is remarkably like the portrait of Locke. He has the same deep eye-sockets." Her choice of details show that she has fastened her fancies onto a projection of her own desire rather than onto the man as he is. She thinks he is distinguished because he has eye-sockets similar to the ones of a distinguished man; a slim reason for adoration. When Celia counters with "Had Locke those two white moles with hairs on them?" Dorothea is reduced to sniffing "'Oh, I daresay! when people of a certain sort looked at him,' [and] walking away a little" (42). In exploring every aspect of Dorothea's attraction to Casaubon, the choice of words indicates less than overwhelming affection for the character; the opening section of the sentence sets up a premise which the latter part of the sentence wittily subverts. We discover, for example, during one of Casaubon's early visits to Dorothea that "He was all she had at first imagined him to be," only to learn that to Dorothea such an expectation translates into: "almost everything he said seemed like a specimen from a mine, or the inscription on the door of a museum" (55).

Casaubon is no better. In the foolishness of their expectations and projected desires these two are well-matched. He believes that "a man of good position should expect and carefully choose a blooming young lady" (312), which again seems reasonable because, despite his age and general unhealthiness, the desire for a young and beautiful wife seems inbred. But we find that Casaubon does not want a "blooming young lady" for even these reasons, but because "the younger the better, because more educable and submissive" (312). The coda is what is unforgivable. To give him credit, he does not disguise his wishes and explains fairly early on to Dorothea what he finds most attractive in women: "The great charm of your sex is its capability of an ardent, self-sacrificing affection" (73).

As she becomes progressively drawn to him, Dorothea's relationship with Casaubon parodies the teacher/lover duet and shows the fissures and faults inherent in such a plot. When Dorothea gushes that "there would be nothing trivial about our lives. Everyday-things with us would mean the greatest things," we find what she means is that "it would be like marrying Pascal. I should learn to see the truth by the same light as great men have seen it by" (51). Loving Locke's eye-sockets and living with someone like Pascal is hardly typical of love's young dream. Such a sentiment will be echoed in Virginia Woolf's *The Voyage Out*, when Rachel is both attracted and repelled by Richard Dalloway's kiss and when we are told that "there must be something wrong in this confusion between politics and kissing politicians" (83).

Dorothea is making the mistake that will color all feminine affection for the teacher/lover: confusing scholarship with kissing a scholar. If a man is loved not for himself alone but for his access to knowledge prohibited to women, he is in danger of becoming merely metonymic. He will be discovered like the Wizard of Oz, yelling for Dorothy/ea to ignore the man behind the curtain. If he is loved for any form of power—and knowledge is the most seductive of all these, thus rendering the teacher/lover a most enticing figure—he is in danger of losing that love once the source of power is discovered. If she realizes that he is not as intelligent, as informed or even as unique as he first appeared, he is lost.

We recognize that Casaubon is lost from the beginning, given the narrator's guiding commentary. Heading the chapter in which Casaubon proposes to Dorothea is the following excerpt from Burton's *Anatomy of Melancholy*, the irony of which is not even disguised, let alone concealed:

> Hard students are commonly troubled with gowts, catarrhs, rheums, cachexia, bradypepsia, bad eyes, stone, and collick, cruditites, oppilations, vertigo, winds, consumptions, and all such diseases as come by overmuch sitting: they are most part lean, dry, ill-coloured. . . and all through immoderate pains and extraordinary studies. (66)

The chapter then begins: "This was Mr Casaubon's letter" (66). His letter is so pretentious and unappealing to anyone except the heroine herself that it affords an occasion for laughter similar to the one provided by Mr. Collins's proposal in *Pride and Prejudice*. Who could resist love-making, the narrator seems to imply ironically, when it is phrased as lyrically as this: "For in the first hour of meeting you, I had an impression of your eminent and perhaps exclusive fitness to supply that need (connected, I may say, with such activity of the affections as even the preoccupations of a work too special to be abdicated could not uninterruptedly dissimulate); and each succeeding opportunity for observation has given the impression an added depth by convincing me more emphatically of the fitness which I had preconceived, and thus evoking more decisively those affections to which I have but now referred" (66). It is difficult to take such a passage seriously, and there are several comparable passages throughout the "courtship" period. The narrator's rhetorical strategies, however, alert the reader to the ambiguity in the presentation of Casaubon's declarations: he may be sincere, but he is nevertheless found wanting. Once again the first phrase of the sentence indicates a generous sentiment which the second phrase proceeds to unravel: "No speech could have been more thoroughly honest in its intention: the frigid rhetoric at the end was as sincere as the bark of a dog or the crowing of an amorous rook" (73). (In *The Madwoman in the Attic* Gilbert and Gubar

103

comment that Casaubon's "frigid rhetoric" seems no less impotent than his "stream of feeling" which is "an exceedingly shallow rill" [505].)

In a later chapter, the narrator challenges us to shift our focus and become more sympathetic towards Casaubon. In what again seems like an apparently generous gesture towards an unattractive character, we are told that he "was spiritually a-hungered like the rest of us" (312). This comment seems to open up the possibility that we will discover in him a reflection of ourselves and thereby necessarily be more disposed in his favor. But when the underpinnings of his philosophy concerning romance and marriage are explored, we come to respect and like him, if anything, rather less. This occurs despite the fact that the narrator claims to protest "but why always Dorothea?" and so appears to be giving us a sympathetic treatment of Casaubon. We then learn that "in spite of the blinking eyes and white moles," he is not truly objectionable. This is hardly a compliment; in a passage posing as a panegyric, the narrator incorporates a great deal of unsavory information concerning Casaubon's beliefs:

> It had occured to him that he must not any longer defer his intention of matrimony . . . [Dorothea] might really be such a helpmate to him as would enable him to dispense with a hired secretary. . . . His soul was sensitive without being enthusiastic: it was too languid to thrill out of self-consciousness into passionate delight; it went fluttering in the swampy ground where it was hatched, thinking of its wings and never flying. (313)

To be told that his soul flutters about the swamp from which it "was hatched" hardly provides us with a new perspective on the charms of this character. The description is constructed so that the apparent counterbalancing of perspective only truly serves to assure us of the validity of our initial reading. We return to the position from which we began, more assured of our original estimation of Casaubon, especially if we had, like Celia, regarded his learning "as a kind of damp which might in due time saturate a neighboring body" (311).

It is clear, then, that Dorothea must invent and project whatever passion she reads onto Casaubon, much as a child projects personality and responsiveness onto a wooden doll, "showering kisses on the hard pate of her bald doll, creating a happy soul within that woodenness from the wealth of her own love" (230). The narrator unevasively portrays the play of textual strategies present in Dorothea's "reading" of Casaubon: "Dorothea's faith supplied all that Mr Casaubon's words seemed to leave unsaid: what believer sees a disturbing omission or infelicity? The text, whether of prophet or of poet, expands for whatever we can put into it, and even his bad grammar is sublime" (74). In his marriage to Dorothea, Casaubon comes to separate further and further the spoken word of affection from the manifestation of it until we hear that when Casaubon answers his wife's conversational gambit with "What is that, my love?" "(he always said 'my love,' when his manner was the coldest)" (257).

Everyone except Dorothea realizes that her dream of marrying the teacher/lover will fail because Casaubon can barely fulfill the first part of the definition while being practically incapable of coming to grips with the second. He concludes that "the poets had much exaggerated the force of masculine passion" since he feels so little of it; the narrator even points out that it "had once or twice crossed his mind that possibly there was some deficiency in Dorothea to account for the moderation of his abandonment" (87). Casaubon's lack of passion is, in fact, the subject of his neighbors' broadly comic commentary. "He has got no good red blood in his body," remarks Sir James, to which Mrs. Cadwallader responds: "No. Somebody put a drop under a magnifying-glass, and it was all semicolons and parentheses" (96). In fact, Mr. Brooke is concerned about the old scholar's abilities to keep watch on his employees once he installs his new wife at the suitably titled estate of Lowick: "There may be a young gardener, you know—why not? . . . I told Casaubon he should change his gardener" (102). The subtext to Brooke's remark is as unsubtle as a D. H. Lawrence novel.

If Casaubon is an old fool to have taken a young wife, he is nonetheless a dangerous fool. To make him an object of fun makes him all the meaner and all the more ready to avenge himself on those who would dare laugh. He suspects that his nephew Will, for example, does not treat him with unswerving respect. On at least one occasion Casaubon "had a suspicion that he was being laughed at. But it was not possible to include Dorothea in that suspicion" (246). Will regards his uncle not as a dragon who had carried a maiden off to his lair, but rather as "something more unmanageable than a dragon: he was a benefactor with collective society at his back" (241). Will is right to locate Casaubon's danger in his position as one of society's elders, as the representative of a host of patriarchal structures: the church, the academy, the gentry. To defy his wishes is to put oneself in jeopardy, since by implication one then defies the institutions that act as his aegis.

But Dorothea does defy her husband's will and gets her "Will" in the bargain, as Boumelha points out (16). Despite the fact that Casaubon's wills —both the literal and figurative ones—attempt to control Dorothea's fate after his death, she throws off the harness and makes her own attachments. She refuses to capitulate to convention, having learned the disastrous results that come from following the script. At one point, she is determined to stop Will Ladislaw from confining her in one of the metaphors that would entangle her. Will had listened to Dorothea and then wants to translate her experience into his terms: "That is a beautiful mysticism—it is a—." But

Dorothea interrupts him before he can affix his label to her experience: "Please not to call it by any name. . . . You will say it is Persian, or something else geographical. It is my life" (427). Here Dorothea is resisting the impulse to be controlled by the established grooves—or ruts—of destiny as defined by language. She does not want to be trapped inside his adjective like a fly inside a tumbler because she might then feel herself compelled to act by the script attached to such a trait. Eliot makes this point most clearly when she earlier describes "poor Mr Casaubon" who "had imagined that his long studious bachelorhood had stored up for him a compound interest of enjoyment, and that large drafts on his affections would not fail to be humoured" (111). The narrator goes on to make explicit that we construct our versions of reality based on these received ideas, and that "all of us, grave or light, get our thoughts entangled in metaphors, and act fatally on the strength of them" (111).

It is important to note that one of the dangers in having one's life reduced to a word or two rests in the impossibility for language to be objective. There is no language that is not in some manner subjective, just as there can be no "neutral transcription" of reality. An exchange between Rosamond and her brother conveniently illustrates this point:

> "Are you beginning to dislike slang, then?" said Rosamond, with mild gravity.
>
> "Only the wrong sort. All choice of words is slang. It marks a class."
>
> "There is correct English: that is not slang."
>
> "I beg your pardon: correct English is the slang of prigs who write history and essays. And the strongest slang of all is the slang of poets." (126)

Eliot places language in a context dominated by an awareness of the ways in which it is owned by various groups. That there is no "correct" language allows Eliot to explore extensively the possibilities of a splintered reality. This recognition also allows her to avoid the confines of certain prescribed literary conventions—even more so than she had done in her earlier works. Tellingly, Eliot uses humor to frame this central passage; the proclamation of language's subjectivity is characteristically undercut by framing it as a discussion of "slang."

Certain words appear neutral but carry the weight of social baggage only the narrator can unpack. "Candor" is such a word, one that appears unambiguously positive. Yet Eliot explains that "To be candid, in *Middlemarch* phraseology, meant, to use an early opportunity of letting your friends know that you did not take a cheerful view of their capacity, their conduct, or their position and a robust candor never waited to be asked for its opinion" (798). In addition, there is "the love of truth," another phrase that seems to have wide appeal until we are told that it translates into "a lively objection to seeing a wife look happier than her husband's character warranted, or manifest too much satisfaction in her lot: the poor thing should have some hint given her that if she knew the truth she would have less complacency in her bonnet, and in light dishes for a supper-party" (798). Even sanity is defined by the correct use of language. When Mrs. Cadawallader insists that Dorothea will "see visions" living alone, and that "We have all got to exert ourselves a little to keep sane, and call things by the same names as other people call them by. To be sure, for younger sons and women who have no money, it is a sort of provision to go mad: they are taken care of then. But you must not run into that" (581). But Dorothea is happy to break ranks with her behavior and language. Her response is significant: "'I never called everything by the same name that all the people about me did,' said Dorothea, stoutly" (581).

But despite her declaration that she never called things by the same name as others, Dorothea has a facility for language and an admirable ability to defend herself when necessary. She can certainly out-argue her uncle and guardian, Mr. Brooke, whose "masculine consciousness" is often "in rather a stammering condition under the eloquence of his niece" (425). At first glance, Brooke might seem a harmlessly comic figure, a verbal buffoon. But Gilbert and Gubar argue that "Brooke is a dark parody of Casaubon," whose "classical allusions, literary gossip, and scientific platitudes are as dated and undigested as Casaubon's notes. As the reform candidate for Parliament and the owner-operator of *The Pioneer*, moreover, he parodies political provinciality the way Casaubon parodies literary provinciality. Thus he is well represented by the buff-colored rag effigy of himself that echoes his words at the political rally, for his own repetitive, derivative, and basically unintelligible speech" (*The Madwoman in the Attic* 507). Like Casaubon, Brooke is a man undone by his own pretensions. Eliot is unsparing and unwavering in her comic use of this character because he holds great power, and yet he is clearly a fool. For Brooke, language is a kind of barbed-wire in which he becomes increasingly tangled as he struggles to free himself. His beliefs are riddled with a dangerous combination of self-interest, ignorance and indecision, forcing him into declarations such as "the Reformation either meant something or it did not, that he himself was a Protestant to the core, but that Catholicism was a fact; and as to refusing an acre of your ground for a Romanist chapel, all men needed the bridle of religion, which, properly speaking, was the dread of a Hereafter" (41). It is important to note that Eliot, while engaged in the particularly feminine habit of making jokes at the expense of others, chooses to ridicule a powerful figure. She does not ridicule the ignorance of the untaught or the indecisions of the powerless but instead chooses as the target for her satire a man with position, education, and money.

It has been said that, like Rosamond, Eliot "never attempted to joke, and this perhaps was the most decisive mark of her cleverness" (188), but it is clear that Eliot uses humor as a cornerstone in her novels. I would risk comparing Eliot, not to aloof and sanctimonious Rosamond, but to the unlikely character of Mrs. Garth. Mrs. Garth has to do everything at once: instruct, entertain, nurture, create and so "she had sometimes taken pupils in peripatetic fashion, making them follow her about in the kitchen with their book or slate. She thought it good for them to see that she could make an excellent lather while she corrected their blunders 'without looking,' —that a woman with her sleeves tucked up above her elbows might know all about the Subjunctive Mood or the Torrid Zone—that, in short, she might possess 'education' and other good things ending in 'tion" (275). Like one of Mrs. Garth's pupils, Eliot's readers must follow her as she attempts—and accomplishes—everything at once.

Paradoxically, a passage from Virginia Woolf's *A Room of One's Own* makes a fitting final comment on the way humor functions in Eliot's novels. Woolf explains that when women write their own texts, they infringe upon the ability of a man "to believe in himself" (35). Men depend on women to reflect the world they create by reproducing it "faithfully"—mimetically. "Women," claims Woolf, "have served all these centuries as looking-glasses possessing the magic and delicious power of reflecting the figure of man at twice its natural size. . . . For as she begins to tell the truth, the figure in the looking-glass shrinks; his fitness for life is diminished. How is he to go on giving judgment, civilising natives, making laws, writing books, dressing up and speechifying at banquets, unless he can see himself . . . at least twice the size he really is?" (35–36). Eliot answers, with her characteristically dry, caustic and understated humor, the question that Woolf rhetorically poses. This, Eliot answers in *The Mill on the Floss* and *Middlemarch*, is what the world looks like when the Bluebeards are shown to be pretentious little boys, when little girls are not St. Theresa, and when the scholar-gentleman turns out not to be Casanova but Casaubon. This is a mirror held up not to flatter or distort, but rather to cause the *reader* to reflect.

A conventionally "faithful" reproduction, Eliot shows us, would necessarily mean the reproduction of a fantasy world wrought by masculine tools and ruled by masculine values: women "echo" reality with a difference; women repeat words but mock them at the same time. When women writers such as George Eliot refuse to be contained within mimesis, they shatter the textual looking-glass.

5

"The Joke or Agony": Elizabeth Bowen's Comic Vision

Humor is being satisfied you are right, irony, being satisfied that they should think you wrong. Humorous people know there is nothing they need dread.

Elizabeth Bowen, *The House in Paris*

Elizabeth Bowen's sharp and acerbic humor cuts through the authority of everything from the Irish "Big House," to the insanities of two world wars, to the intimate parlor games of a society redefining itself sexually and psychologically. Bowen's prose is emblematic of the way women's humor questions, mocks and demystifies the world of inherited and institutionalized power. Already jealously guarded by scholars and critics of Irish as well as English literature, I want to claim Bowen's short stories, novels, and essays for the study of women's humor.[1] Like her predecessors, particularly Austen and Eliot, Bowen is deeply concerned with the way that humor at once deflates and invigorates social intercourse. Humor in Bowen deflates both pretensions to greatness, the narcissism of the perpetual victim, and the self-conscious moral superiority of the chronic do-gooder. In contrast to her relentless refusal to supply the usual feminine applause for the important man or woman, the poor soul, and the good Samaritan, she illuminates instead the workings of the heart and minds of the outsiders and social outlaws who must nevertheless live inside society.

Bowen focuses her attention on the dangerous orphan, the young woman of no social standing who is trying to decide on a fixed persona in *The Death of the Heart* and *Eva Trout*; she focuses on the passions of brothers-and sisters-in-law in *Friends and Relations*; she focuses on the sexually passionate but insecure woman in *The Heat of the Day* and *To The North*. Most centrally, she focuses her attention on the structuring and importance of the way women use language in her work, and her dry, sometimes didactic, always dangerous humor allows her to say damning things obliquely. Humor is a vehicle for truth in Bowen, and like "Love, drink, anger," humor causes something to "crumble . . . the whole scene" of social convention so that "at once one is in a fantastic universe" of which both its "unseemliness and its glory are indescribable, really" (*Death of the Heart* 270).

Victoria Glendinning argues that Bowen's writing is "what happened after Bloomsbury," and that she is the "link that connects Virginia Woolf with Iris Murdoch and Muriel Spark" (xv). Writing from 1923 until 1968, Bowen received cautious applause during her lifetime, but much of it was muffled by condescension and shadowed by reproach, in part because she deploys a form of what Judy Little calls "renegade humor," a term which succinctly establishes the characteristically rebellious nature of comedy created by writers such as Virginia Woolf and Muriel Spark.[2] Bowen's comedy recognizes experience as arbitrary and subjective, and declares that the ordering of it is illusory.

We create order in order to perceive order the way a skeptic might pray *in order* to believe rather than as a result of belief; the question of cause-and-effect is always at the heart of Bowen's fiction and at the center of her humor. We see patterns in order to convince ourselves that chaos is not triumphant, Bowen implies, which delegates the ordering of experience to the merely ritualistic rather than fundamentally important. "Everything can be shifted, lock, stock and barrel" observes a character from *The Heat of the Day*, "Like touring scenery from theater to theater." "Everything" here encompasses the full range of human experience, from war and history, to love, to fear and rage. "Reassemble it anywhere; you get the same illusion. . . . [W]hat else but an illusion could have such power?" (133).

Only illusion, Bowen implies, can instill in an inhabitant of the twentieth century a sense that life has any meaning whatsoever. Once, when there was a sense that life was endowed with a significance beyond the everyday, perhaps there was a sense of hope. A sense that the past held a sort of promise obliterated by modern life is summed up by a comment from *The Death of the Heart*, when Thomas tells his half-sister Portia that perhaps earlier in history people were tougher: "There was a future then. You can't get up any pace when you feel you're right at the edge" (30). Bowen's characters live in the liminal world charted by Judy Little in *Comedy and the Woman Writer*; they cross and recross the boundaries delineated by Cixous and Clement. Bowen's humor is the humor of the ruthless observer.

And yet the exposure of order as illusion, and the subsequent anger at the earlier efficacy of the illusion is at the heart of Bowen's comedy. Hers is the humor of one who has bought experience at a high market price, and she often structures metaphors for emotion by juxtaposing the heart with the wallet by discussing love and affection in terms of investment and repayment. "Not for nothing do we invest so much of ourselves in other people's lives—or even in momentary pictures of people we do not know," argues the narrator in *The Death of the Heart*. "It cuts both ways: the happy group inside the lighted window, the figure in long grass in the orchard seen from the train stay and support us in our dark hours. Illusions are art, for the feeling person, and it is by art that we live, if we do. It is the emotion to which we remain faithful, after all: we are taught to recover it in some other place" (95). Clearly, however, Bowen's frustration with the world cast in such terms remains paramount. As Nancy Walker has shown, women's humor "is frequently a means of dealing with frustration or anger, rather than simply celebratory or fun" (*A Very Serious Thing* 106). Bowen is especially compelling because her works skillfully intermingle the apparently contradictory forces of anger and humor. Her anger is not the explosive, cleansing humor of some other women writers, but is instead a warning shot fired once in the dark.

Satire created by Bowen does not have a corrective function; indeed, her work remains fascinatingly problematic because while she mimics the accents of the ruling class, she mirrors power only to ridicule it. In so doing, she illustrates the argument made by Rachel Brownstein that women writers of humor often "mime so as subtly to mock the certainties of authoritative discourse" ("Jane Austen" 65). Here Brownstein tailors to comedy the larger claims made by theorists such as Sandra Gilbert and Susan Gubar concerning the way women writers unapologetically exploit the "very conventions [they] expose as inadequate" (*The Madwoman in The Attic* 121). When, for example, sixteen-year-old Portia from *The Death of the Heart*, goes through the motions of romance with the damaged and damaging family friend Eddie, Bowen exploits the usual conventions of girlish love (including secret phone calls, upsetting letters, trysts, and secret diaries) but does so in a way that exposes the mechanisms of romance as at best foolish and at worst, profoundly corrupting. She gives Portia the foil of a friend, Lilian, who is a caricature of the literally love-sick adolescent.

Described by the narrator as walking through London "with the rather fated expression you see in photographs of girls who have subsequently been murdered," (51) Lilian is given to such affectations as washing her long blond hair to the accompaniment of Stravinsky played on the gramophone. Possessed by the very thought of melancholy romance, Lilian has been removed from one school for falling in love with the 'cello mistress only to develop a crush on an actor once she is in London. Self-absorbed and radiating a sense that "tomorrow, anything might happen," Lilian is an exaggeration of Portia, and by extension, an exaggeration of all conventional romance. At one point, Portia is discovered by Lilian weeping in the cloakroom at school, and "at once" she is brought "inside that sub-tropical zone of feeling:

nobody can be kinder than the narcissist while you react to life in his own terms" (291). The narrator further describes the scene by declaring that "To be consoled, to be understood by Lilian was like extending to weep in a ferny grot, whose muggy air and clammy frond-touches relax, demoralize and pervade you" (291). This description serves to frame Portia's genuine dismay and sense of dislocation within the distasteful exaggerations of Lilian's world, since "Factitious feeling and true feeling come to about the same thing when it comes to pain. Lilian's arabesques of the heart, the unkindness of the actor, made her eye Portia with doomful benevolence" (291). Lilian is the comic version of Portia because she is two-dimensional; Portia fears being laughed at, but the narrator invites us to laugh at Lilian, not because she is pathetic but because she is so clearly a survivor. She can afford to be laughed at; Portia cannot.

Bowen's humor also works by announcing to the world that which usually remains hidden. Characters "call" one another in her works on those very aspects of personality or patterns of behavior one would expect to be ignored or overlooked in so-called "polite" society. When Portia, her face buried in Eddie's shoulder as they ride in a taxi says "No, don't kiss me now," Eddie—quite expectedly—wonders "Why not now?" Portia—quite expectedly—replies "Because I don't want you to." Surprisingly, Eddie then "calls" her on her answer by pushing her response to its deeper level of meaning "'You mean,' he said, 'that I didn't once when you did?'" (296). It's a delicate moment, done with extreme caution and expertise, like the balancing of an orange on the rim of a plate (a trick we hear much of in *The Death of the Heart*). Portia and Eddie form a sort of unholy alliance, since they are both intemperate in their desire to speak the truth as they see it. The world, Bowen indicates, cannot accommodate such truth-tellers. "You've got a completely lunatic set of values, and a sort of unfailing lunatic instinct that makes you pick on another lunatic—another person who doesn't know where he is," wails Eddie, seeing himself mirrored by this girl seven years his junior. "You know I'm not a cad, and I know you're not batty. But, my God, we've got to live in the world" (302). Portia doesn't know "what is unspeakable," and so lives in a socially prelapsarian world.

For Portia, the worst possibility the world holds is to be the object of ridicule. The daughter of a woman who married a divorced man after she became pregnant, Portia grew up living in hotels as a sort of refugee, fearing always that she and her mother would be the object of someone's derision, made fun of for not understanding the unspoken rules. Portia learns at an early age that it is her small gestures that most truly betray her since "Sins cut boldly up through every class in society but mere misdemeanours show a certain level in life" (56). Portia is, therefore, most upset when she thinks that her half-brother, Thomas, and sister-in-law Anna, are laughing at her.

Hoping to enlist his aid in an emotional coup, Portia tells Major Brutt, an unemployed friend of Portia's sister-in-law, that he, to, is the object of laughter; "'You are the other person that Anna laughs at,' she went on, raising her eyes. 'I don't think you understand: Anna's always laughing at you. She says you are quite pathetic. She laughed at your carnations being the wrong colour, then gave them to me'" (309). Like Austen's heroine in *Mansfield Park*, Portia is often the unlaughing figure, not because she lacks a sense of humor (despite the fact that she doesn't laugh at the Marx Brothers, but instead looks "appalled") but because what passes for humor in her circle is simply social savagery dressed up as comedy. Eddie does a vicious version of her sister-in-law for Portia's benefit, and is angry when she doesn't laugh on cue. "Darling, didn't you think me being Anna was funny?" asks Eddie. "No, not really. I didn't think you enjoyed it," answers Portia, with Bowen once again underscoring Portia's instinctive understanding of people's hidden lives and motives. "Well, it was: it was very funny, asserts Eddie, defiantly. At which point Eddie begins to make "several faces, pulling his features all ways, as though to flake off from them the last figments of Anna. The impersonation had (as Portia noticed) had fury behind it: each hypothetical arrow to him from Anna had been winged by a demoniac smile" (109).

Bowen's works consistently demonstrate the effectiveness of the comic as a strategy of subversion by employing what she might term "an irony which is seldom gentle, and is in the long run deadly to what it attacks" (*Collected Impressions* 124). Certainly the conventions of ordinary life are called into question by *The Death of the Heart*, to the extent that we are told that if Portia were to meet her dead father she would have to tell him "That there is no ordinary life" (313). Humor in Bowen's writings embodies a profound awareness that the accepted pattern has no necessity, and her female characters are particularly aware that life is a series of arbitrary, closely guarded assumptions based on the most flimsy and transient foundations. Women, like all marginalized or exiled groups, live under only assumed boundaries; they understand the arbitrary construction of history and reality. They realize that not only is everything possible, but this is so because "nothing is really unthinkable; really you do know that. But the more one thinks, the less there's any outside reality—at least, that's so with a woman," as one character puts it in *The Heat of the Day* (214). Women understand that only illusions can have real power, and that, conversely, power is itself an illusion, realizing like the title character in *Eva Trout* that "there was no 'real life'; no life was more real than this. This she had long suspected. She now was certain" (216). Women have "no scale," according to Bowen. They are therefore unlikely to accept some things as great and others as small. They are, by extension, unlikely to accept hierarchies where the great and small are put in so-called natural order. Rather, women chart their growth from the day they arrive at the inevitable "belief that nothing real ever happens" (*The House in Paris* 191).

Although one might be tempted to describe Bowen's humor the way she characterizes Emmeline in *To the North*, as a means of brightening a "drawing-room with . . . satirical gentleness" (16), Bowen's tone is, clearly, more of a presence and more demanding. It should be emphasized that the rejection of commonality and normality has always presented a risk for writers, especially women writers. "To write is always to rave a little," Bowen explains in *The Death of the Heart* (7). In Bowen we see clearly how apparent madness and writing are linked to magic for the figure of the hysteric, the witch, and the matriarchal comic. Bowen allies herself in this company by seeing "magic" that "emanate[s] from words" (*Collected Impressions* 101). The magic inherent in language cannot be fixed by a series of absolutes; to fix or stabilize things through language is to attempt to force them into stasis and, by implication, an attempt to limit their possibilities. The impulse to reject these limitations might, however, be both frighening and necessary; in fact, recognition of what is necessary is often terrifying and often resembles madness. Within the paradigmatic figure of extremes, the hysteric, there is still what Bowen might call "the sidelong glitter of reason, the uncanny hint of sanity" (*The Heat of the Day* 214). We are presented with the sidelong glitter of understanding, the hint, a suggestion of the hidden subversion, the idea that success lies only in circuit, as we had suspected. Bowen's texts often contain unparalleled subversions of conventional forms and her humor is inextricably linked to her belief that there is "no longer the safety of a prescribed world, of which the thousand-and-one rules could be learnt, in which one could steer one's way instructed and safe" (*Collected Impressions* 67).

Eva Trout, for example, has been seen as "a metaphor, represent[ing] a sense of life, large, awkward, always out of kilter, unable to find a form" (Gindin 32). Eva is a giant, literally and figuratively, a physically large, overwhelming presence. She cannot be contained by forms which fail to encompass such a creature; she remains outside the realm of the expected, as do so many of Bowen's characters. But their strength, ultimately, like Eva's, lies in the fact that they remain on the periphery of social and cultural structures, undermining these structures by their very presence. They are unassimilable. Yet they remain the central figures of Bowen's comedy, never actually the creators of vicious humor, but still the catalysts initiating recognition of the absurdity of the absolute. Chaos, violence and anger are associated with the feminine position of symbolic mobility within the system. The feminine here is not unimportant and frivolous, but volatile, the figure of unexpected and unlimited power. Lee's observation that "there is a close relationship in all [Bowen's works] between violence and humor" (144) is worth pursuing. Humor is the mainstay of all of Bowen's fictions, italicizing the effects of dislocation and loss rather than expelling them through catharsis or resignation. Bowen provides a ruthlessly deft assessment of characters. We know, for instance, that Iseult Smith of *Eva Trout* had been "a D. H. Lawrence reader and a townswoman" so her husband was "lucky not to come out worse than he did" (16); that "all young men [are odd].... no sooner were their lips unstuck from your own than they began to utter morality," according to Louie in *The Heat of the Day*.

In the modern world of *The Death of the Heart*, we are to understand that "arts and crafts had succeeded Sturm and Drang," and that a middle-aged adulterous husband, in confronting his understanding wife, "looks impressive, silly, intensely moral and as though he would like to denounce himself. [The wife] would never let him denounce himself, and this was rather like taking somebody's toys away" (14). We learn in *The House in Paris* that a child is "not yet ripe for direct sex-instruction yet, though [his father] is working towards this through botany and mythology" (33). In *The Hotel* we see that sensitive people "fee[l] spikes everywhere and rush to impale" themselves (77), that a clergyman holds an idea of God as "an enormous and perpetually descending Finger and Thumb" (89). We are instructed that a British outing usually consists of having "motored twenty-five miles [to sit] on a stump of the Roman villa, their feet in a pit" (*To the North* 59). Bowen explores "the joke or agony" (*The Heat of the Day* 322) without seeing anything odd about the juxtaposition of these elements. When women recognize the uncertainty of what has been passed off as certain, rational and absolute, they begin "under this compulsion . . . to laugh too, though rebelliously, with bewilderment and uncertainty" (322). The rebellion, bewilderment and uncertainty remain beneath the most decorous of surfaces, however, because, as Bowen comments in *The Heat of the Day*, "to be abandoned you must be respectable" (165).

Bowen's comedy has been contextualized within the framework she herself created for the absurd in *The Death of the Heart*. The following passage indicates her fascination with and ability to work with the monstrous, the unassimilable: "each of us keeps, battened down inside himself, a sort of lunatic giant—impossible socially, but full-scale—and that it's the knockings and batterings we sometimes hear in each other that keep our intercourse from utter banality" (333). A few critics, including Lee and Gindin, have categorized Bowen's work as "comedy of manners" with an "underlying pull of fatality" (Lee 49). This view of Bowen's novels, while partially effective, does not deal with the subversive aspects of her comedy. It does not acknowledge the circuitous, hidden "resistance writing," or the way "she looks wildly sideways" (*Collected Impressions* 5), manipulating conventions even as she employs them incontrovertibly. In particular, the critics do not explore in detail Bowen's refusal to supply a "normal" happy ending because she revises and redefines the concept of a happy ending.

For the women Bowen creates in her works it seems "that while people were very happy, individual persons were surely damned" (*The Death of the Heart* 61). Happiness is linked more closely to damnation than to marriage. Certainly, a happy ending is not equated with marriage. Cecilia in *To the North*, for example, seems to have escaped a fate worse than death "when, within less than a year, Henry died of pneumonia," because, as a sympathetic relative muses, "given Henry's nervous make-up and Cecilia's temperament, there had been no time for worse to come of it" (12). Marriage often provides "little more than the shell of a happy ending" (*Collected Impressions* 5) and is itself the source of much of Bowen's satire. Newlywed Gerda Bligh from *To the North* is described by Bowen as "not really a fool, she was an honest girl . . . with a tendency to hysteria. Having read a good many novels about marriage, not to speak of some scientific books, she now knew not only why she was unhappy but exactly how unhappy she could still be" (51). As Gerda and her young husband argue bitterly during a weekend in the country, "their attention to one another was almost lover-like. They broke off conversations at dinner to glare compellingly at one another across the table; they dogged one another about the house and garden to see what the other was doing and interfere. . . . The Blighs . . . were taking up more than their share of the week-end programme: like a pair of indifferent arobatic dancers they came bounding again and again from the wings without an encore" (60). If this is marriage, it is not surprising that Bowen's women seek alternative endings.

Marriage and death, the two acceptable endings for a female character, are wryly confronted by Bowen in a number of her short stories. The vain, immature ghost of "Green Holly," who wears a feather boa and flirts with the boring civil servants now occupying her house, wishes desperately to join the paltry Christmas festivities of the living who inhabit the house. She does not wish to do so for any religious or "spiritual" reason; she does not wish to join church services; she wants to join their party simply so that she might have a good time. As she walks past the eternally silent figure of her husband's corpse, we gather that he shot himself through jealousy of her. She exhibits no remorse, even in her immortal state: "It was too bad. She had been silly, but it could not be helped. They should not have shut her up in the country. How could she not make hay while the sun shone?" (723). Trapped inside the house where she had committed the follies of her life, the ghost continues to speak in the language of bad romance throughout the rest of the story. This ghost has not been granted a dignity in death. Her ability, at times, to transcend her death, to move between the thin walls, has not given her the ability to re-think her position. She is still concerned, for example, with her appearance, except that now the word "appearance" is charged with new implications: she is not only worried about how she will look to others, but whether they will be able to see her: "It was not merely a matter of, how was she? but of, was she—tonight—at all?" (723). Trapped by lack of change, she repeats the follies of her living life, repeating trite refrains. "It's Kismet," she wails "zestfully" to an unnerved young man. "People spoke of love, but I never knew what they meant" (725). This ghost is trapped inside her house but extends her connection through time only to attempt the same misguided flirtations she attempted in life. The life and after-life of this particular young woman are equally bound to keep her foolishly falling in love, trying to escape the boredom of a dull marriage, forever stepping over her husband and his mute reproach. Her ghost life and perhaps her hell, is to be taken up with the same trivial pursuit that controlled her life: "She was left with—nay, had become—her obsession. Thus it was to be a ghost" (724). Bowen realizes that it is difficult to discuss a ghost rationally: "Have you noticed . . . that one may discuss ghosts quite intelligently, but never any particular ghost without being facetious?" ("Foothold" 298). Even when a houseguest is bothered by "that damned woman going in and out," it forces him to wonder, "supposing she really is a damned woman?" (299). A potentially melodramatic encounter is undercut by transforming questions of life and death into a question of social etiquette. The juxtaposition of prosaic detail with both the supernatural and the humorous is part of the dissonance which gives Bowen's stories their power.

Bowen's indeterminate endings disturb many critics, and for good reason. For example, Eva Trout is literally killed by the child behind the gun: her ward shoots her at a railway station as she is about to set out on a mock marriage. Eva's last words are "what is 'concatenation'?" (301) and this is telling. "Concatenation" refers to things linked together in a series or a chain; Bowen makes connections at the ends of her narratives without providing closure. One of the last lines of *Eva Trout* reads: "There is invariably more. Nothing is final, I suppose" (296). The pattern is similar in other novels: *The Hotel* ends with the refusal of a perfectly reasonable marriage and with the major characters finding their ways home separately. Often, as in *The House in Paris*, we are left with the central characters "wildly smiling" and "unserene" (42). Bowen's comedy bespeaks chains of events, not resolution or reconciliation. Because her humor does not have the properties associated with traditional comedy, its hidden and subversive nature has been misunderstood.

In disrupting the pattern, however, Bowen risks being categorized as a writer of "limited appeal." When she is misfiled under an inappropriate heading, the woman writer is in danger of being either drastically misread or passed over altogether. This is, no doubt, one reason why Bowen's humor has been overlooked; she is usually read in light of a masculine tradition. In his introduction to a 1987 collection of essays on Bowen's works, Harold Bloom, for example, explains that her stories "are in the mode of Henry James. . . . But the shadow of the Master flickers uncertainly in these three strong stories. . . . The economy and control of Henry James and James Joyce find a legitimate continuance in Bowen's art. Yet her stories seem to me to touch the sources of their power in ways more analogous to those of Lawrence" (1). Bloom positions her only in relation to male authors and validates her work by comparison to these Masters; he politely ignores her gender, perhaps in order to legitimize her. Her books have also proven difficult for critics like Leon Edel who, while admiring Bowen's work, found it necessary to apologize for woman-centered texts: "I had noted the extent to which some of the male members of my Princeton seminar had actually resented being maneuvered . . . into the mind of an adolescent girl" (3). The Princeton undergraduates are apparently not alone in their resentment. As James Gindin has observed, Bowen is often "relegated by critics to the condescending category of the sensitive female novelist, pushed . . . into the designation of the merely perceptive" (30). Gindin might have had Fredrick Karl's comments in *The Contemporary English Novel* in mind. If he didn't, Karl fits the bill when he characterizes Bowen as "an intensely feminine novelist" (109), who is able to "sensitively depict" a "kind of world," but a world which for the male reader "ultimately remains . . . too overly feminine and gossipy, in a final view, shadowy" (129). In fact, Bowen is unapologetically concerned with a world depicted through the lives of women; it appears shadowy only to critics who fail to see what she is about. By placing women at the center of all of her novels, Bowen irritates critics who cannot accept books about women's lives as important and who consider it a particular affront when the focus of the narrative is a young woman.

If certain critics are unable to become interested in a world created by women, or perhaps frightened by the possibility of its existence, then Bowen resists with equal force the pressure to center her interest in the world of men: "I do think men are pathetic, don't you? If only they were more interesting," suggests one of Bowen's young female characters (*The Hotel* 126). When her friend protests, "I should have said they were interesting," she replies "You wouldn't if you'd had as many as I have. . . . I dare say I thought men were interesting when I was about seventeen. Now I can see they're all exactly the same" (*The Hotel* 126). It is important to state that Bowen incorporates Douglas's strategic joking in this passage; she is using humor to make a point, disrupting the usual balance of power by calling into question the conventionalities of romance, sexual behavior, and the assumptions of male Princeton undergraduates. But when critics claim that "by keeping [a] young girl at the center of the novel, the novelist has forsaken any possibility of enlarging the scope of vision through more demanding personalities" (Karl 110), or that "the mark of the fully mature novelist is his ability to probe emotionally and mentally developed adults" (Karl 129), they are not joking, but are making damning pronouncements about the worth of an author based exclusively on her sex. Bowen, not a "fully mature novelist," has apparently "forsaken any possibility" of making an important statement about the "larger world" because by writing about women she by definition excludes "much that makes life exciting and significant" (Karl 129). To evaluate texts by this definition is to misjudge Bowen's writings as well as women's lives. Historically, critics have equated women-centered texts with insignificant texts. Bowen is an undervalued example of a writer who seeks to undo the universally accepted nature of that equation by making use of the very conventions she sets out to subvert.

Indeed, to value Bowen is to value her humor. Bowen's humorous voice is carefully encoded, depending on the sort of "double voice" suggested by Susan Lanser in her work on the idea of a feminine narratology. Lanser argues that "the condition of being a woman in a male-dominant society may well necessitate the double voice, whether as a conscious subterfuge or as a tragic dispossession of the self" (157). Quite simply, Bowen provides a ladylike cover for her most accomplished heresies. In Lanser's terms, Bowen's "deployment of decorum in staid and elegant drawing-rooms, however, actually challenges the ideology of manners . . . Her female characters both embody and rail against domestic codes" (157). Duplicity is imposed on women, who must learn to conceal their actions under apparent submission. They are then inevitably misread as sincerely submissive; this is at the heart of Bowen's irony. Her female characters are imprinted with the seal of prescribed femininity only to be told that the markings are put there by nature. Women acquire the art of duplicity, according to Bowen, in part because of their problematic relationship to language. Bowen seems to presage contemporary feminists when she explains that:

> people learn to be disingenuous. Finding no language in which
> to speak in their own terms, they resign themselves to being
> translated imperfectly. They exist alone; when they try to enter
> into relations they compromise falsifyingly—through anxiety,
> through desire to impart and to feel warmth . . . . They are
> bound to blunder, then to be told they cheat. In love, the sweet-
> ness and violence they have to offer involves a thousand betray-
> als for the less innocent. Incurable strangers to the world, they
> never cease to exact a heroic happiness. Their singleness, their
> ruthlessness, their one continuous wish makes them bound to be
> cruel, and to suffer cruelty. The innocent are so few that two of

them seldom meet—when they do meet, their victims lie strewn
all round. (*Death of the Heart* 110)

Imposed disingenuousness is literally dangerous beyond words, as Bowen illustrates in a number of texts. "Incurable strangers to the world," (as inevitably women must be, given their exclusion from patriarchal culture) are
bound to bring the world to ruin.

The de-centeredness of her central characters is, in fact, Bowen's signature. Bowen's works map "the region of the immoderate, where we are
more than ourselves. Here are no guarantees. . . . Here figures cast unknown
shadows; passion knows no crime, only its own movement; steel and the
cord go with the kiss. Innocence walks with violence; violence is innocent,
cold as fate; between the mistress's kiss and the blade's is a hair's breadth
only, and no disparity. . . . but who is to say that this is not so?" (*To the North*
193). If we are unnerved by moving dangerously through this world of lim-
inality, Bowen wryly suggests that we deserve what we get.

What do we get? Madwomen and monsters, it seems, but with a Bow-
enesque and comedic twist: these figures are considered mad or monstrous
only because their ideas or actions are unusual; monsters are monsters only
through their rarity. The female figures populating Bowen's works are the
laughing Medusas described by Cixous; they are the women described by
Judith Wilt as hesitating, "laughing at the edge, withholding fertility, humility, community" (180). Wilt goes on to describe female characters in
works by women as crossing "the boundary where comedy ceases to cheer
and succor and becomes violent, destructive, murderous, [and] will tumble
over the edge of myth into madness" (174). If we impose duplicity and disingenuousness, we end up with the most dangerous of figures. "Avenging innocence," for example, could be called one of Bowen's most dangerous
comedic strategies. Hildebidle observes that because "the innocent especially lack the ability or the desire to make human readjustments, when they
act, they can become terrible figures" (118). Eva Trout, for example, like
her counterpart Portia from *The Death of the Heart*, is one of the innocents
who leaves her victims scattered about, leaving "few lives unscathed. Or at
least, unchanged" (196). An astute friend compares Eva to Browning's Pippa who "only had to pass by (though as a matter of fact, she did more than
that, she sang away at some length under people's windows) to leave behind
the most dynamic results," arguing that "you're a sort of Pippa—though in
reverse" (196). In a pattern illustrative of the power of powerlessness as articulated by Elizabeth Janeway in *The Powers of the Weak*, Bowen instructs
that we should all "suspect victims; they win in the long run" (95). Or perhaps it is because others do not consider the strength of refusal which appears like "the patient, abiding, encircling will of a monster" (95). Janeway
argues that "the weak can't initiate alternative action themselves, there is

no apparatus of rule to which they have access, but they can refuse to participate in doomed action, or to add their imaginative supplement to the ongo-
ing process of coping with events. Where once they agreed enthusiastically,
they can simply be silent. They may not be able to formulate realistic goals
and practical techniques for achieving them, but they can erode the virtue
of the goals and techniques set up by the powerful" (115). In this passage,
Janeway outlines the narrative trajectory present in most of Bowen's novels. The "innocent" in Bowen's works confounds those in control because
she continues to stand outside the social order even when invited in; she remains uninitiated, unassimilable and unreliable. She is dangerous because
she cannot be counted upon. Like the witch and the hysteric, Bowen's innocent sees her victim with "pity but without reproach" (*The Death of the
Heart* 111).

Bowen was aware of the ways in which these contradictory forces
figure in much of women's fiction. In an astute observation, Bowen herself
maps the way Austen's novels "locate, and never far from themselves, possible darkness, chaos; they feel the constant threat of the wrong—be this
only a mean act, a callous or designing remark, a subtly deceiving proposition, a lie" (*English Novelists* 25). The method of observation she applies to
Austen reflects back with clarity when superimposed on her own work.
Bowen mentions, for example, that Austen unashamedly presented the
world with which she was familiar as a woman, and "depicted and pene-
trated" it "not just as a world, [but as] the world," by implication, claiming
equal authority for women's experience as for men's (25). Austen's scathing
wit and subversive humor are indeed echoed by Bowen. In both cases their
humor, cloaked at first, is eventually revealed as both deadly and accurate.
The remarks made by G. W. Harding in "Regulated Hatred: An Aspect of
the Work of Jane Austen" can be applied with equal force to Bowen: "To
speak . . . of her work as 'satire' is perhaps misleading. She has none of the
underlying didactic intention ordinarily attributed to the satirist. Her object is not missionary; it is the more desperate one of merely finding some
mode of existence for her critical attitudes. . . . She is a literary classic of
the society which attitudes like hers, held widely enough, would undermine" (167).

Equally resonant are Bowen's own comments on other women writers. When Bowen argues, for example, that Elizabeth Gaskell "was keenly
aware of the injustices done to her sex in the name of morality" (36), and
that Gaskell coupled comedy and outrage in order to create "counterpoise"
in her work (37), we can apply these comments directly to Bowen's own
wryly subversive prose. Perhaps most significantly, Bowen frames Virginia
Woolf in radical terms; Bowen sees Woolf as revising and rebelling against
the conventions she was meant to inhabit. "[Woolf] chooses in fact unlikely

matter to kindle—but, once kindled, how high she makes it burn!" Bowen proclaims that Woolf "has put behind her, having no need of, devices that make all other stories work" (*English Novelists* 48). She writes that Woolf creates characters who appear "conventional and compliant" but who in reality have an "inner strangeness . . . in the manner in which they see and feel" (48). Clearly, Bowen reads in Woolf a characteristic of her own writing: an account of the "century's emotion" which she sees as "dislocated and stabbing" (*Collected Impressions* 46). There is no doubt that Bowen values in a writer the refusal to be guided by patterns already established, which is best illustrated by her own refusal to rework the pattern of anger, for example, into the conventionally feminine habits of forgiveness or passivity. Indeed, of one young woman, her male business partner complains that her manner is "insufficiently feminine; he could have done it better himself" (*To the North* 33). A woman institutionalized as mad in Bowen's *The Heat of the Day* refuses to embroider her roses the way she is told, not because "there is no more pink wool" but instead because "there are purple roses" (240). "Nobody believes me," she acknowledges, and yet she persists in her belief that "I could lead you to the very place in the garden and show you the bush. There is only one; it's not my fault if there are no others in the world" (240). Her refusal to capitulate is a sign of her defiance; her defiance is perhaps her downfall, but it is also her strength.

Defiance forms the bridge between the richness of chaos and the richness of comedy in Bowen's work. Anger and humor establish their own authority, with defiance as the manifestation of rage and humor as its voice: "there is one kind of sublime officiousness, anger's or love's, that is overruling: pure anger crystallizes its object, the seducer becomes the abstract of appetite or the thief" (*To the North* 201). Like cruelty, anger can be viewed as "supremely disinterested as art," and, like art, anger has "its own purity, which could transcend anything and consecrate the nearest material to its uses" (*The Hotel* 150). The "terrible clarity" offered by rage shows clearly that everything totters with a "sense of destruction" which causes one to feel "the whole force of a doubt in that moment: had there ever been anything there?" (*The Hotel* 10). Even "sorrow is anger, of a kind" (*Eva Trout* 281) and loss itself contains the power of "original savagery" (*Eva Trout* 281). However, as one of Bowen's critics noted: "restless anger . . . does not just eventuate into fretfulness" (Glendinning 31). Anger and hate are catastrophic, chaotic and therefore generative. Rage obliterates the need for any presumption of objectivity and can thereby act as a catalyst for inventive action; rage can also be the wellspring of a humor that cuts through conventional practice the way a river cuts through rock. The image is one used by both Bowen and contemporary feminist theorists. Kate Clinton, for example, clarifies the outlines of feminist humor by comparing it to lichen, which by "growing low and lowly on enormous rocks, secreting tiny amounts of acid, year after year, eating into the rock [makes] places for water to gather, to freeze and crack the rock a bit. . . . It is the lichen which begins the splitting apart of the rocks, the changing of the shoreline, the shape of the earth" (39). The implications for a discussion of Bowen's humor are clear: in her texts, anger and humor destroy limits and dismantle systems, allowing for growth. Anger can cause "the whole scene" to "crumble" and "at once one is in a fantastic universe. Its unseemliness and its glory are indescribable, really" (*The Death of the Heart* 270). Indeed, for Bowen the very act of thinking is itself linked to anger, and anger to glorious, limitless and joyous possibility: "to think may be to be angry, but remember, we can surmount the anger we feel. To find oneself like a young tree inside a tomb is to discover the power to crack the tomb and grow up to any height" (*The House in Paris* 202). The desire and ability to break apart without the need to repair or rebuild is emblematic of Bowen's work.

Bowen instills her young women with a special talent for such rebellions. The young female central figure subtly undermines the world from which she is excluded. Like a combination of the sorceress and the child, the Bowen protagonist is all the more dangerous because of her apparent vacancy, her evident innocence and what appears to be her talent for submission. The nature of a young woman's power, however, derives in part from her rejection of its acknowledgment by others. Acknowledgment is dangerous; it gives body to the insubstantial. She will refuse to accept prescribed definitions of herself in order to remain "unfixed" and unassimilable. Lois in *The Last September*, for example, will not be defined by someone else's language: "But when Mrs. Montmorency came to: 'Lois is very—' she was afraid suddenly. She had a panic. She didn't want to know what she was, she couldn't bear it: knowledge of this would stop, seal, finish one. Was she now to be clapped down under an adjective, to crawl round life-long inside some quality like a fly in a tumbler?" (70).

Even the apparent innocence of children is open to Bowen's satiric gaze. Under her scrutiny, it becomes clear that their so-called innocence is more a function of their exile from the world of power than a function of their age. "There is no limit to the terror strange children feel of each other, a terror life obscures but never ceases to justify. There is no end to the violations committed by children on children, quietly talking alone," Bowen wryly observes in *The House in Paris* (23). Indeed, children's games are, when viewed without sentimentality, vast ceremonies of ruin. A group of photographs, described by Bowen with signature wickedness, portrays every child as "engaged innocently in some act of destruction—depetalling daisies, puffing at dandelion clocks, trampling primrose woods, rioting round in fragile feathered grown-up hats . . . or knocking down apples from the bough" (*The Heat of the Day* 234).

Bowen's fiction resembles the duplicity of the child and the innocent by disguising its shocking, dislocating and rebellious aspects beneath acceptable, even decorous, layers. Bowen's decorous rhetoric covers the discrepancy between what is acceptable and what actually exists as one might conceal a loaded weapon beneath chiffon. *The Little Girls* clearly demonstrates this irreducible distance between what is permitted and what exists: "I happened to know there was that drawer full of I don't know how many pair of long, long gloves, folded up and beautifully put away," explains a woman, describing a scene from her childhood. She continues, "so then I lifted the gloves up, to stow my sugar mice underneath, and there was the pistol or revolver" (207). Here is a perfect dramatization of Bowen's awareness of the way subversion is concealed behind apparent orthodoxy; Bowen knows well how the multiple levels of meaning operate. The powerless have an outsider's perspective, and under a superficial capitulation to convention, they might well possess a knowledge which could cripple the system. Those who nurse a fundamental hostility towards the powerful, whether consciously or unconsciously realized, pose the greatest threat.

Bowen asks in *The House in Paris*, "The child at the back of the gun accident—is he always so ignorant?" (221). Bowen provides one answer to this question when she ends *Eva Trout* with a child shooting his adoptive mother. What are the implications for a writer whose humor is bound up with such awkward questions—and even more awkward answers? Answers, for one thing, can never provide a guarantee of correctness. Like Alice in Wonderland, Bowen's heroines move through a world created by "magic, the Eden where fact and fiction were the same" (*Collected Impressions* 269). In such a world, truth is reduced "to a slogan, desperately reworded to catch the eye" (*The Heat of the Day* 100). To assert that "common sense" is often neither common nor sensical, is to risk misunderstanding and rejection. Bowen, who Leon Edel said had "a genius for unreality" (Cited in Miles 55) sees, as does one of her characters, "what a fiction was commonsense" (*The Death of the Heart* 315). Her undercover narrative strategies dismantle conventional authority while taking aim at, for example, orthodox history. The catechism laid out in *The Heat of the Day* offers the conventional question "But isn't much to be learned from the lessons of history, Connie?" The question is answered by an unconventional response: "In my experience one thing you don't learn from is anything anyway set up to be a lesson; what you are to know you pick up as you go along" (172). And, after all, Bowen writes, as if in response to the critics who claim she writes about too limited a world, "what people call life's larger experiences . . . are so very narrowing" (*The Hotel* 165).

Given that Bowen's comedy does not fit traditional categories, it is not surprising that men in Bowen's novels often have radically different concepts of humor from women. Men voice the authoritative directive "that's not funny," the characteristic rebuke thrust forward by the oppressive nature of the dominant ideology. For Bowen, men simply do not understand why women find certain things funny, and do not approve of women's humor. Like Leopold in *The House in Paris* who cannot begin to understand foreign jokes in his comic magazine, men are rendered uncertain, disturbed and disquieted by the "Martin ideology" of comedy beyond their comprehension (31). To Leopold, "The funny stories and pictures brought him to a full stop. His passionate lack of humor was native and untutored; no one had taught him that curates, chars, duchesses, spinsters are enough, in England, to make anyone smile. The magazine perplexed Leopold with its rigid symbolism and Martian ideology. A veil of foreign sentiment hung over every image, making it unclear" (31). Most men in Bowen's novels do not understand women in precisely the same way that Leopold does not understand. When Sir Mark, "who did not detach himself easily from a topic," speaks condescendingly to a young women at a party about the Channel tunnel, only to have her offer the information "but I am a shipping agent," he can only assume that she is making a joke. It does not occur to him that she is indeed a businesswoman. "'Ha-ha,' said Sir Mark. 'Hum. Very good, yes, ha-ha!' Thumbs under his lapels he looked, however, rather anxiously round the room. Conversation with someone at whose joke you have heartily laughed without seeing the point is apt to become precarious" (*To the North* 130). The precarious nature of any humorous exchange is repeatedly highlighted by Bowen.

Bowen sees that men's humor rarely leaves women unscathed and that women must create their own humor in contrast to the conventions of comedy. Women must see men's humor as the weapon it usually is: "she now saw his smile as the smile of one who has the laugh" (*The Heat of Day* 310). Women come to equate the serious acceptance of reality with absurdity because "to be serious is absurd; it is useless" (*The House in Paris* 109), and therefore comedy offers one of the few possibilities for useful discourse. Women must respond to the charge that they use comedy wrongly (the perennial "that's not funny"). When a man says to his female companion "What you say is deadly. Must everything be funny?" she has no choice but to respond that "[o]ne's life is" (*The House in Paris* 109). Though women are frequently accused of being humorless and unlaughing in Bowen's fiction, their wicked humor remains, nonetheless, the most keenly subversive, most potently dangerous and most necessary of rebellions even at those moments when it is "fatal to laugh" (*Eva Trout* 187).

Emmeline from *To the North* discovers the fatality of laughter when she becomes sexually involved with Markie, a slightly profligate young man "whose sense of humor [is] not agile." In a conventionally masculine manner, Markie is "accustomed to lead laughter rather than be surprised by it" (68). In part, Markie is attracted to young, independent, and inexperienced Emmeline, who owns a travel agency boasting the slogan "Move Dangerously," because his intelligence and wit are "badly needed for Emmeline" (19). All too easily pleased by most women, only to find himself subsequently all too easily bored, Markie initially values Emmeline's apparent disdain of his superficial sociability: "Evidently his . . . manner did not go down well with her; she made him feel foolish, as though he were wearing a paper cap" (22). He values her precisely because she seems not to value him. Described by Emmeline's sister-in-law Cecilia as "not nice really, though he made me laugh; he was self-satisfied and looked rather sensual" (18), Markie is the embodiment of the man who cannot decipher or even fully appreciate distinctively female sensibilities, particularly female humor. He is too busy making an impression himself to register an impression made by someone else; he is too busy being amusing to be amused.

His lack of understanding or appreciation of anyone's humor other than his own is a fault of extreme narcissicism, and it is an error which will lead him to underestimate catastrophically the complex and unconventional nature of Emmeline's character. It would appear that Markie is more accustomed to the usual run of young women, those who are "intense in their interest, unflagging in their responsiveness, punctual with their laughter" (128) and yet it is Emmeline who arouses his interest because, in part, she does not laugh along with the laugh track provided by the genteel society in which they live. Markie, whose appetite for sexual adventure belies a deep conservativism, believes that everyone apart from himself should follow the rules, unless he instructs them otherwise. He holds dear the notion that he is the only one to observe clearly—and so have the right to alter—existing circumstances. He wants complete control over any situation he is in, and does not see that Emmeline, for all her desire to please him, is as far beyond his control as a falling star or a wild animal.

In a passage illustrative of the delicate sexual mechanics behind the perception and use of humor, Bowen shows us that Markie's wit, because of "its very nature, blunted or splintered against a quality that he called [Emmeline's] divine humourlessness" (190). Contrary to Markie's estimation, Emmeline has an exquisite and finely tuned sense of humor, what the narrator calls "a profound irony." Markie's error is that he regards Emmeline as "amusing" because he believes she is the object of his humor: "He found her—like all naive and humorless people who did not in any way represent themselves by a manner but had to be taken as they were found—funny; she seemed adorably comic" (190).

Markie's mistaking profound irony for humorlessness will be more than problematic for both characters; with increasing frequency and emphasis as the novel progresses, we see that any misreading of humor proves in some measure disastrous for all of those involved. Especially dangerous is the fact that Markie finds Emmeline a sort of "adorably comic" object instead of seeing her as an instigator of her own wry humor; he sees her as someone who does not act, but who is acted upon. This is a grave error on Markie's part.

Determined to win her, Markie presses Emmeline for both emotional and physical intimacy. The eccentricities of his personality are initially "lost on Emmeline: he might have been quite ordinary" (68), which is one reason he becomes obsessed with possession of her. When he asks her to tell him her thoughts, for example, Emmeline, "with a surprise so mild as to be either innocent or satirical . . . said: 'Do you want to know?'" (68). Appearing to be innocent, she is instead satirical; although she seems self-effacing and is often accused of being vague, Emmeline is more astute and insightful, not to mention determined and dangerous, than Markie imagines possible for a woman. When Emmeline asks him about various male and female companions to whom he refuses to introduce her, she wonders: "'Are most of your friends amusing?' 'No,' he said, definite. Emmeline responds, 'I expect they are. But as you're amusing yourself you might not notice'" (182).

By accusing Markie of being unable to see any humor except that which he initiates, Emmeline provides him with an opportunity for self-reflection which he fatally ignores. In fact, Markie consciously rejects the need to engage Emmeline as anything except a charming audience for his own performances. He writes a letter insisting that "I would do anything to amuse you, but the fact is you are so dazzlingly beautiful I really don't care if you're amused or not" (45). Yet at the outset of their relationship, Emmeline declares that "I like Markie [because] he's so funny" (48), only to have Cecilia counter that listening to Markie be clever is "like watching something catch too many flies on its tongue" (49). Markie's conversation is unapologetically built on ridicule; he has an "intelligence both ravenous and satirical" (142). He wittily attacks working women, of which Emmeline is a successful example, so effectively that even "Emmeline had to admit that this whole affair of careers for women did sound rather funny, the way Markie saw it, not unlike a ladies' race at regimental sports" (185). Yet he continues to resent the possibility that she will laugh when he does not. When a ghostly whistle floats up the inside of a wall from the basement to indicate that Markie's cook has prepared their meal, Emmeline is at first understandably startled and then enormously amused. "This seemed to Emmeline funny, she laughed immoderately. 'Why does she do that? What an extraordinary cook! Our cook doesn't whistle'" (69). Markie, however, is not amused; it is one of the earliest instances of the disjunction between Emmeline's immoderation and Markie's rage for control. Where Markie wants to control every situation, Emmeline builds even her business by supplying uncertainty: "we give clients their data: they have to use their own wits. 'Of course'—we always say to them—'you may not enjoy yourselves'" (23). Emmeline understands, as Markie does not, the power of instability. "Move Dangerously" is not an idle advertising poster. It is actually how Emmeline and her partner run their business, and, to Markie's great astonishment, it turns out to be how Emmeline lives her life. Where Markie, the unconventional man, longs for control, Emmeline, the self-conscious young woman, longs for abandonment.

This disjunction between them widens, paradoxically, as their sexual relationship progresses, until Markie is overwhelmed by Emmeline's capacity for sheer abandonment. When Emmeline organizes a flight to Paris for herself solely for the purpose of setting up a branch office in France, Markie insists upon joining her. As she waits for Markie at the aerodrome, "such an exalting idea of speed possessed Emmeline that she could hardly sit still and longed to pace to and fro—but that would annoy Markie who did not like to be made to feel late," and this passage dramatizes the tension in Emmeline between her desire for escape and her desire to please Markie (135).

Significantly, Markie's response to flight is directly contrasted to Emmeline's: for "Markie the earth was good enough, he could have asked no better; he observed, however, from Emmeline's face of delight that something had happened: earth had slipped from their wheels that, spinning, rushed up the air. They were off. Dipping, balancing, with a complete lack of impetus" (135). Unlike a number of other fictional heroines, Emmeline has no fear of flying. She enjoys the rush of power, and the disassociation from ordinary life. She likes, in short, being out of control for the moment.

Even as she leaves ordinary life behind, however, Emmeline does not lose sight of the original purpose of the visit: to contact a travel agency in Paris in order to establish a business relationship. As they fly over the channel, Emmeline writes on a napkin "What is the French for 'Interplay'?" because she is considering the way in which she will present her project to potential business partners. Markie becomes jealous of her attention to her work, since he demands always to be the focus of all emotional energy and resents any attention paid to anyone apart from himself. He begins to write flirtatious notes to Emmeline since the noise of the airplane makes it difficult to speak. Markie is, in fact, quite taken with this manner of correspondence because it involves a "deliberation unknown in speaking, boldness quite unrebuked by its own vibrations and, free of that veil of uncertainty and oblivion that falls on the posted letter. . . . The indiscretions of letter-writing, the intimacies of speech were at once his" (137). He takes advantage of the possibility for indiscretion, and scribbles to Emmeline that "you must know what I want: all I want: If I COULD marry, it would be you" (138). But he also makes it clear that he does not intend to marry her.

Emmeline loses her virginity to Markie in a Paris hotel. Instead of feeling triumphant in his conquest, however, Markie feels conquered by Emmeline's passion and, in an echo of their respective responses to the plane journey, oppressed "by sensations of having been overshot, of having, in some final soaring flight of her exaltation, been outdistanced: as though a bird whose heart one moment one could feel beating had escaped from between the hands." Markie is profoundly disturbed by the "passionless entirety of her surrender, the volition of her entire wish to be his had sent her a good way past him: involuntarily, the manner of her abandonment had avenged her innocence" (147). The joke is, in a significant way, on Markie. Once again, Emmeline proves to be more than the passive audience he expects. She is in control of her own capacity for passion and pleasure. And yet she is devastated when, almost immediately, Markie wants to put distance between them. Emmeline recollects "How Cecilia had told her men always chose to explain things at the most curious times" when, after once again emphasizing that people "like you and me" do not marry, Markie says "much more cheerfully: 'If I shot anyone, I am the sort of man I should shoot'" as if this line exonerates him for all responsibility towards the woman who has just become his lover (150). It is important to note that Emmeline likes Paris taxis because "'they're like the Last Ride Together'"[3] and then immediately reminds Markie of the moment when she laughed and he did not: "'Do you remember your cook that night? How annoyed you were'" (147). The twinning of the Browning poem and Markie's petulant refusal to appreciate Emmeline's laughter reflects the importance of the disparity between their responses. Both Emmeline's laughter and anger grow more self-conscious as the relationship with Markie deteriorates, so that it is as if "something restlessly ate up the air, like a flame burning" (180).

Markie senses the turn in her from delight to fury and is "much afraid for himself. He was afraid, as she stood there so gently beside him, as much *of* as *for* Emmeline: it was almost physical" (my italics; 193). He does not know how to break things off, and so is ruthlessly cruel to her on the second journey upon which they embark as lovers. At one tense moment, Emmeline perceives with all the "lucidity of a nightmare" the "dead stop of his tenderness [which] flicked off sharply as electricity," and "his incomprehension and ice-cold anger" (209). When Emmeline becomes upset at his inappropriate behavior, he declares her mad and indicates "that her madness was nothing to him" (210). Emmeline recognizes "a profound and slighting contempt for her point of view, that must have underlain at all times his tenderness" (210). When she admits her vulnerability to Markie by asking him to spend the night, he declares "Quite frankly, I don't care to stay in a cottage this size with a cold and hysterical woman." Emmeline, who has told Markie that she feels as if he will kill her with such unkindness, says in response only "I see," and drops her voice suddenly, whereupon Markie, "fixing her eyes with his cold eyes . . . had that uneasy feeling, that quick touch of physical fear again, as though something were going to spring" (212). Emmeline's anger is not irrational: she is right to be jealous and to be angry. Markie has, by this point in the novel, been drawn back into an earlier relationship with a "rather lowish" woman who provides the empty-headed audience for which he truly longs.

In one of the scenes most characteristic of Bowen, and one which links her back to Lennox, Austen, Bronte, and Eliot, Emmeline shatters the thin shell of her conventional femininity by refusing to muffle her desires and fears. Not being able to reach her lover, Emmeline telephones Daisy in the middle of the night to ask if Markie is there. She overhears Daisy's foolish whisper as well as Markie's muffled and irritated response. After this incident, Markie decides that he is through with Emmeline because "a woman who rang up Daisy would stop at nothing; things began to be dangerous. . . . He loathed suffering, out of place in the rational scheme" (233). Even before this indiscretion, "her wildness appalled Markie. And to this wildness, this flood, this impetus that he could not arrest, there appeared no limit" (185). He is most appalled, in other words, by the fact that he cannot control her.

Markie finds her immoderation in anger as unnerving as immoderation in laughter and so refuses to continue their relationship. As Emmeline becomes increasingly distraught, a close male companion considers forcing Markie to accept responsibility for his injury to Emmeline. Julian, however, decides in a particularly insightful moment that to do so is to deny Emmeline the right to her own destiny. "Championship has to discount in the woman anything but passivity," decides Julian; "to deny that she could not have been undone without some exercise, however fatal, of her discretion and was in fact her own to ruin" (191). Emmeline abandons hope of seeing Markie again.

Yet, after months of silent rejection, when Markie sees Emmeline at a dinner party, he is enchanted by the way she has resumed her aloof and impenetrable manner. He is flooded with renewed desire to possess her, and when she offers to drive him home, he accepts gladly. Still believing that he can control her, he belatedly and offhandedly offers marriage by asserting that "here I still am. And you're something I can't get past. In a sense, I'm done for" (241). Bowen's irony here makes a profound point in much the same way as the earlier reference to "The Last Ride Together": the stress falls on Markie's sense of entitlement being undercut by Emmeline's refusal and anger. "[W]e'll have to be on a footing: we'll have to marry," Markie jokingly taunts Emmeline. She now rejects him by explaining, while with "pressure from her silver slipper" the speedometer needle creeps up, "I can't marry anyone now." Bowen explains that Emmeline's speed "had the startled wildness of flight" (243).

As she follows the motorway signs "To the North," Emmeline arrives at the territory of exile familiar to women: "the North laid its first chilly fingers upon their temples, creeping down into his collar and stirring her hair at the roots. . . . [T]his icy rim to the known world began to possess his fancy, till he half expected its pale reflection ahead. Cut apart by cold singing air he and she had no communication" (238). "There's no truth left," Emmeline observes, as she drives more recklessly, "ignorant of their lives" and then offers "[o]r is it I that am mad? There seems to be no truth anywhere" (239). In an ironic echo of Markie's earlier rejection of her as hysterical, Emmeline is now calmly playing his description of her as the madwoman as her little car, "strung on speed," swerves progressively closer to danger. Rushing at increasing speed towards the outer boundaries of the possible, Markie insists that Emmeline may "[k]eep driving all night, angel: you won't get away from this!" (243). Emmeline, however, does get away by keeping them on the course she alone has set; having made herself vulnerable to Markie once, she is now literally in the driver's seat. When he at last calls her name, "dazzled, she turned to smile," while driving them into the headlights of an oncoming car (259). Coupling the ecstatic experiences of sex and death, Bowen illustrates the way in which the female figure embodies passage from one point to another. For Bowen's female characters, humor, sex and death depend on the breaking down of established patterns as well as the refusal to accept the constrictions of conventional femininity.

Women's positions are indefinite within the dominant ideology. They therefore entrust themselves to chance, having learned that what appear as choices for them are deceptive at worst and severely limited at best; they are hardly choices at all. The forces of chaos offer the preferred options. Bowen's characters realize that they are "entrusted to one another by chance, not choice. Chance, and its agents time and place. Chance is better than choice; it is more lordly. In its carelessness it is more lordly" (*Little Girls* 252). Bowen explores "a rising tide of hallucination" (*Collected Impressions* 49) in her fictions, because the "small worlds-within-worlds of hallucination" are "in most cases, saving hallucination" (50). Hallucination is no more imaginative than the so-called stability of the everyday because "once a board gives, the raft begins breaking up. Were not awaited people killed in the streets every day?" (*House in Paris* 127).

But change, as Bowen writes in *The Little Girls*, is almost never "convulsive"; rather, "what is there is there; there comes to be something fictitious about what is not" (166). Revolutionary change appears only as the most remote of possibilities, but it nevertheless holds a glittering, seductive charge. For Bowen's female characters particularly, the burning down of the old order holds enormous appeal. In *The House in Paris*, a young woman explains how she wishes "the revolution would come soon; I should like to start fresh while I am still young, with everything that I had to depend on gone." She continues to explain that those with position in society, counting herself among them, are "unfortunate" because "we have nothing ahead. I feel it's time something happened. . . . I should like it to happen in spite of me" (82). One critic writes of this character that "she wants a conflagration: it will mean change, at least. . . . Lois's wish to be violently precipitated into her future is granted with a vengeance: it is as though her restlessness in part wills the end" of the dominant ideology (Lee 45).

Longing for the revolution is rather different from longing for the prince on a white horse; longing for revolution is different from longing for refuge. In traditional comedies, refuge offered by the prince (or whatever representative form he should take) is considered a happy ending, a fulfillment of the heroine's deepest wishes. In Bowen, revolution offers the possibility of real joy because it holds the promise of continued change, yet all too often the revolutions of history move only in full circles. The system revolves, only to stay within the same circle of conventional history which ensures continuation rather than actual change or destruction. Women are taught not to expect very much, then, from minor alterations in the order from which real change is excluded: "People must hope so much when they tear streets up and fight at barricades," comments one of Bowen's older women, who goes on to explain "but, whoever wins, the streets are laid again and the trams start running again. One hopes too much of destroying things. If revolutions do not fail, they fail you" (*House in Paris* 151). This displacement of the politics of government by the politics of gender is central to Bowen. The boundaries remain in place in the narratives constructed by these writers because subversion takes place on a more subtle level. More dangerous perhaps for the traditional order than war and the destruction of literal walls is the recognition by women, silently, among themselves, that the walls are arbitrary, and that these walls can be brought down by the powerful, heretical, and subversive laughter of women.

6

The Ancestral Laughter of the Streets: Humor in Muriel Spark's Earlier Works

It is known as a scrambler, because the connection is heavily jammed with jangling caterwauls to protect the conversation against eavesdropping; this harrowing noise all but prevents the speakers from hearing each other, but once the knack is mastered it is easy to hear the voice at the other end.

Muriel Spark, *The Hothouse by the East River*

Since she started writing in the early 1950's, Muriel Spark has received enormous critical attention. Evelyn Waugh called her first book "highly exhilarating" (*Spectator*, 22 February 1951) and her subsequent work "dazzling" (*Spectator*, 7 July 1961). She has been called "the reasonable recorder of unreason" and likened, of course, to Jane Austen—"the Jane Austen of the surrealists," according to one critic (Hoyt 280).

Spark's work, like Elizabeth Bowen's, has a wide appeal and has spanned over forty years. David Lodge has called Spark "the most gifted and innovative British novelist of her generation, one of the very few who can claim to have extended and altered the possibility of the form for other practitioners" (Lodge 1). Frank Kermode has said of Spark's novels that "some literate people dislike them, though not, so far as I know, for decent reasons" ("The Prime of Miss Muriel Spark" 397). The reasons some people dislike them may be more or less summed up by the following comments on Spark's works by Frederick Karl, which appear in *The Contemporary English Novel*:

> [Spark's] novels . . . are so involved with the eccentric event and the odd personality that they have virtually no content. Miss Spark's novels are a sport, light to the point of froth. She can write about murder, betrayal, deception, and adultery as though these were the norms of a crazy-quilt society. (126)

Karl concludes by saying that she "lacks penetration." But, to apply to his opinion of Spark what another critic has concluded concerning Karl's remarks about Iris Murdoch: "Karl's misunderstanding . . . is so radical as to be helpful" (Kuehl 38). Peter Kemp has offered the following explanation for the perception of Spark's work by some critics—including but unfortunately not limited to Karl—as "lightweight": "books so entertaining, it is felt, must be proportionately trivial" (8). Novelist John Updike, not surprisingly, has difficulties with Spark, though he admires what he calls the "ominous . . . witchcraft" of her work: "The undercurrents of destruction [and] madness . . . are allowed to run unspoken, welling up here and there, as they do in life, with an unexpectedness that would be comic if we could laugh" (192). Updike may seem sympathetic, but he *cannot laugh* and this is perhaps the most illustrative of the remarks made by male critics concerning comedic works by women writers. Women's writing, they claim, would be comic if "we" (sic) could laugh. It is my argument that *we* are indeed laughing. *They*, including Updike, are not.

For women writers, including Spark, undercurrents of destruction and unexpected wellsprings of madness are more a definition of women's comedy than an argument against it. These unspoken currents act like the jumbled text put through on the scrambler: they are there but difficult to perceive without initiation. However, Spark's subversive comedy, like the submerged text, is "easy to hear" "once the knack is mastered," in other words, once the dislocating, encoded aspects of comedy can be perceived within the more conventional comedic context.

Spark deals with what Kermode rather neatly termed "a radically non-contingent reality" (*The Sense of the Ending* 131), and these aspects of her work as the "surrealist Jane Austen" have been discussed with more attention than the parallel aspects of Bowen's apparently more conservative fiction. V. B. Richmond, for example, writes that Spark's fiction "mirrors the uncertainty, confusion, infidelity, and violence that are ordinary characteristics of contemporary society" (106). In contrast, Faith Pullin claims that Spark's severe editing of her text "encourages the reader to suspend his belief, not his disbelief" (76). Quoting from *Loitering with Intent*, Pullin contextualizes Spark's gift for unreality: "complete frankness is not a quality that favours art" (76). Striking a similar note in her article "The Canonization of Muriel Spark," Sharon Thompson says that she counts "Catholics, feminists, misogynists, postmodernists, Fowlerites, and those with a simple taste for a wicked tongue among Spark's supporting factions" (9).

Spark does not seem to write for the "general reader" despite her wide audience. It may be instructive to take note of how two of her characters discuss this very issue in *Loitering with Intent*:

"Fuck the general reader," Solly said, "because in fact the general reader doesn't read."

"That's what I say," Edwina yelled. "Just fuck the general reader. No such person" (56).

Pullin makes an important point linking Spark's refusal to create so-called realist fictions for the "general reader" and her position as a woman writer. In "Autonomy and Fabulation in the Fiction of Muriel Spark," Pullin argues that the subtlety of Spark's work "is nowhere more evident than in the treatment of her women characters. . . . Her women are initiators, actors, magicians whose 'real' nature, like that of life itself, can never be known" (91).

Judy Little provides what is the best feminist criticism of Spark in her book juxtaposing the works of Spark with those of Virginia Woolf. Little examines their use of comedy in terms similar to those which we have established:

> When Spark and Woolf evaluate relationships between the sexes, and use such an ascetic norm to do so, their laughter is not content to tease follies and flail vices, or to urge a little common sense. Their laughter instead demands a radically "new plot." Woolf and Spark, from different directions, approach the four-thousand-year-old secular scripture and rip the temple curtain from top to bottom. (178)

Little's recognition of the ways in which Spark seeks to destroy the "secular script" of patriarchal authority through comedy implies the use of aggression and anger as weapons of comedy. Peter Kemp has noted the way "multiple instances of malice and aggression crowd the narratives" of Spark (7), but even his use of the verb "crowd" indicates his inability to see this malice and aggression as the encoded forces that will "rip" through boundaries to allow for the limitlessness, the non-closure of Spark's comedy.

Kemp is not the only one to see Spark's anger. Sharon Thompson provides a provocative discussion of the effectiveness of Spark's undercurrent of rage as women's subversive discourse in her comments on *The Driver's Seat*, pointing out those very elements that seem to make Updike too nervous to laugh: "It takes an iron stomach to write a plot like that. I've read angrier rhetoric in fiction by women, but . . . no angrier plot. It's stunning—actually scandalizing. In comparison, Rhys's novels, which I love, snivel and Lessing's slop" (9). Indeed, Spark's portrayal of anger and refusal characterizes both her short stories and novels. In *The Girls of Slender Means*, Spark explores the imposed disingenuousness of women who are dangerously ruthless—while never forfeiting their role as ingenue. Spark explains at the beginning of the novel that, as the girls realize themselves to "varying

degrees": "Few people alive at the time were more delightful, more ingenious, more movingly lovely, and, as it might happen, more savage, than the
girls of slender means" (6). Spark herself has defended literature of aggressive intent claiming that: "the only effective art of our particular time is the
satirical, the harsh and witty, the ironic and derisive. . . . We have come to a
moment in history when we are surrounded on all sides and oppressed by the
absurd" (Cited in Kemp 14). In keeping with our argument that women's
comedy re-doubles anger rather than expelling it, Kemp remarks, "glycerine
soothes, but acid galvanizes" (114).

Even the most "innocent" figure in a Spark novel is capable of savagery; in *The Comforters*, one character notes that "everyone can do harm,
whether they [sic] mean it or not" (128). Often the most innocent figure in a
Spark fiction is also the most savage, having been denied access to more acceptable forms of refusal or even participation within the dominant society.
Spark's characters, in particular her women characters, are marginal, peripheral, exiled from all acceptable systems of power. These marginal
figures attempt to hide their anger under conventional behavior. They try
to "say anything beside the point rather than what [one] might say, at such
moments, pointedly" when they "have a sharp tongue" (*Robinson* 73). But often their anger emerges, like the clear message through the scrambler, for
those willing to hear.

On the one hand, a number of Spark's heroines are believed by the
members of their immediate community to be suicidal, depressed, mad, engaged in espionage, possessed or even, in one extreme instance, already
dead. On the other hand, a number of characters who in fact are murderous,
insane, or even dead are not recognized as such. Spark does not shy away
from extremes; she can be compared to the sensationalist novelists discussed
by Showalter who inverted the stereotypes of traditional novels and paro-
died the conventions of their male contemporaries. Spark follows the same
route, it can be argued, and her novels express "female anger, frustration,
and sexual energy more directly than had been done previously. . . . women
escape from their families through illness, madness, divorce, flight, and ultimately murder" (Showalter 160). As Kermode argues in "Sheerer Spark," the
very plot of *The Driver's Seat* is an inversion of a conventional comedy. The
narrative can be reduced to its essentials: girl meets boy, girl loses boy, girl
finds boy. Happy ending? When that plot is carried out to its typical (what
Frye would call its "normal") conclusion, perhaps, but Spark's results are
rape, murder and deviance. What is normal becomes corrupt in Spark's
fiction. Lise, the main character, "is looking for her type," Kermode summarizes, "seeking on her vacation a murderer as other girls might seek a lover.
She finds him on the plane, loses him, and recovers him," but the confusion
dislocates comedy, dislodges it from any possibilities of stasis, comfort, rec-

onciliation or social acceptability. Spark reshapes expectations in order to introduce the forces of chaos and non-closure, as well as her particular perfection: surprise.

Spark writes from what she calls the "nevertheless" principle, a principle which is based on the overturning of expectations. She remarks: "In fact I approve of the ceremonious accumulation of weather forecasts and barometer-readings that pronounce for a fine day, before letting rip on the statement: 'Nevertheless, it's raining'. I find that much of my literary composition is based on the nevertheless idea" (Cited in Kemp 7). "There is more to be had from the world than a balancing of accounts," Spark writes in *The Only Problem* (44), underscoring her refusal to supply conventionally happy, tidy endings. Ruth Whittaker writes that Spark "has an impatience with mimesis since her real concern is with the inimitable" (168). Kemp argues that Spark keeps to "her own axiom that if fiction is not stranger than truth it ought to be" (8). These comments point to the fact that Spark systematically refuses to accept the "absolutes" encoded within man-made cultural systems. It is significant that in *Robinson*, January Marlow, the only female character, keeps a journal even though she remarks that "through my journal I nearly came to my death" (7). Marlow suggests why her writings are important even though she does not consider herself an objective recorder of "reality": "though I know it to be distorted, never quite untrue, never entirely true, [my journal] interests me. I am as near the mark as myth is to history, the apocrypha to the canon" (137). January argues that writing "fetches before me the play of thought and action hidden amongst the recorded facts" (7), and it is what is hidden among recorded fact that Spark considers necessary to explore. "The secret play of thought and action" (7) is for Spark the most important aspect of comedy.

Spark draws heavily on the multiplicitous structures of mythology. Fleur Talbot of *Loitering with Intent* comments on the necessity of the mythological in literature and argues persuasively against the systematic application of convention and closure: "Without a mythology, a novel is nothing. The true novelist, one who understands the work as a continuous poem, is a mythmaker, and then wonder of the art resides in the endless different ways of telling a story, and the methods are mythological by nature" (*Loitering with Intent* 100). The heroine of *The Abbess of Crewe* explains that as far as she is concerned "history doesn't work. . . . We have entered the sphere, dear Sisters, of Mythology" (16). Perhaps this is because Spark links women with mythology and in doing so reaffirms the value of the illogical, irrational and disruptive. "And it is said the pagan mind runs strong in women at any time," writes January Marlow, the only woman to survive the plane crash in *Robinson*, "let alone on an island" (9). *Robinson* is Spark's most explicit exploration of women's link with mythology and sorcery. Hoyt writes in an essay subtitled "The Surrealist Jane Austen" that Spark "understands that the artist traces his [*sic*] descent from the sorcerer" (130), and as we see from January's own perceptions, her writing is connected to the "whole period's," being "touched with a preancestral quality, how there was an enchantment, a primitive blood-force which probably moved us all" (9). Particular characters, like Georgiana Hogg of *The Comforters*, can have "turbulent mythical dimensions" (154) and characters like Dougal Douglas from *The Ballad of Peckham Rye* are out-and-out inhabitants of the fabular dimension.

Spark's use of mythology embodies the insight of the Italian proverb of which Spark is fond: "if it isn't true, it's to the point" (*Public Image* 43). Spark's fictions work towards unveiling the nature of truth as itself the deliberate construction of, in the words of one critic, "a supreme fiction." Her narratives operate by "cutting through the barriers of overused language and situation a sense of reality true to experience, an imaginative extension of the world, a lie that shows us things as they are—a supreme fiction" (Malkoff 3). Spark concerns herself with the ways in which innocence, particularly the innocence imposed on women, is a danger to the symbolic, patriarchal order. David Lodge has written, for example, that "Miss Brodie was not a wicked woman, but a dangerously innocent one." He quotes from a scene in *The Prime of Miss Jean Brodie* in which Sandy, one of Brodie's former pupils, now a nun in a convent, speaks to a former friend: "'Oh, she was quite an innocent in her way' said Sandy [to Jenny], clutching the bars of her grille." Lodge argues that innocence is "dangerous and volatile because [it is] ignorant of real good and evil" ("Uses and Abuses of Omniscience" 60).

One of the more dangerous ways innocence transfigures itself in Spark is through the creation of apparently material reality initiated by belief or thought; Spark's works are informed by the "transfiguration of the commonplace," a phrase taken from the title of Sandy Stranger's (or, as she becomes in the convent, Sister Helena of the Transfiguration) treatise on psychology. Spark emphasizes the ways language shapes and creates reality since there is no objective reality; she focuses on "the ways fiction can body forth the shape of things unknown" (*The Prime of Miss Muriel Spark* 397). An example of this transfiguration occurs in *The Hothouse by the East River* where Elsa and her husband Paul are dead and living in New York. Paul believes they exist because of Elsa's will: "His heart thumps for help. 'Help me! Help me!' cries his heart, battering the sides of the coffin. 'The schizophrenic has imposed her will. Her delusion, her figment, her nothing-there, has come to pass'" (14). Spark's phrase "her nothing-there" highlights the use of absence, empty space, and the "hollows" of language and reality in women's writing. In *The Driver's Seat*, for instance, Lise's room is described in terms of absence: "the lines of the room are pure; space is used as a pattern in itself" (11). The same can be said of Spark's prose. Art is, in fact, linked to the noth-ing-there element of language, as one of Spark's characters explains in her short story "The Playhouse Called Remarkable": "And if ever you produce a decent poem or a story, it won't be on account of anything you've got in this world but of something remarkable which you haven't got" (*The Stories of Muriel Spark* 103). In perhaps her most elegant use of absence as pattern, Spark ends *The Public Image* with an image of space, but space which con-tains the infinite. The main focus of the book, Annabel, has been described by her vicious husband as all surface, an empty shell. But Spark revises the damning phrases of the husband with his limited vision to create a benedic-tion of the limitlessness contained within Annabel and within all women: "She was pale as a shell . . . [and had a] sense weightlessly and perpetually within her, as an empty shell contains, by its very structure, the echo and harking image of former and former seas" (192).

Absence, echo, space and the hollows of things supply meaning. In contrast, substance, the material manifestation of apparent reality, can be misleading and should not be trusted. In a brief essay on a fresco by Piero della Francesca, Spark comments that "today we know more about sub-stance than ever before, but the more we know the more it is recognized that we know nothing" ("Spirit and Substance" 103). Spark claims, in the third act of her play *The Doctors of Philosophy*, that "realism is very flimsy." The only difficulty for the characters, usually women, who realize the flimsy nature of reality, is convincing others, usually men, of what they have discovered. Elsa of *Hothouse by the East River* argues to her husband Paul that while he might seem to accept what she says, he will refuse to accept her truth. It becomes useless, according to Elsa, to attempt explanation: "[y]ou'll believe me, yes, but you won't believe that it really happened. What's the use of telling you?" (4). However, women who recognise the flimsy nature of reality learn, like Elsa, to use the power of their own beliefs to revise the pliable substance of reality.

Everything created by language "involves a tangled mixture of damag-ing lies, flattering and plausible truths" (54). Kemp notes that in her study of John Masefield, Spark exclaims: "how sharp and lucid fantasy can be when it is deliberately intagliated on the surface of realism" (Cited in Kemp 40). According to Kemp, Spark is writing not primarily as social chronicler but as "an artist, a changer of actuality into something else" (85). Things can be transfigured, as we have noted, through language.

Through a sort of language-transubstantiation, the "real" can be cre-ated. In *Robinson* we learn that "the awful thing about . . . insinuations" is that "you never know, they might be true," (123) or they might become true through sheer belief. For example, we learn in *Hothouse* that if "Paul could

be induced to believe this man's somebody else, then he will become somebody else. It's a matter of persevering in a pretense" (38). *The Comforters*
contains the most consistent playing out of the idea of the transubstantiation of the apparent absolutes of reality, such as material existence. In a
telling remark, Carolyn, the novel's protagonist, explains to her fiancee
(who believes in "objective existence") that things "might have another sort
of existence and still be real" (70).

Spark's female characters initially spend a great deal of energy attempting, like Elsa, to convince those around them that what we perceive as
real is no more substantial than the imaginary. These characters abandon
the attempt after realizing that they are in fact in control of situations that
they had originally perceived as outside of their sphere of influence. This is
the pattern of comedy in Spark's novels: the gradual knowing of the absurdity of the absolute by male as well as female characters. Spark's central characters come to understand that so-called reality can be revised, reshaped and
undermined by the power of the peripheral, powers more accessible to wom-
en than to men. Men and women, explains January of *Robinson*, can be "on
the same island but in different worlds" (144). Women characters, like Carolyn of *The Comforters*, have a unique understanding of the multiple layers
forming apparent reality. Like Carolyn, they understand that "the voices
are voices. Of course they are symbols. But they are also voices. There's the
typewriter too—that's a symbol, but it is a real typewriter. I hear it" (75).

It is not surprising that Carolyn, who is writing a book on twentieth-
century fiction entitled "Form in the Modern Novel" is "having difficulty
with the chapter on realism" (62). Kermode comments that "[t]he relation of
fiction and reality is uniquely reimagined" in Spark's novels, claiming that
Spark requires the reader to undergo "a radical re-appraisal of this relation."
Kermode argues that Spark accommodates "different versions of reality, including what some call mythical and some call absolute" ("Prime of Miss
Muriel Spark" 131). Spark rarely deals in absolutes. Like other women writers, especially writers of comedy, she refers to the subjective nature of even
the most superficially objective "givens." Very little indeed is universally
perceived: "There were other people's Edinburghs quite different from hers,
and with which she held only the names of districts and streets and monu-
ments in common. Similarly, there were other people's nineteen-thirties"
(*Jean Brodie* 50). Spark's fictions depend on our perception and understanding of what she calls the "shifting ground" of reality (*Comforters* 107). The
"picture" or subjective reality replaces the "truth," or objective reality. For
example, in *Hothouse by the East River*, someone wants "the picture, the
whole picture and nothing but the picture" (17). Spark articulates through
her novels the concept that the conventional pattern has no authority and
must be understood to be the dominant fiction rather than the "truth." This

leads, as we should expect, to the refusal to portray, even in the comedic context, a secure world. "Nowhere's safe," says a character in *The Girls of Slender Means* (155). The implications of non-closure, subversion and revision for comedic narrative are clear.

One critic, for example, castigates Spark for "her refusal to be committed, to solve her fictional situations, for her readiness to abandon all for a jest, for her random satire" (Stubbs 33), for precisely those elements which we now see are functional determinants of women's comedy. Spark explores the peripheral boundaries of fiction and is unapologetic about refusing to supply conventional comedic closure. Spark links the forces of creation and chaos with her usual (and much discussed) economy of method in a number of novels. In *Robinson*, for example, a character explains that "if you choose the sort of life which has no conventional pattern you have to try to make an art of it, or it is a mess" (84). The ability to overcome conventional patterns is of enormous importance in Spark's fictions. She views the writer as anarchist, as a subversive figure, armed with humor against the dominant ideology: "There is a kind of truth in the popular idea of an anarchist as a wild man with a home-made bomb in his pocket. In modern times this bomb, fabricated in the back workshops of the imagination, can only take one effective form: Ridicule" (*Girls of Slender Means* 69).

Kemp quotes Spark on the subject of writing-as-subversion: "I would like to see," she writes, "a more deliberate cunning, a more derisive undermining of what is wrong, I would like to see less emotion and more intelligence in these efforts to impress our minds and hearts" (114). He presents her views on fiction as undermining or at least forcing us to recognise the "ridiculous nature" of what is passed off as reality: "'We have come to a moment in history,' Mrs. Spark claims, 'when we are surrounded on all sides and oppressed by the absurd': and what this means for literature, she argues, is that 'the rhetoric of our times should persuade us to contemplate the ridiculous nature of the reality before us, and teach us to mock it'" (146).

It is worth considering in brief the manner in which Spark's subversion of realism has been handled critically. Spark often displays the destruction of boundaries between the "real" and the imaginary through events of great emotional violence, by which she shifts our perspective and reveals what Malkoff has categorized as the "bizarre underpinnings of the superficially conventional" (3). Kemp argues, noting the dialectical interplay between the apparently acceptable/conventional and the subversive/chaotic in Spark: "Many of [Spark's] fiction's features are immediately recognizable: what makes its effect disorienting and, indeed, almost hallucinatory is that the pattern into which they would normally fall has been violently deranged" (141).

Faith Pullin characterizes Spark's fiction in the very terms we have established for women's comedy when she argues that "the nature of Muriel Spark's fiction is its duplicity; she specializes in the subverting of expectations. As she herself claims, in the well-known "House of Fiction" interview, "what I write is not true—it is a pack of lies" (71). Valerie Shaw agrees, in her article on Spark entitled "Fun and Games with Life-stories." Shaw proposes that there is "clearly a strong case to be made for [Spark's] work as being actually subversive of realism" (46). Vera Richmond calls Spark's central characters "shape shifters" (74). Caroline of *The Comforters* asks at one point, "Is the world a lunatic asylum then? Are we all courteous maniacs discreetly making allowances for everyone else's derangement?" (196) and Spark answers, with a smile, "yes."

Spark's comedy in fact rests on being able to undermine the valid currency of the dominant ideology by "shifting the ground" of her narrative discourse. "Once you admit you can change the object" of a belief, she writes in *The Girls of Slender Means*, "you undermine the whole structure" (23). Spark depends on the traditional systematic acceptance of convention, it is true, because otherwise she would be unable to subvert expectations as regularly as she does. This point has been noted by a number of critics, although few of them link the undermining of convention directly with comedy. Rosalind Miles, for example, writes that "convention . . . has to be understod as the basis for nearly all of Muriel Spark's fiction; she assumes our familiarity with its precepts in order to be able to undercut and diminish them" (58), while Hoyt sees in Spark "an almost irresponsible impertinence towards everyday reality" (128). Alan Bold believes that Spark "confronts realistic detail with surrealistic tension, invests natural incidents with supernatural overtones. Her fiction is not contained by a rigid narrative framework; it unfolds in a visionary dimension" (9).

Spark's uncanny ability to make ordinary conversation take on a surrealistic quality has received much attention. The "visionary dimension" in her work can quickly accommodate the commonplace by illustrating the ways simple misreadings take place, the ways in which those uninitiated in language systems and thereby uninitiated in the language of authority attempt to find meaning. Lise of *The Driver's Seat* is probably Spark's most marginal figure in that she is on the very periphery of social acceptance. She has no friends, no family, no socially prescribed role except the one supplied through employment. She cannot recognize deviance when she meets it since she has little sense of the norm. In the following exchange, for example, Lise attempts to hide her marginality, not even aware of the marginal nature of the man's own discourse. She thinks he must be making sense because he is a man. Lise believes she should understand him, and so, illustrating the most damaging sort of duplicity, she pretends that she does:

"You know what Yin is?" he says.

She says, "Well, sort of . . . but it's only a snack, isn't it?"

"You understand what Yin is?" "Well, it's a kind of slang, isn't it. You say a thing's a bit too yin. . ."; plainly she is groping.

"Yin," says Bill, "is the opposite of Yang." (33)

Even the health-food addict appears more in control than Lise because he perceives himself as an authority; Lise, however, ultimately controls the actions of the novel, despite her inability to grasp the concept of yin and yang.

Judy Little provides one of the few arguments defining the comedy in Spark's narratives as gender-based. "In Spark's fiction possibility is assured," Little argues, "in effect, guaranteed—by an absolute, eternal openness that judges and shocks any human effort at easy closure" (187). This, of course, supports the theory that women's comedy is itself characterized by the limitlessness of its endings, by the refusal to construct a conventional sense of finality at the end of the narrative. "Knots were not necessarily created to be untied," writes Spark, and continues: "[q]uestions were things that sufficed in their still beauty answering themselves" (Cited in Kemp 156).

But Spark does not only provide passive resistance to the narrative conventions which she refuses to employ; she sees in non-closure possibilities beyond those usually identified with the twentieth-century British novel. Returning to the figure of the writer as bomb-throwing anarchist, she writes that: "Any system . . . which doesn't allow for the unexpected and the unwelcome is a rotten one. . . . Things mount up inside one, and then one has to perpetrate an outrage" (*Robinson* 162). We must remind ourselves often that, as Spark writes at the end of *Robinson*, "all things are possible" (174). We must retain, she insists in *The Prime of Miss Jean Brodie*, "a sense of the hidden possibilities in all things" (119) and even the ability to be "unnaturally exhilarated," like Caroline in *The Comforters*, "by a sense of adventure" (64).

Spark informs her readers about "a lot of subjects irrelevant to the authorised curriculum," as one character calls alternatives to the prevailing authority-system in *The Prime of Miss Jean Brodie*. Spark herself teaches the literary equivalent of the "rudiments of astrology but not the date of the Battle of Flodden" (10) by providing narratives that undercut the system while remaining within it, much as Brodie teaches astrology while the girls in her class hold up their history textbooks in case the headmistress should walk by the class. Spark provides a narrative "cover" for her subversive text similar to the one Brodie uses when she keeps a multiplication question on the board during math hour while she speaks to her girls about art, sex and how witch-hazel is better for skin than soap and water. Sandy, Brodie's star pupil and ultimately her betrayer, learns to uncover the subtext of the most apparently innocent utterance under Miss Brodie's influence: "Sandy, who

had turned eleven, perceived that the tone of 'morning' in good morning
made the word seem purposely to rhyme with 'scorning,' so that these colleagues of Miss Brodie's might just as well have said, 'I scorn you,' instead
of good morning" (79). And even as Miss Brodie encouraged her girls to re-
cite, with feeling, "The Lady of Shalott," she also assured them that "the
people perish" and bids Eunice to "come and do a somersault in order that
we may have a comic relief" (13). Comedy is the mainstay of Spark's fiction.
In fact, Spark has described her experience of writing full-length fiction after the poetry and criticism she had earlier attempted by saying, "the novel
enabled me to express the comic side of my mind and at the same time work
out some serious theme" (Cited in Kemp 11).

In "Muriel Spark's Fingernails," Malcolm Bradbury discusses Spark
primarily as a writer of comedy. He sees the precision and economy of
Spark's comedy as shaped by a "tactic of indifference" which provides
"poise" for her aesthetic manner. He writes of Spark's "splendid impudence"
in creating a "decidedly strange view of the world and of human potential
and the human condition" (138), but like Hoyt, who sees Spark's "uncomfortable and distinctive humor" as a departure from the "humane world of
the traditional, realist novel" (169), Bradbury perceives Spark as providing
clever but not particularly revolutionary texts.

Kemp's framing of Spark's comedy provides, with the exception of Little's, the only viable way to accommodate the non-closure and consistent
use of subversive humor throughout Spark's texts. Kemp quotes the response of one critic to *The Girls of Slender Means*: "I enjoyed it as a joke until it stopped being a joke" (8). Kemp argues:

> To read Muriel Spark in this way is to mistake the varnish for
> the picture. Her books are never simply jokes, though they in-
> variably contain them; they are not eccentric jeux d'esprit,
> ephemeral and whimsical. Comic, it has to be stressed in any ap-
> proach to these novels, does not equate with trivial, any more
> than solemn does with valuable. It is a commonplace to describe
> certain works as deeply serious: the books of Mrs. Spark are
> deeply funny. (8)

The "deeply funny" nature of Spark's work draws on the power of the marginal and the magical. In obvious parallel to what Updike called Spark's
"ominous . . . witchcraft," (which, as we noticed, prevented him from laughing) stand the figures of the hysteric and the sorceress, urging laughter and
abandon. Spark's comedy is tied in some way to the primitive ritual of exor-
cising evil, a number of critics have claimed, but what might appear evil to
Spark and other women writers might be the very thing which to others is
the embodiment of good. Spark does not accept convention, she mocks the

most strongly accepted norms. Like one of her own favorite writers, John Henry Newman, Spark could reply to critics who criticize her for being overly satirical that "what they think is exaggeration, I think truth" (Cited in Bold 61).

The inevitable (male) criticism, "that's not funny," and its response, appears as follows in *The Hothouse by the East River*:

> "I don't see what there is to laugh at," Paul tells her. . . .
> "it has it's funny side," she says. (133)

Lodge writes that "it is perfectly true that [Spark's] imagination is fascinated by revenge, humiliation and ironic reversals, and that she looks upon pain and death with a dry, glittering eye" (Omnipotence" 169); nevertheless, he also sees Spark as primarily a writer of comedy. Her comedy is undeniably informed by her anger. She presents us with "something between a wedding and a funeral on a world scale" (*Girls of Slender Means* 16). Richmond calls it "hilarity and rueful recognition" (79). Instead of leading us to reconciliation and regeneration, Spark's comedy, like that of other women writers, is directed towards recognition and realization, even if this process marginalizes the characters even further from the dominant ideology. Perhaps the process of moving further from the vortex of power, the pull of false "reality" as the most desirable choice should be couched not in terms of "even" but of "especially."

"If it were only true that all's well that ends well," writes Spark at the beginning of one novel, "if only it were true" (*Hothouse* 3). Spark dislocates our expectations continually, rebelling against the cyclical nature of traditional comedy which reaffirms the standing order. "Spark uses laughter as a dynamic . . . weapon," asserts Hoyt.

Spark addresses the issues of language and creation through the reworking of "givens" or cliches such as the "all's well" and "I wish I were dead" syndrome. For example, in her story "The Go-Away Bird," a young woman who is unhappy in both her African and her English existences cries "God help me, life is unbearable" and is promptly shot dead. Words have enormous power, as we have seen, especially for someone like the inescapably self-reflective figure Spark creates during a brief aside in *Robinson*, "MURIEL THE MARVEL with her X-ray eyes" who can "read your very soul" (61). Like MURIEL, who has "dozens of satisfied clients," Spark is concerned with her audience's reactions and has said she likes to "make them laugh and to keep it short" (Cited in Lodge 60).

Comedy is, of course, a defense as well as a weapon. Often intelligent women like Caroline Rose or Sandy Stranger resort to humor as the only way to make sense of an obviously ridiculous reality. For Sandy, "fear returned as soon as she had stopped laughing" (*Jean Brodie* 60).

There is another form of comedy for women, usually exhibited by minor characters in Spark's novels but nevertheless acting in significant counterpoint to the more subtly dangerous mocking of the protagonists. This form of comedy is the laugh of the hysteric, the "cackle" of Wilt's matriarchs. The non-participatory women in Spark provide the broadest broom to sweep away convention. They can barely contain their laughter at the absurdity of the universe before them; one such figure from *The Driver's Seat* "gives out the high, hacking cough-like ancestral laughter of the streets, holding her breasts in her hands to spare them the shake-up" (176).

Spark's comedy forces the very issue of the "happy ending" that has so unnerved critics of her work and of the works of so many women writers of comedy. In *The Only Problem*, she considers the question explicitly, wondering if "Job would be satisfied with this plump reward, and doubted it. His tragedy was that of the happy ending" (176). "Make it a straight old-fashioned story, no modern mystifications," is the advice given to Caroline at the end of *The Comforters* as she sets out to begin her novel. "End with the death of the villain and the marriage of the heroine." Caroline laughs and replies, "Yes, it would end that way" (222). *The Comforters* itself ends with the marriage of an elderly couple, not the marriage of Caroline herself. A religious woman is drowned and Caroline can only manage to save herself by allowing the woman to go under. Hardly the "normal" happy ending. Yet the book finally ends with a framed "look of one who faces an altogether and irrational new experience; a look partly fearful, partly indignant, partly curious, but predominantly joyful" (74) and this emphasis on the play of emotions, rather than the unity of emotion, is characteristic of Spark and of women's comedy in general. Spark's comedy presents "a series of pictures, distinct, primitive, undisdainful, without hope, without pain, without any comment but the grin and laugh of a constitutional survivor" (*Hothouse* 58).[1]

7

"Let Us Now Praise Fallen Women": Hate and Humor in Fay Weldon's Novels

She laughed and said she was taking up arms against God Himself. Lucifer had tried and failed, but he was male. She thought she might do better.

Fay Weldon, *The Life and Loves of a She-Devil*

Women are taught to mask their anger, their sexuality and their humor, yet women writers nevertheless successfully weave together carnage, carnality, and the carnival. The connection is not coincidental; these three forces are dangerous to conservative structures of authority. When women begin to explore their own uses for sex, hate and humor, they are often seen, quite correctly, as making trouble. Few contemporary writers make trouble as expertly as Fay Weldon. Weldon, whose novels have received wide critical acclaim in Great Britain and have been translated into twenty-four languages, puts women at the center of her fictions, focuses on the peripheral, apparently powerless nature of women's position in the cultural structure and sees the phrase "universal truth" as a contradiction in terms. While she has become one of the most significant feminist authors in England (as well as in countries such as Sweden, where her novels are examination set-texts at the secondary school level), her work has been relatively neglected in the United States, this despite the fact that such important theorists of women's comedy as Judy Little and Nancy Walker refer to Weldon as part of their larger arguments. Weldon's comedy, like the comedy of other women writers, is characterized by its refusal to supply conventional comedic closure and by its emphasis on the non-absolute nature of the universe. Judy Little comments that "[a]t its best, feminist comedy deals with absolutes, but not absolutely" (187). Weldon's work provides an equally striking example of this particularly feminist form of comedy.

Typical of how women's humor functions, according to Emily Toth, is an emphasis on the delineation and importance of female experience in a world where that experience is devalued. According to Toth, "women's wisdom and wit have created bonds and community ties; they have also enabled women to be (in Adrienne Rich's phrase) 'disloyal to civilization'" (14). This is equally characteristic of Weldon, who links comedy to the forces of anger, refusal and rebellion insofar as she writes humorously about apocalyptic rage. Ruth's declaration in *The Life and Loves of a She-Devil* is emblematic of Weldon's twinning of hate and humor: "Hate obsesses and transforms me: it is my singular attribution. I have only recently discovered it. Better to hate than to grieve. I sing in praise of hate, and all its attendant energy. I sing a hymn to the death of love" (12). Ruth's cool consideration of her own hatred, the coupling of hymnals with revenge, and the transfiguration of the heroine through recognition of her own anger are all patterns characteristic of Weldon's comedy.

I want to argue that Weldon is a novelist, short story writer, and essayist who sees herself as writing "rather wicked" material, and who believes that humor is the most effective tool against deeply embedded forms of cultural and personal repression. When I asked her about her narrative style and her apparent commitment to writing a particularly lethal form of deadpan humor, Weldon declared that "it would not be fair to make people feel safe when safety is, in fact, an illusion. It is dangerous to be reassuring" (interview with the author 27 April 1984). She further explained that "humor allows the reader to feel pleasure even as something important is being passed on to them." Women have been driven so far from their genuine centers of pleasure that, according to Weldon, they must be introduced to the obvious audience for their particular humor: themselves. And that is why, as Weldon writes in *Letters to Alice*, "any seminar on Women and Writing, or Women Writers, or the New Female Culture, or whatever, is instantly booked up. . . . [W]e are not alone in the oddity of our beliefs. Our neighbour, whom we never thought would laugh when we laughed, actually does" (74).

At what do women laugh? They laugh at the way women are systematically trained to misread their own perceptions of the world, as well as the way that they are simultaneously encouraged to ascribe power to any man, however feeble, dull or impotent. For example, twenty-one-year-old unwed mother Scarlet of *Down Among the Women* misreads her response to Edwin, an appalling man nearly forty years her senior. She kisses his dry, thin lips and feels something, but Weldon tells us that "[i]t is not desire that is stirred, it is her imagination; but how can she know this? She feels she loves him. When she thinks of him kissing her, she is simply enchanted" (110). In this novel, which the author regards as her most autobiographical, readers are encouraged to laugh at the disjuncture between Scarlet's romantic script and her choice of a leading man, but the laughter is not directed at Scarlet. Significantly, the humor of the passage resides in the cultural structure that would quite naturally pair an old man with a young woman. In this respect, Weldon echoes Eliot's treatment of Dorothea in *Middlemarch*. Weldon's humor does not reject Scarlet but instead questions the conventional notion of desire. Weldon instructs us that "we see the world as we are taught to see it, not how it is," implying that if we are taught to find old men attractive, then we will seek them out and subsequently rationalize our attraction (*Down Among the Women* 34).

Even beautiful, successful and worldly Mary Fisher, in Weldon's well-known *The Life and Loves of a She-Devil*, falls from worldly and wordy success the moment she relies on her new lover's opinions of her writing. Bobbo, once only Mary Fisher's accountant but now her lover—and, by extension, the supreme critic of her work—suggests that her wildly successful novels should be written with an eye towards the presentation of reality. Mary shows her manuscript in progress to Bobbo, "as any loving woman would her man, and he had even helped her with it. He'd wanted her heroes to be a little graver, a little less tall" (103). Not seeing that Bobbo wants all heroes to be created in his image, Mary Fisher listens and subsequently tailors her writing to fit Bobbo's tastes. She gains his grudging approval but nearly loses her publishing contract.

How and why does this happen: why are women so willing to forfeit success and personal happiness? Or, as Weldon asks, "Why does it take so long? Why do we stay so stubbornly blind to our own condition, when our eyes are not only open, but frequently wet with grief and bewilderment?" (*Praxis* 229). Perhaps it is "our passivity" that "betrays us, whispering in our ears, oh, it isn't worth a fight! He will only lie on the far side of the bed!" (*Praxis* 229). "Whereas the male humorous figure . . . seeks escape from the moral domination of women," argues Walker in her article "Humor and Gender Roles," "the female figure in women's humor struggles vainly to live up to expectations for her behavior emanating from a culture dominated by men" (101). Weldon shows the impossibility of achieving perfection in the eyes of a man who will only lie on the far side of the bed when confronted with any requirements from his partner. In addition to passivity, in women's disparagement of their own sex lies powerlessness. "We prefer the company of men to women," wryly observes one of Weldon's characters (*Praxis* 229). Women's identification with and desire to please men even as they fear them, coupled with an inherited fear of independence, keep women at one another's throats. "We betray each other," writes Weldon in an early novel. "We manipulate, through sex: we fight each other for possession of the male—snap, catch, swallow, gone! Where's the next? We will quite deliberately make our sisters jealous and wretched" (*Praxis* 229).

As Judith Wilt has noted, women have also been encouraged to turn humor against themselves in order to render neutral an experience which might otherwise cause them to act to the detriment of the system. Women in Weldon's novels do so at their own risk (usually high) and then only for those periods in which they are going through what Weldon calls a "stupid patch" of attempting to live "an agreeable fiction" (*Down Among the Women* 127). Praxis, for example, at her most self-denying stage, "turned the meeting with the Women's Libbers into a joke, into a dinner-table story, and presently could stop trembling when she thought about it" (237). When Gwyneth in *Female Friends* uses the cliche "you have to laugh . . . it's a funny old life," the third person narrator responds only with an ironic "Ha-ha" (47). Gwyneth is using the phrase as the system would have her use it, to continue justifying her own powerlessness.

It is when women begin to use comedy not to justify the ways of god/man but rather to expose the folly of such ways, or when women's comedy is misread by convention, that it gains its real power. By understanding the social and economic basis for women's exclusion from the patriarchal structure or, as Weldon defines social structure, "the government, the church, the civil service, educational and caring organizations, lobbies, societies for this and that, quangos and so forth and so on" (*Darcy's Utopia* 18), women can undermine the system by refusing to participate within their assigned roles. Weldon humorously but unrelentingly exposes the myths that have helped keep women in their place. For this reason, in part, she establishes her right to be called a feminist author. Indeed, Weldon has been said to "create a work whose very structure is feminist." In "Feminism and Art in Fay Weldon's Novels," Agate Krause goes on to say that Weldon "may be unique among the new feminist novelists in developing such a structure" (5). Weldon's carefully constructed characters rarely present themselves as role models. Weldon is not of the let's-present-the-best-possible-images-of-the-modern-woman school; her women are, well, no better than her men, although they are usually more complex, interesting and important. Her novels are intricate weavings of politics, aphoristic commentary, romance and satire.

A recent novel, *Darcy's Utopia*, published in 1990, fulfills expectations for a Weldon work: the reader must pay attention to every curve in the narrative to stay in control of the tale or risk being taken in by the false prophets whose words line the pages. *Darcy's Utopia* is a disturbing and fascinating comic novel requiring enormous attention. Weldon's particular brand of humor laces these pages in a particularly wicked manner, to borrow the author's own term, because it plays on the role of the reader as well as the roles of the character. On the face of it, the novel deals with Eleanor Darcy and her ideas for a new society where "we have to start again, rethink everything, from how and why we brush our teeth to how and why we bury our dead" (185). Eleanor is an example of the sort of ambitious, if not ruthless, protagonist Weldon created in *She-Devil*, but instead of changing herself to suit the world, Eleanor wants to change the world to suit herself. The characters who meet her are uneasy in her company and their experience mirrors our response as readers: Eleanor is hardly a heroine, given to pronouncements such as "all babies will be automatically aborted unless good reasons can be shown why they should be allowed to proceed to term" (133), and "it's only women who can't find lovers, who only have husbands, who have to make do with babies" (163). This is hardly the talk of a heroine; Eleanor commands center stage, but Weldon offers the reader clear caveats concerning the various seductions of her vision. In other words, it is dangerous to approach this novel believing that Weldon is providing a blueprint for a desirable social order, however superficially appealing Darcy's thought of a "unicultural, multi-racial, secular society" (135) might be; seeing the split between the author's voice and the voice of the protagonist was never more important than in this ironic tour-de-force.

Eleanor Darcy preaches in order to convert journalists Valerie Jones and Hugo Vansitart to her doctrine. Like Weldon's other works, *Darcy's Utopia* concerns itself with the distribution of, right to, and uses of power. Like her other works, humor undercuts what first appear to be the most serious declarations; Eleanor's closest friend tells the journalists that it's "hard to tell when she's joking and when she isn't" (188), a comment reminiscent of the last line in *She-Devil*: "A comic turn, turned serious" (241). Nearly every character in these novels ends by questioning the right of any society to govern; indeed, questioning the very idea of society itself: "Rules? You want rules? You really can't survive without a book of rules? . . . Can't you decide, one by one, what's right, what's wrong? Do you have to continue to believe in groups?" (225). Weldon's satire encompasses everything from high culture ("museums will be very boring places indeed. If you want to subdue the children you only have to take them on a visit to a museum, and they will behave at once, for fear of being taken there again" [171]) to elections ("there will be elections, but people will be expected merely to vote for people they personally like. It will be a popularity contest. An annual 'boy or girl most likely to run the country' jamboree" [87]). A structuring principle for all Weldon's fiction is an unevasive acknowledgment of the mutability of perception and definition. Only the worst are full of unconsidered conviction.

Individual characters in Weldon's fiction more than announce prepackaged convictions; they attempt to live by such falsehoods. When a physical education teacher announces proudly that "female fidelity . . . is the cornerstone on which the family, the heredity principle, and the whole of capitalism rests" (*Down Among the Women* 196), we hear echoes of Cixous and Clement, as well as echoes of Marx and Levi-Strauss. Tellingly, Weldon, who can certainly be identified as a writer concerned with materialist analysis, holds degrees in both economics and psychology, and her novels reflect both these influences. In addition, Weldon writes frequently on the hard sciences, and offers conclusions drawn from her knowledge of structural anthropology (Weldon, "Thoughts We Dare Not Speak Aloud"). In fact, Levi-Strauss's concept of woman as sign is converted into everyday language by Weldon when a character from *The President's Child* explains that "men . . . pass girls on, you know. They're forever doing each other favors. They like to share the good things of life, whilst making sure the less privileged don't get a look-in. They're the same sexually as they are financially. Capitalist to the core. They hand around the wives too" (74). This may be the point at which we should qualify Aristotle's claim that comedy typically "aims at representing men as worse . . . than in actual life" (*Poetics* 2.4). Though Weldon's comedy is often described as an exaggerated and humorously distorted picture of our culture, it offers an unnervingly accurate portrait of contemporary life. Weldon's humor, like the humor produced by other women writers, often works by providing what at first might seem like hyperbole ("men pass women around") which is then revealed to be a transcription of the everyday life of a number of her characters. Those characters or actions that would seem to be "an imitation . . . of a lower type" turn out to be simply median (*Poetics* 5.1). What is perceived as exaggeration is actually the product of an uncensored vision; the lower types are indeed running the system.

Comedy, however, can also disrupt the system by providing a context for women's refusal to participate while allowing them to remain within the confines of accepted discourse. Weldon gives evidence of a woman's power, through sexuality and through humor, to refuse to be part of the masculine game. For example, the following anecdote from *Down Among the Women* prompts us to laugh at the figure of authority, not at the sexually active, socially marginal woman: "Reminds me of the story of Royalty visiting the maternity hospital. Royalty inclines towards young mother. 'What lovely red hair baby has, mother. Does he take after his father?' Answer: 'Don't know, ma'am, he never took his hat off'" (21). Weldon implies women refuse to act as the currency of the dominant system when they realize the system has been constructed on a false basis. When women understand, as Elsa does in *Little Sisters*, that for them, at least, sex is "not for procreation, it is for the sharing of privilege," they can abandon the rules and seek their own limitless pleasure and power (134). Elsa, in fact, realizes that sex, outside the rules laid down for women's morality, proves fortifying rather than depleting, proves exhilarating rather than shameful. It proves, in fact, comedic. Shame, perhaps, is the province of the male, since sex proves to be his "loss" under these terms: "Man! Come to bed. Handsome, young, rich, powerful, or otherwise fortunate—is that you? Excellent? Come inside. Because what I know and perhaps you don't is that by some mysterious but certain process of osmosis I will thereupon draw something of these qualities into myself . . . gaining my pleasure through your loss" (134).

This realization, Weldon suggests, is what has created the figure of the sorceress, the hysteric, the witch. Once the first rule is broken, all rules crumble. For Weldon, "the first step . . . the breaking of the first rule" (*She-Devil* 54), is often the rejection of discrimination: one learns to reject the false assembly of values. The second step is realizing that "when male power and prestige are at stake the lives and happiness of women and children are immaterial" (*President's Child* 163). This leads to the ultimate realization that the public world, which is supposedly created in order to protect the vulnerable, actually sets about systematically to destroy the powerless, but only after those in authority have profited from them. "Let us now praise fallen women" demands Weldon in *Down Among the Women*, "those of them at any rate who did not choose to fall, but were pushed and never rose again . . . truckloads of young Cairo girls, ferried in for the use of the troops . . . lost to syphilis, death or drudgery. Those girls, other girls, scooped up from all the great cities of East and West, Cairo, Saigon, Berlin, Rome. Where are their memorials? Where are they remembered, prayed for, honoured? Didn't they do their bit?" (185). The most significant part of women's recognitions in these matters is to see that reality and nature are arguments used by men against women, used by men to enable themselves to keep the power they have asserted—and, most importantly, that power and authority are constructs of language, not forces reflecting the inherent order of the universe.

Language permits those in authority to do exactly as they please. Even women's understanding of themselves has often been designed by men who have been "prepared to generalise about women, and women would not argue, but would simper, and be flattered by the attention paid" (*Praxis* 217). The cost of this attention, however, is astronomical. Weldon writes in *The President's Child* that men "murder and kill with impunity: not so much in the belief of the rightness of their cause, or even telling themselves that ends could justify means, or in their own self-interest, but simply not realizing that murder was what they had done" (62). This occurs, as Isabel says, because they have the authority enabling them to change "language itself to suit their purposes. If . . . anyone had to go, she would not be killed, let alone

153

murdered; she would be liquidated, wiped out, taken out, obliterated, dealt with" (*President's Child* 62).

Women's marginality is written into the language, as feminist critics have pointed out. Monique Wittig, for example, writes that personal pronouns are "pathways and means of entrance into language," and that they mark gender through all language, "without justification of any kind, without questioning" (65). Weldon confronts this in her fiction. "I know you have a low opinion of your own sex," says one woman in *Praxis*, "it is inevitable; our inferiority is written into the language: but you must be aware: you must know what's happening" (54). In *Life and Loves of a She-Devil*, Ruth indicates that it is not surprising that women are not offered easy access to traditional authority, given their exclusion from language: "we are powerless, and poor, and have no importance. We are not even included in everyone" (50).

If women subscribe to the conventional role assigned to them within the traditional system, they are stripped of their humanity. "Human beings rant and roister, fuck and feed, love and smother, shake their fists at the universe in thunderstorms and defy a creator who is sure to get them with the next lightning bolt," explains Weldon in *Female Friends*. "These little English girls, with their soft, uncomplaining voices, and their docile hearts, whose worst crime has been a foul on the hockey pitch, are quite alien" (130). Women have not been permitted to participate as human beings and so are perpetually alien to the world of men while creating distance between themselves and other women. On the other hand they can realize that, as Esther says to Phyllis in *The Fat Woman's Joke*: "Any woman who struggles to be accepted in a man's world makes herself ridiculous. It is a world of folly, fantasy and self-indulgence and it is not worth aspiring to. We must create our own world" (83). While not a separatist feminist in her personal politics, certainly Weldon would advise women to leave behind the masculine model and find a vision that accommodates a woman's perspective. Women must, to begin with, see themselves and all women as human beings, and as guardians of their own integrity and fate. This simple agenda is at the heart of Weldon's feminism.

This leads to Weldon's assumption that although "you could advance the view that all good writing is bound to be feminist . . . it depends on how you're going to define feminist." She adds, "I was brought up in an all-female household, went to a girls' school, was supported by my mother. The world is female, as far as I'm concerned. Most people believe it to be male" (Barreca, *Belles Lettres*). As Weldon illustrates in her novels, however, the apparently vigorous world of men pales in comparison to the world of women: "affairs of state . . . are child's play compared to the affairs of the home . . . of the intricacies of a marriage and the marriage bed" she writes in *Remember*

Me 203). In this way, Weldon illustrates one element identified by Nancy Walker as characteristic of women's humor, that "[m]en are nearly extraneous to the 'real' lives of women; their experiences outside the home are so remote as to seem nonexistent, and their lives within the orbit of the home are trivial, insignificant, or mysterious" (13). Weldon sees the tasks designated as women's work—the primary responsibility of caring for other human beings on a day-to-day basis—as far more dangerous than work in the corporate world. Weldon argues convincingly that "if a corporation had to decide at what point it was feasible for a small child to ride its bicycle in the road, they would hire a dozen consultants and probably be unable to arrive at any conclusion. A mother has to make that decision in one afternoon based purely on her good sense and instinct. And she has to accept responsibility for her decision herself" (interview with the author 14 January 1992). The real weight of the world's work falls on women.

If women are able to cope effectively with the world's emotional work, why are they so often so ill-prepared to care for themselves? Where did they learn to see themselves as failures or victims? From Mary Fisher, for one, who "writes a great deal about the nature of love. She tells lies" (*She-Devil* 1). If we examine the philosophy of aging barmaid Gwyneth of *Female Friends*, we see that she absorbs her platitudes from "dubious sources, magazines, preachers and sentimental drinkers," and that these "often flatly contradicting the truths of her own experience, are usually false and occasionally dangerous" (45). And, of course, women get instructions directly from the state: "There was much talk of 'the bond' down at the clinic and a good deal done to foster it. It was less taxing on welfare funds to have mothers looking after their own progeny than leaving the state to do it" (*She-Devil* 180). Weldon points out that women often begin from a false point if they start by "supposing there's a world in which there's a right way to do things" (Cited in Haffenden 306). Nothing is obvious, least of all the truth. When Ruth of *She-Devil* takes her whining, clinging children to the high tower where Mary Fisher lives with Ruth's adulterous husband in order to leave the children there ("the only place they'll have a chance to witness" the primal scene, she drily offers), she is confronted with a stock truth: "It is obvious that the children can't stay here. They must go home where they belong, with their mother." "Why is it obvious?" Ruth responds (72).

Just as there is no hard core of reality, since truth, as Weldon describes it, is like an onion where you simply peel away layer after layer only to find that there is no heart of the matter, there is also "no such thing as the essential self." So admits one of Ruth's many doctors when she asks about changing the physical self: "It is all inessential, and all liable to change and flux, and usually the better for it" (*She-Devil* 221). When women recognize that the apparent orthodoxy is upheld by mere consensus, they can begin to acknowledge the powers of subversion which they have within them. Every prevailing notion is then held up for questioning, especially those as fundamental as the concept of nature itself. In one quintessentially Weldon passage, the author vivisects the conventional bond between women and nature by at first declaring that "[i]t is nature, they say, that makes us get married. Nature, they say, that makes us crave to have babies. . . . It's nature that makes us love our children, clean our houses, gives us a thrill of pleasure when we please the home-coming male," but then undoes the rhetoric by asking "Who is this Nature?" (*Praxis* 147). "Nature does not know best, or if it does, it is on the man's side. . . . [W]hen anyone says to you, this, that or the other is natural, then fight. Nature does not know best; for the birds, for the bees, for the cows; for men, perhaps. But your interests and Nature's do not coincide. Nature our Friend is an argument used, quite understandably, by men" (*Praxis* 147). Weldon's humorous framing of such universals as "Nature our Friend" indicates the way women's comedy borrows cliches only to undercut them, and her off-handed remark concerning the nature of oppression ("an argument used, quite understandably, by men") calls our attention to her understanding of the social and cultural basis for the powerless position of women. There is nothing inherently natural any more than there is any inherently right answer or right way to live. And besides, as Ruth petulantly declares, women-as-she-devils are "beyond nature: they create themselves out of nothing" (*She-Devil* 133). Women have to invent themselves from the beginning if they reject the sexual script prepared for them by the self-appointed guardians of righteousness.

The righteous view of the world set forth by the status quo would, for example, have women understand and forgive what should remain monstrously baffling and unforgivable. If the cultural catechism would have us "understand furcoated women and children without shoes," we will then be taught to rationalize "Hitler and the Bank of England and the behaviour of Cinderella's sisters" (*Female Friends* 53). Constructing a classically Weldon mosaic of politics, economics and emotion, the author underscores the reason we must combat the forces of generalization and justification. In addition, Weldon's unapologetic coupling of the supposedly important (Hitler, the Bank of England) with the supposedly trivial (Cinderella's sisters) is emblematic of the way her very prose encompasses her refusal to accept standardized systems of value.

Weldon's moral framework is based on the concept of situational morality, validating the multiplicity of experience against a drive for a unified vision. There is no one right way to live, women realize, if they do not accept the absolute, codified systems of their culture. Praxis recognizes this, for example, when she argues that there are a number of "different" worlds, "each with its different ways and standards, its different framework of normality" (*Praxis* 190). This recognition eventually leads to laughter at standards arbitrarily imposed on women who can never meet them. But, significantly, these recognitions then lead to anger at the typically strait-jacketed definitions of femininity. Nancy Walker presents a map for the layers in which women's humor emerges and grows. Humor, Walker argues, may originate in a benign form of appreciation which then quickly becomes "a strategy for coping with frustration, and the reader feels a bond with the writer who can simultaneously delineate and rise above a familiar, uncomfortable situation. Finally, and most important, the reader is subtly invited to agree with the writer about the source of discomfort—to assent to the proposition that someone or something is at fault in a culture that isolates or trivializes women's experience" (*A Very Serious Thing* 101–2). In other words, humor is not merely a cathartic experience which purges anger or frustration. Instead it is a catalyst, urging women on to anger and action. In Weldon novels, certainly, women are encouraged to harness and redouble their refusal and anger until it becomes an unholy transfiguration. They must see, like Ruth, that "it is not easy . . . to forgo the reassuring pleasures of servitude, to face the unknown. Don't think it doesn't hurt. The first sea animals crawling up onto dry land must have had an agonizing time: struggling for breath, burning in the primeval sun" (*Remember Me* 246). As if formulating a mathematical equation for a child, she explains: "if everything is inexplicable, anything might happen" (*Praxis* 19). And if everything is open to question, then women should question the basis for their institutionalized oppression. There are several ways to question and disrupt the system, with the creation of art being one among many. Art, for Weldon, "is invention and distillation mixed . . . it is fundamentally subversive."

Art, given its subversive roots, may well provide a more effective tool against the dominant order than politics, whose fundamental nature is conservative. Weldon insists that the possibilities for overturning the system lie not in political revolutions but in revising the entire concept of power and construction. "You could go to Israel and fight Arabs and really start something. Build a new country," suggests Elaine to Praxis, who replies that "new countries are in your mind." Elaine, although she acknowledges Praxis's point, suggests that "they have to be, if you're a woman. . . . Personally, I'd rather carry a gun" (*Praxis* 171). Carrying a gun is the easiest and least dangerous option; women are far more dangerous than weapons. As Cixous and Clement argue, women "represent the eternal threat, the anticulture" to men because they challenge the masculine structures of logic, reason and nature (67). When faced with the maxim "one comes to terms with this kind of thing in the end," in response to a miserable situation, a woman should reply "I come to terms with nothing" (*Fat Woman's Joke* 10). When truly marginalized, or in other words, when they have abandoned the attempt to naturalize their lives, women inevitably gain power from their exiled position. They secure for themselves the right to outright laughter and obvious outrage.

"Anger was better than misery" decides Praxis (253). Weldon expresses her characters' rage through the apparently conventional forms of the domestic novel, but with subversive results. Weldon provides equally detailed recipes for dinner and for conflagrations. As one critic comments, Weldon "describes the modern all-electric kitchen with deadly accuracy, then invests it with the occult resonance of a magic cave. Suburban dinners do of course get fixed, between bouts of hysteria and plate-throwing, but behind them you can hear the thunder and smell sulphur" (Caldwell 52). Ruth's sorceress-recipe from *She-Devil* illustrates this union:

> I make puff pastry for the chicken vol-au-vents, and when I have finished circling out the dough with the brim of a wine-glass, making wafer rounds, I take the thin curved strips the cutter left behind and mold them into a shape much like the shape of Mary Fisher, and turn the oven high, high, and crisp the figure in it until such a stench fills the kitchen that even the fan cannot remove it. Good. (*She-Devil* 10)

In this passage, Weldon's humor is at its best: she is irreverent toward domesticity and is shamelessly furious, yet relates everything in deadpan-clean prose. In making a kitchen the scene of her anger, Ruth is playing out an argument by Helene Cixous and Catherine Clement, who assert that "Cooking badly is also being badly married . . . there is a family, household, intimate stench hanging over it all" (37).[1] Ruth also acts out Cixous and Clement's directive that the hysteric weeps but the sorceress does not when she reveals that "I ran upstairs, loving, weeping. I will run downstairs, unloving, not weeping" (*She-Devil* 24). Indeed, Weldon creates a number of characters similar to those described by Cixous and Clement in *The Newly Born Woman*, women who "revolt and shake up the public, the group, the men, the others to whom they are exhibited. The sorceress heals, against the Church's canon . . . the hysteric unties familiar bonds, introduces disorder into the well-regulated unfolding of everyday life, gives rise to magic in ostensible reason" (5). Ruth becomes expert at healing physical, emotional and spiritual woes as she progresses through her unholy transformation. She forces science to bend to her wishes and relies on magic to secure her eventual triumph. She is a great force of disorder and a powerful adversary to received wisdom. Ruth, as a result of her triumphs, recognizes, however, that the usual field of battle is misleadingly reductive. To reduce all women's struggles to a mere fight between the sexes is to unify it into an absurdity of the sort propagated by the dominant culture. It is a more complex battle than that because "it is not a matter of male or female, after all; it never was: merely of power" (*Praxis* 241).

It is the structure of power itself that needs subverting; men, deluded and decorative, are dangerous to women because they try to make women into the sign that will permit the system to flourish. One of the ways, as we have seen, that women revise the constructed order is by rejecting the typically happy ending and by implication, rejecting the rewards for behaving within the rules. Yet happy endings in women's writing, as we have also seen, are the triumphs of non-closure, multiplicity and limitlessness. Happy endings in women's writings often replace "integration" and "reaffirmation" with recognition and realization. As Weldon writes in *Letters to Alice*, happy endings do not mean "mere fortunate events" but a reassessment or reconciliation with the self, not with society, "even at death" (83). But part of women's defiance, and one of Weldon's strongest comedic structures, is the refusal of women to accept finality, even the finality of death or marriage. Her novels often end with the dissolution of a marriage, with the defeat of reason, with the triumph of the female Lucifer, with the abandonment of children or with the laying to rest of a ghost. Weldon systematically inverts the normal happy ending, so that we applaud Chloe's abandonment of her husband at the end of *Female Friends*. Chloe's triumph rests on the fact that she has finally stopped understanding and forgiving her infuriatingly narcissistic husband. "As for me," she says at the novel's conclusion, "I no longer wait to die. I put my house . . . in order, and not before time. The children help. Oliver says 'But you can't leave me with Francoise,' and I reply, 'I can, I can, and I do'" (311). Similarly, at the end of *Praxis*, we have an old woman with a broken toe, who laughs in delight at her own triumph. "Even here," says the heroine, "in this horrible room, hungry and in pain, helpless, abandoned by the world in general and the social worker in particular, I can feel joy, excitation and exhilaration. I changed the world a little: yes, I did. Tilted it, minutely, on its axis. I, Praxis Duveen" (50).

Triumph at undoing the structures, undermining the system, likens daily life to a battle, "an exhilarating battle, don't think it wasn't. The sun shone brightly at the height of it, armour glinted, sparks flew" (*Female Friends* 309). Weldon sheds her particular light on what has remained shadowed in the typical happy ending, the acceptance of mutability and possibility. As she instructs her female reader: "days can be happy—whole futures cannot. This is what grandmama says. This moment now is all you have. These days, these nights, these moments one by one" (*Female Friends* 310). Therefore, she insists that women—and men as well—must "treasure your moments of beauty, your glimpses of truth, your nights of love. They are all you have. Take family snaps, unashamed" (*Remember Me* 310). Madeleine, soon to die in a car crash on the A-1, buys heather from a poor woman, taking coins from the milk money: "'Never mind,' says Madeleine from her heart. 'Never mind. Good times will come again. Or at any rate, we had them once'" (18).

It is in *Remember Me* that Weldon's refrain "recognition, realization!" so very emblematic of women's comedy, occurs. What should women realize? For a start, they should pay careful and constant attention to the stories of their sisters, mothers and grandmothers. Women must learn to validate and value the experience of other women, patterning their lives and thoughts from the alternative text feminine wisdom provides. Weldon counsels that if attention is paid, then the listener, sitting on her grandmother's cushions, "may not end as tired and worn and sad as she. Be grateful for the softness of the cushion, while it's there, and hope that she who stuffed and sewed it does not grudge its pleasure to you. The sewing of it brought her a great deal of pain and very little reward" (*Female Friends* 309). Significantly, the validation of relationships apart from those of the usual pair of lovers is the hallmark of Weldon's endings. This validation can concern, as does Elsa's in *Little Sisters*, a woman who finally sees the full range of emotions she holds for her mother. Elsa realizes that she "loves her, fears her, pities her, resents her, escapes her, joins her, loves her" mother and therefore "is saved" (137). The traditional happy ending of boy-gets-girl-and-forms-a-new-society is at best "'*like* a happy ending,' Scarlet complains" (*Down Among the Women* 183; my italics). Weldon, like other women writers, has cause to complain about the traditional happy ending and the subsequent fate of women at the hand of conventional comedy. The heroine of conventional comedies appears to be in as insecure a position as the one in which Gemma finds herself in *Little Sisters*:

> Silence. The knife blade trembled at her throat. Mr. First sighed and put the knife down.
>
> A joke, after all.
>
> Of course. Employers always joke with typists. (94)

In Weldon, however, there is no such thing as "only" joking. "'I was only joking,' she says. But of course she isn't," Weldon writes in *Down Among the Women* (88). Joking is an important business for the very fact that comedy is part of the survival process for women. Praxis goes through the full range of responses when she "wrote, she raged, grieved and laughed, she thought she nearly died; then, presently, she began to feel better" (280). Comedy and power are interlocked in Weldon's writing: the power of comedy is to undo expectations and revise women's view of themselves in the system.

Most significantly, joking is a divisive, not a unifying experience. Chloe's laughter at the end of *Female Friends* is the laugh not only of the

Medusa, of Medea, and of Clytemnestra, but is also the laughter heard in the wake of every woman's escape from any form of confinement: "Chloe finds she is laughing, not hysterically, or miserably, but really quite lightly and merrily; and worse, not with Oliver, but at him, and in this she is, at last, in tune with the rest of the universe" (259). Seven pages later, Weldon, as if to double-check, asks: "is she laughing at him?" The answer is "yes, she is. Her victory is complete" (267). It is no small victory. Why is comedy so important? Because laughter is as obvious a manifestation of refusal as the bite or the kick. The whole system of society and culture may, in fact, be set up by men in order to keep "women occupied, and that's important. If they had a spare hour or two they might look at their husbands and laugh, mightn't they?" (*Down Among the Women* 54). And that laughter, Weldon implies, would bring down the house.

8

Metaphor-into-Narrative:
Being "Very Careful with Words"
in Texts by Women Writers

Yes, run along," says Victor, as he used to say . . . run along,
from the very first day she rose from crawling position to sway
on her tiny feet. Eventually she became good at running, and
made a very fine wing at hockey, and even later, occasionally
captained the school team.

Fay Weldon, *Words of Advice*

I want to suggest that there is a pattern woven into women's writing, particularly women's comedic writing, which I can most easily call metaphor-into-narrative. The basis of the strategy relies on re-literalizing
what has become merely symbolic. Rather than creating a word/object/ac-
tion that accrues meaning through repeated appearances in a text, metaphor-into-narrative illustrates the stripping away of symbolic or over-deter-
mined meaning in order that the "original" significance of the word/object/
action should dominate. It involves a linguistic strategy that takes a metaphor, simile, perhaps a cliche, and plays it out into the plot of the text. We
do not expect, in reading *The Comforters*, that Muriel Spark will present us
with Georgiana Hogg, a character described as "not all there" (169). Georgiana gradually disappears—she doesn't metaphorically disappear, she
"really" vanishes from the backseat of the car where she is napping. Fay
Weldon writes of a certain character that "presently he will get into the
habit of saying he's going to die of boredom, and presently indeed he will"
(*Down Among the Women* 30).

Metaphor-into-narrative works something like an optical illusion, like
the patterns used in psychology classes to illustrate false perception and
with a view towards the same end: perspective is all and all in our

definitions of reality. Conflicting contexts, weighted equally, disturb our prepared interpretive strategies. We might misread a phrase because our perceptions code the metaphor as a "category mistake" when it is in fact an accurate statement. People can't die of boredom, we say, and so we read the phrase wrongly until this radical narrative strategy initiates us into a new code that revives the "dead" metaphor. This is nothing new to the idea of comedy; Henri Bergson and others have discussed the concept of the comic mis-reading of words.[1] Freud, in *Jokes and Their Relationship to the Unconscious*, seems to argue that comedy is made during the process whereby we attach meaning to the meaningless, only to delight in discovering our mistake.[2]

There is however a significant difference in the metaphor-into-narrative strategy: by attaching a buried, literal meaning to what is intended to be inert and meaningless, women writers subvert the paradigmatic gesture of relief that characterizes comedy. A joke usually depends on the equation between initial error (taking something literally) and final pleasure (discovering that it is only meant figuratively). Here the process is reversed; the joke depends on the error of believing language to be used figuratively when it is used literally. There is little relief in this comedy; it is more apocalyptic than reassuring.

Metaphor-into-narrative links language with magic, and not only in its ability to bring the "dead" back to life. This strategy illuminates the manner in which discourse has the power to shape the way things happen, not just the way things are seen or the way they are described. Language has a formative, not merely an evaluative, function. As Fay Weldon states in *The Fat Woman's Joke*: "One must be careful with words. Words turn probabilities into facts and by sheer force of definition translate tendencies into habits" (24). Words are alchemical, transforming one order into another, and they function as a fundamental link to the supernatural. That something is said, as well as the manner in which it is said, becomes crucial. In many works by women writers, particular words are volatile, infused with power: "Acknowledgement is dangerous; it gives body to the insubstantial" ("Watching Me, Watching You" 75). Reality is encoded in language; language shapes rather than reflects an otherwise substantial, otherwise authorized universe.

Metaphor-into-narrative is Margaret Atwood's *Edible Woman*; it is the basis for Doris Lessing's story "How I Finally Lost My Heart;" it is the fact that Fay Weldon's novel *Life and Loves of a She-Devil* plays out quite literally the changes Ruth must go through in order to "look up to men." It is what May Sinclair does in *The Three Sisters* when the vicar, bothered by his daughter's renditions of Beethoven and Chopin, forces Alice to literally change her tune. In its lowest key, it is Marianne's fall when she sees

Willoughby; it is at the heart of many of Flannery O'Conner's stories and some of George Eliot's most salient remarks. Metaphor-into-narrative is a ritual, linguistic, and I believe, feminine transubstantiation that makes a word the thing itself as well as the representation of the thing. When a character in these stories says "over my dead body," it usually means just that. The disenfranchised language of the dead metaphor or cliche provides a narrative structure for the stories themselves.

To focus on metaphor and the woman writer is not new. Margaret Homans has brilliantly discussed in a number of texts the psychoanalytic aspects of the feminine literalization of metaphor. In "Dreaming of Children: Literalization in *Jane Eyre* and *Wuthering Heights*," for example, Homans introduces this argument by pointing out that "the literal is traditionally classified as feminine," drawing on Nietzsche's identification of "truth" as woman (257). Gilbert and Gubar write in *The Madwoman in the Attic* that "women seem forced to live more intimately with the metaphors they have created" (87). Donna Stanton's important discussion of metaphor, "Difference on Trial," included in *The Poetics of Gender*, asks whether "metaphor itself must be interrogated to see whether it provides the best means for exploring the many aspects of the female unknown" (159). Stanton mentions Cixous's remark that metaphor is "desirable and efficacious" for women writers because it "presupposes faith in its capacity to transform existing meanings," and quotes Irigaray's statement that "analogy, in contrast to the rigor/rigidity of male geometricity, 'entails a reworking of meaning'" ("Difference on Trial" 161). Perhaps Mary Jacobus's argument in "The Question of Language" concerning George Eliot's use of maxims provides the most provocative discussion of women, "dead" metaphors, and cliched wisdom. Jacobus argues that "impropriety and metaphor belong together on the same side as a fall from absolute truth on unitary schemes of knowledge" (48). She states, echoing from Maggie's remarks in *The Mill on the Floss*, that "if words may mean several things, general rules or maxims may prove less universal than they claim to be and lose their authority" (44). This is applicable to the question of metaphor-into-narrative, I think, because Jacobus argues that it is the "special cases or particular contexts" that "determine or render indeterminate not only judgment but meaning, too" (44). As Maggie can revive the "dead language of Latin" through her decision to "skip the rules in syntax" because the examples became so absorbing, so do the women writers of metaphor-into-narrative revive so called "dead metaphors" by breaking the code that killed them. Jacobus argues that Eliot's use of metaphor can undermine "the realist illusion of her fictional work, revealing it to be no more than a blank page inscribed with a succession of metaphoric substitutions" (47).

It is this transformation of "the familiar into the exotic and strange"

(45) that is at work in the comedy of metaphor-into-narrative in writers such as Muriel Spark. Spark's works often turn on the axis of this strategy. Her literalization of metaphor has been noticed although not explored by a number of critics who see that, as one reviewer mentioned in a rather throwaway remark, Spark "contrives to work a metaphor, a conceit into a narrative. . . . Spark is the John Donne of English fiction, a few centuries behind her time, but nonetheless interesting for it" (Thompson 9).

One of Spark's short stories, "Portobello Road," is a linguistic tour-de-force, making a most obvious and deliberate use of metaphor-into-narrative. It is a translation of metaphor from image to structure. Spark makes literal what has come to be disregarded as simply conventional, reconnecting the signifier and the signified in order to explode meaning. "Portobello Road" seems to be a working out of metaphor-into-narrative, if the term can be permitted to embrace the wider concepts of simile, cliche and even an occasional broader rhetorical device such as a maxim. The narrator of Spark's story, for example, is nicknamed Needle because "One day in my young youth at high summer, lolling with my loveley companions upon a haystack, I found a needle" (7).

This, she says, confirms her idea that she was "set apart from the common run." Immediately we are given a shock both to our powers of belief and disbelief: finding a needle in a haystack is a stock phrase used to describe the impossible, but this is both the opening and the "legend" for mapping the rest of the story. We must take this literally to be able to proceed with the story at all. Needle, by the way, is a ghost. She was murdered in, as might be expected, a haystack. She was missing several days before her body was discovered; the newspaper headlines read " 'Needle' found in haystack" (7).

There is more. The reader is unaware that Needle is a ghost, and is only informed of this fact several paragraphs into the story. When she greets a friend who is surprised to see her, the reader cannot yet fully comprehend the extent of this friend's surprise, and Needle's comment—"I suppose . . . that from poor George's point of view it was like seeing a ghost when he saw me standing by the fruit barrow"—seems to be a simple cliche (11). Only after the reader is initiated fully into the ghostly significance of such apparently casual remarks does the playful and deadly meaning become evident.

Needle often says that she saw George "just before my death five years ago" (29). George, in fact, is the one who kills Needle, his childhood friend, and so the phrase "just before my death" also takes on renewed meaning. What we believe may be read over lightly suddenly begins to tug at us, forcing us to read more slowly in order to recognize the implications of almost every word. There is nothing too ordinary to be important, Spark indicates, and readers cannot consume her sentences all at once, but must weigh and consider each phrase.

Needle describes her living life (to take a cue from her phrase "young youth") in the following manner: "I was not conscious that I, Needle, was taking up any space at all. I might have been a ghost" (14). Once again, such usage of conventional phrases, always regarded metaphorically, begin to make us question, consciously, the very premise of conventional language. Commonplace phrases and metaphors are no longer inert. They have meaning in terms not only of imagery, but of narrative; they are no longer mere rhetorical devices, but the very 'stuff' of the stories themselves. This phenomenon is synthesized most elegantly at the climax of the story when Needle says, in one short sentence, "He looked as if he would murder me, and he did" (29). The wild power and meaning behind the conventional "he looked as if he would murder me" is restored. There is an implication that the world of "as if" and the world of "as is" are not, in fact, separated by anything except perception and acknowledgment.

In Fay Weldon's *Remember Me*, Jarvis, Madeleine's ex-husband, spurred on by too much drink and his second wife's remarks concerning Madeleine, offers the following toast to his guests: "Death and damnation to all ex-wives. Down with . . . the succubi" (90). Jarvis speaks at ten to one in the early morning. At nine minutes to one Madeleine's car "veers off through the dividing rail, hits a post, carries on, crumbling as it goes" (93). The clocks in Jarvis's house stop at the moment of Madeleine's death, the very moment that Jarvis is wishing her dead. Second-wife Lily, feeling vicious on the morning after all this, states " 'She must have died about the time you were wishing her dead,' says Lily unforgivably, 'so I think you're being very hypocritical . . . and what's more, the clock stopped at the time she died.' She says it in triumph, as if this last fact somehow proved her value and his worthlessness" (123). Jarvis responds that if they are to get through the experience she can "start by not implying that it was I who killed Madeleine" (123). But even Lily, so out of touch with anyone's emotions but her own, realizes that by stating "Madeleine, die," Jarvis' words have in some way affected reality.

Jarvis continues to name events that he calls "the farago of superstitious nonsense" which are, in fact, a fairly accurate summation of the previous night's events: "It was Madeleine's ghost swept through the house last night, opening the windows, sticking a cosmic pin into Margot Bailey's leg, another into Jonathan and another into Hilary" (123). What Jarvis sees as hyperbole and hysteria, what he states, certain that his statement is rhetorical, is really a description of the narrative. It is precisely what Weldon has encouraged the reader to believe. That words do not simply describe but instead actually define a world is a central focus for the writings of these authors.

As women writers explore the links between the symbolic and literal uses of language, they do so in a way that reflects their "engendered" position as speakers of the necessarily patriarchal discourse. Feminist critics, as we have seen, suggest that women somehow live more deeply with the metaphors they create. I would like to take this idea a step further and suggest that women live more deeply, or even live out, the metaphors that control the systematic constructs labeled as the natural world. They live out the metaphors they inherit, but they live them with—quite literally—a vengeance. Discussing the displaced daughter in *Words of Advice*, Fay Weldon tells us that Wendy takes her father's words literally. In doing so, she dislodges them from their intended context and therefore subverts his meaning. Paradoxically, she invests his trite comment with a power that then enables her to transform his off-hand dismissal into a catalytic dictum: " 'Yes, run along,' says Victor, as he used to say . . . run along, from the very first day she rose from crawling position to sway on her tiny feet. Eventually she became good at running, and made a very fine wing at hockey, and even later, occasionally captained the school team" (54). Wendy both does and does not do what her father intends. She takes his language and literally runs away with it.

In *The Girls of Slender Means*, Spark gives us a group of women living in the May of Teck Club for young ladies in London at the very end of the second world war. Spark describes them as follows: "[a]s they realized themselves in varying degrees, few people alive at the time were more delightful, more ingenious, more movingly lovely, and, as it might happen, more savage, than the girls of slender means" (6). The prettiest and most popular girls live on the top floor and compare waist and hip measurements as if their lives depended on them. . . . Which, as it turns out, they do. There is a fire in the Victorian house, and only those slender enough to pass through the bathroom window survive.

In *The Life and Loves of a She-Devil*, Weldon offers us Ruth who laughs her grating, uncomfortable laugh and explains that she wants only "to look up to men. . . . Little women can look up to men. But women of six feet two have trouble doing so" (22). Initially, we find it merely amusing to learn that Ruth's problem is literal: she is an enormous woman, altogether bigger than her husband Bobbo. But Weldon plays out the looking-up-to-men cliche to the point where Ruth has major surgery to reduce her overwhelming stature: she has inches of bone removed from her legs in an operation. We follow Ruth's picaresque journey across continents in creation of a more publicly acceptable self, one who need no longer look down on men. Looking up to men is neither an extended metaphor nor a leitmotif: it is the central structure of the plot and the catalyst to action. You can't use these phrases and not expect us to take them seriously, Ruth's actions imply. When Bobbo calls her a she-devil for the first time (for having done nothing

167

but weep at his infidelity and drop the chicken vol-au-vents), there is "a change in the texture of the silence" (42) that comes from Ruth's closed door. Ruth wonders whether "it was possible by mere words, to influence the course of events" (23) while Weldon illustrates with savage precision exactly how possible it is for Ruth—and the rest of us—to do this.

By defining a situation, by limiting it and categorizing it through language, the words themselves are clearly both manipulative and powerful. It is a return to an almost primitive and superstitious belief in the magical powers associated with language. Every word has a formative purpose. These writers forge a complex narrative structure that appeases our desire for verisimilitude while simultaneously forcing us to question the very nature of truth. By encoding a system of language shifts that continually displace us from the fixed, naturalized meanings of commonplace phrases, our 'naturalized' mythology is called into question. If we wish to call their style or tone ironic, we must see that irony here means a juxtaposition between an initial truth and a final truth: the concept of a unified reality is constructed word by word.

There is no going back because once words are said, they stick; they become opaque, a presence. When Ruth is left by her accountant husband, she cries out "What about me?"—a phrase which will connect, Weldon tells us, "myriad other women, abandoned that very day by their husbands. Women in Korea and Buenos Aires and Stockholm and Detroit and Dubai and Tashkent, but seldom in China where it is a punishable offense. Sound waves do not die out. They travel forever and forever. All our sentences are immortal. Our useless bleatings circle the universe for all eternity" (46).

The acknowledgment of the central role of language is linked, by these authors, to the acknowledgment of the validity of female experience. Actions themselves do not offer definitions: the words describing the actions become the central factor in the text. The manner in which language frames a situation determines that situation. During times of war, for example, women like the protagonist Stella from Bowen's *The Heat of the Day*, are engaged in the work of the world from which they have traditionally been barred. Seeing clearly, and often for the first time, the uncertain and tautological nature of the structures on which political and social reality is in fact based, these women must begin to redefine their vision and their roles. One thing is certain: words matter. This is a rejection of traditional concepts of wartime experience, which tend to privilege only violent action. Faced with the assertion that what someone says (as opposed to "does") can hardly be of much importance, a Bowen character argues that: "conversations are the leading thing in this war! Even I know that. Everything you and I do is the result of something that's been said" (67). In *The Heat of the Day*, a young woman named Louie is in a state of dislocation for much of the war because she is unable to find the words to describe herself and her situation: "Look at the trouble there is when I have to only say what I *can* say, and so cannot ever say what it is really. Inside me it's like being crowded to death—more and more of it all getting into me. I could bear it if only I could say. . . . I would more understand if I was able to make myself understood" (275). Words—cliches and trite phrases—offered by the press eventually construct Louie's view of herself and the world around her. Louie embraces newspaper stories about the war because they make "people like her important." Perhaps it can be argued that women embrace comedy for the same reason. Louie takes at face value what she reads in the paper and so creates an acceptable character by piecing together bits of typeface in much the same way as Ruth takes at face value the dictum that shapes her life and so creates a desirable creature out of herself.

Bowen states explicitly the relationship between language and reality: "One can live in the shadow of an idea without grasping it. Nothing is really unthinkable; really you do know that. But the more one thinks, the less there's any outside reality—at least, that's so with a woman" (*The Heat of the Day* 214). The sense that language is self-referential and that the apparently immovable structures of reality can be undermined and shaken apart: these are the lasting effects of metaphor-into-narrative.

In Spark's "The House of the Famous Poet" (Collected in *The Stories of Muriel Spark*) there is a focus on the metaphoric versus the literal use of words. For example, the narrator is concerned with the current adoption of the word "siren" for the purposes of war: "I was thinking of the word 'siren'. The sound [of the warning siren] became comical, for I imagined some maniac sea nymph from centuries past belching into the year 1944" (196). Perhaps the narrator's concern also arises from the gender implications of the word, as well as from the obvious but unstated change in role: "warning siren" seems to be an oxymoron. The Sirens lured people to their deaths, their feminine voices seducing sailors away from reason; the sirens set up during war were meant to drive people from danger, an almost maternal "voice" calling all to safety. Certainly the meanings overlie and reflect back on one another: is the safety offered by sirens, in fact, safe? "Actually," admits the narrator, "the sirens frightened me" (196).

The unnamed narrator of "House of the Famous Poet" agrees to accompany a young woman to the house where she works as a caretaker. The narrator explains her action: "It had the element of experience—perhaps, even of truth—and I believed, in those days, that truth is stranger than fiction" (193). At one distinct point, however, the story pivots and swerves on its axis: this twist is more than a blurring of distinctions. It becomes a deliberate 'tangling' of language: it becomes a challenge. Through this narrator, Spark addresses the reader directly: "You will complain that I am withholding evidence. Indeed, you may wonder if there is any evidence at all. . . . You will insinuate that what I have just told you is pure fiction. Hear me to the end" (197). After a fairly conventional story about a young woman describing how she suddenly finds herself in the house of a famous writer, and who is thrilled and appalled that she did not realize this sooner, Spark introduces a surreal element. A soldier, who has appeared briefly in the first few paragraphs, tracks the narrator down in order to get some money. He doesn't want to borrow it, he tells her; rather, he has something to sell: " 'It's an abstract funeral,' he explained, opening the parcel. . . . I handed over eight shillings and sixpence. There was a great deal of this abstract funeral. Hastily, I packed some of it into the hold-all. Some I stuffed into my pockets, and there was still some left over" (197). This passage illustrates the way in which Spark cleaves the absurd and the surreal onto apparent realism. The "hold-all" is now really holding all, since it holds this abstract notion. The abstract funeral, sold to the narrator's companion and to the famous poet is responsible for their deaths; only because the narrator throws her notion out of a train window, wanting instead "a real funeral . . . one of my own," (199) does she survive. Getting rid of certain notions does make the difference. The story resembles Doris Lessing's "How I Lost My Heart" in its refusal to back down from manipulating the "real" into the "surreal" without apology.

It might be thought that this strategy is particular to twentieth-century novelists who have read Freud, Bergson or Nietzsche on the use of metaphor in comedy and elsewhere. I would like to suggest that while metaphor-into-narrative can be read in light of, as well as being reflective of, the work on metaphor done by Searle, Ricoeur and so many other linguistic theorists, it should also be seen as a structure employed particularly by women writers, and particularly by women writers of comedy, because of their engendered relationship to language. A general discussion of the use of metaphor does not consider the very aspects most in need of exploration, those concerning gender.

Women's use of metaphor, as well as their use of comedy, is disruptive in its refusal to accept the conventions which propagate the language of the father. This is emblematic of the fact that women are not offered the possibility for full initiation into the symbolic order, but still maintain a level of power to affect the cultural codes because of their position on the boundaries. "Societies do not succeed in offering everyone the same way of fitting into the symbolic order," explain Cixous and Clement, "those who are, if one may say so, between symbolic systems, in the interstices, offside, are the ones who are afflicted with a dangerous symbolic mobility" (7).

The phrase "dangerous symbolic mobility" is significant for a study of comedy by women. It echoes the earlier phrase "all laughter is allied with the monstrous" and reflects Kristeva's assertion that woman as "semiotic" space is allied with pre-Oedipal discourse that does not accept the absolutes of language but rather plays with language, using non-sense and puns, as part of its refusal to embrace initiation into the symbolic order. Metaphor-into-narrative can be seen as an effect/indication of this relationship between women and language.

At the risk of repeating what is already established, women and words form a problematic alliance within the symbolic order. This is important to keep in mind in any discussion of women and comedy, but particularly for the discussion on metaphor and comedy. Women are not meant to give utterance: when they do, they step out of their function as sign. When they create comedy, they are stepping out of their destined communication and are deviating from it in order to transform their position. They are also risking the maintenance of the system of exchange because they are shifting the ground on which the system rests. Should women remove themselves or "devalue" themselves in terms of exogamy, the system is in danger of collapse:

> Ultimately one might even think, as we know, that the woman must remain in childhood, in the original primitive state, to rescue human exchange from an imminent catastrophe owing to the progressive and inescapable entropy of language. Words have been able to circulate too much, to lose their information, to strip themselves of their sense. At least let women stay as they were in the beginning, talking little but causing men's talk— stay as guardians, because of their mystery, of all language. Levi-Strauss calls what they are thus able to retain "affective wealth," "fervor," "mystery," which at the origin doubtlessly permeated the whole world of human communications. (Cixous and Clement 28)

Women writers are able to make use of the shiftings of the system. The symbolic dimension, as Juliet Mitchell describes it, enables the subject/child to disentangle words from the snares and fascinations of the imaginary. The child's accession to language coincides with the advent of the Oedipus complex, according to Lacan, and through this process women can be defined "as excluded by the nature of things which is the nature of words" (Cited in Gilbert and Gubar, *Sexual Linguistics* 536). The symbolic order— the "highest" order—is linked to the masculine and to language. To play with language, then, seems to be to play with the authority of the symbolic/ masculine view. There is a renewed exploration of the comedic in the exploration of play with language, of the use of non-sense and pun and, finally, of metaphor-into-narrative, to undermine the authority of language itself.

The symbolic order is what allows for unification of perspectives through an apprehension of the so-called authority of language, that attaches one meaning eradicably to one word; the problem in this equation arises when the instability of language is brought to the forefront. This links logocentrism with phallocentrism, according to a number of writers: looking for the one, unchallenged, "correct" point is common to both. Metaphor-into-narrative, then, becomes emblematic of women's refusal to accept this inherited, codified understanding. Like George Eliot's Maggie Tulliver in *The Mill on the Floss*, women writers play with the syntax and focus on the particular. We will take the instruction to "run along" quite literally. In the haystacks created by these writers we *will* indeed find needles; big women are indeed prohibited from looking up to men. We read wrongly if we read with an eye towards automatic correction. This should be stressed. There is no "mistake" in these metaphors; they are accurate namings insofar as any naming can be accurate. It is we who initially mis-name by looking for the single correctly symbolic reading, unable to see the play with meaning that paradoxically offers a subversively "literal" reading in place of the traditional, symbolic ones. We will read women writers best when we allow for their humor, their laughter, and their appetite for dislocation.

Notes

Chapter 1

1. For excellent discussions by these authors on comedy see Bakhtin, Mikhail. *Rabelais and His World* trans. Helene Iswolsky, Bloomington: Indiana University Press, 1984; Eco, Umberto. "Frames of Comic Freedom." *Carnival!* ed. Thomas Sebeok. Berlin: Mouton, 1984: 1–9; and Robert Polhemus. *Comic Faith: The Great Tradition from Austen to Joyce.* Chicago: University of Chicago Press, 1980.

Chapter 2

Katharine Rogers, whose work on eighteenth-century women writers inspired my own interest, greatly helped to influence the design and argument of this essay when I began it several years ago. Her essay in *Last Laughs* on "Deflation of Male Pretensions in Fanny Burney's *Cecilia*" has been important in the development of my essay, as has Rachel Brownstein's essay, "Jane Austen: Irony and Authority," from the same volume.

1. Joanna Russ argues in an article on the modern gothic entitled "Somebody Is Trying To Kill Me and I Think It's My Husband" that "the Gothics are a kind of justified paranoia: people *are* planning awful things about you; you can't trust your husband (lover, fiance); everybody's motives are devious and complex; only the most severe vigilance will enable you to snatch any happiness from the jaws of destruction" (681).

2. For a fuller discussion of Austen's use of "modal auxiliaries"—can/could, may/might, will/would—see Zelda Boyd's "The Language of Supposing" in *Jane Austen: Women and Literature* Vol. 3, edited by Janet Todd.

Chapter 4

1. See, for example, Peggy Ruth Fitzhugh Johnstone, "Narcissistic Rage in *The Mill on the Floss*," in *Literature and Psychology* 36 (1990): 90–109; also see Carol Christ, "Aggression and Providential Death in George Eliot's Fiction," *Novel* 9 (1976) 130–140.

2. It should be mentioned, however, that although his wielding of the sword is

funny, the weapon he possesses is no joke. Dressing as Bluebeard, Tom can only disguise himself as a murderer of women and act as one "for fun." But this is really more than play acting: it can also be read as dress rehearsal. I am indebted to Lee Jacobus for raising this issue.

3. See, for example, Gillian Beer's examination of Eliot's beginnings and endings in the essay "The Dark Woman Triumphs": Passion in *The Mill on the Floss*, in *George Eliot* (Key Women Writers Series), ed. Sue Rose, (Brighton, Sussex: Harvester, 1986) 123–51.

Though it deals specifically with Daniel Deronda, Ellen B. Rosenman's "Women's Speech and the Roles of the Sexes in *Daniel Deronda*," *Texas Studies in Literature and Language* 31 (Summer 1989) raises similar issues.

Chapter 5

1. It is also crucial to place Bowen within the tradition of Anglo-Irish women writers who, marginalized by ethnicity, gender, and choice of genre, have developed specific strategies for confronting and subverting oppressive and prevailing literary conventions. Janet Egleson Dunleavy and Rachael Lynch argue that until 1960, Bowen was identified primarily as a step-child of the Bloomsbury group, but that after 1960 "both critical and popular attention turned increasingly to her novels and stories that explore contradictions in traditional roles based on sex, challenge concepts of children and adolescents, and depict the ambivalent family structure of the Chekhovian Anglo-Ireland" (93). Dunleavy and Lynch present a framework for Irish women writers into which Bowen's work gracefully falls. Irish women writers, they suggest, present "a male-centered, male-dominated universe, a woman's world in which men are but unwitting props and bit players in the archetypal dramas" (99), and where writers move beyond the subject of "fundamentally incompatible male-female relationships to probe the reasons why otherwise sensible and capable women allow themselves to be trapped in marriages that predictably prove unhappy" (101). Finally, and convincingly, they argue that "women do not have to write as men or about men to take their place in the mainstram of contemporary Irish literature" (106). And it is clear that one of the most representative ways in which these women writers distinguish their work from their male contemporaries is through the creation of a particular tradition of humor.

2. Fortunately, contemporary critics such as Harriet Chessman, John Hildebidle and Thomas Dukes are in the process of constructing a feminist analysis of Bowen's work, and their insights are of considerable importance (even though they differ radically in their conclusions). Chessman's article "Women and Language in the Fiction of Elizabeth Bowen" demonstrates convincingly that women are presented as "outsiders to discourse, unless they turn traitor and defect to the other side" (124). She describes Bowen's use of what she calls "unarticulated and inchoate femaleness" (125); drawing on Irigaray's theories concerning the unbridgeable gap between the masculine subject and the feminine object, Chessman suggests that Bowen delineates a world where what "resides in a femaleness . . . asks to be

expressed, but . . . can find no expression" (138). In contrast to Chessman, Dukes maintains in "The Unorthodox Plots of Elizabeth Bowen" that women in Bowen's fiction are driven to speech, that "having to speak is, in fact, at the heart [of her works] and forms the core of the 'second' or subversive plot" (13). (It is interesting to note, however, the way in which Bowen satirizes a number of characters who explain at length why they are silent: "'Oh dear no,'" says Miss Tripp from *To The North*, "smiling bitterly. 'I find it hard to express my own point of view,' she went on fluently" [120].) Dukes's concentration on the "unorthodox plot" is useful when considering Bowen's use of humor. Of particular interest is John Hildebidle's comments in his *Five Irish Writers* concerning Bowen's "reliance upon the stuff of melodrama and of romantic comedy" (115) and his belief that "her work is, from beginning to end, an effort to write the modern *tragedy* of manners" (italics mine; 128). Perhaps Hildebidle assumes Bowen writes tragedy rather than comedy because he regards as tragic the realization that "any belief in order [is] at best an illusion" (127).

3. See *Eva Trout* for a strikingly similar passage:

> "Before we said goodbye, I wanted to ask you—"
> "This is not 'The Last Ride Together,' is it?"
> "Unless you kill me" (265).

Chapter 6

1. For an excellent discussion of Spark's humor, see John Glavin's "Muriel Spark's Unknowing Fiction" in *Last Laughs: Perspectives on Women and Comedy* ed. Regina Barreca (New York: Gordon and Breach, 1988), 221–241.

Chapter 7

I would like to thank Fay Weldon for her generous, warm responses to my innumerable inquiries about matters professional and personal. I could not have dreamed of a better subject for women's humor.

1. See Nancy Walker's description of mad cooking: "Marge Piercy's poem 'What's That Smell in the Kitchen?' both illustrates and partially defines this kind of humor. Piercy uses the metaphor of women burning what they are cooking to stand for the anger women feel about their subordinate status and the steps they feel they can take to express that anger. The poem ends with the following lines: 'If she want to serve him anything it's a dead rat with a bomb in its belly ticking like the heart of an insomniac. Her life is cooked and digested, Nothing but leftovers in Tupperware. Look, she says, once I was roast duck on your platter with parsley but now I am Spam. Burning dinner is not incompetence but war'" (*A Very Serious Thing: Women's Humor and American Culture* 146).

Chapter 8

1. See Henri Bergson's "Laughter. An Essay on the Meaning of the Comic." For a good recent discussion of comedy, see Scott Cutler Shershow, *Laughing Matters*.
2. For example, Freud writes that "Words are a plastic material with which one can do all kinds of things. There are words which, when used in certain connections, have lost all their original full meanings, but which regain it in other connections" (*Jokes and their Relation to the Unconscious* 34).

Bibliography

Aristotle. *Poetics*. In *The Rhetoric and the Poetics of Aristotle*, 223–66. New York: Random House, 1984.

Armstrong, Nancy. *Desire & Domestic Fiction*. Oxford: Oxford University Press, 1981.

Auerbach, Nina. "The Power of Hunger: Demonism and Maggie Tulliver." In *George Eliot's "The Mill on the Floss,"* ed. Harold Bloom, 43–60. Modern Critical Interpretations. New Haven: Chelsea House Publishers, 1988.

Austen, Jane. *Jane Austen's Letters*. Ed. R. W. Chapman. Oxford: Oxford University Press, 1979.

———. *Emma*. Intro. by Ronald Blythe. New York: Viking Penguin, 1966.

———. *Mansfield Park*. New York: Penguin, Signet Classics, 1970.

———. *Northanger Abbey*. London: Oxford University Press, 1971.

———. *Pride and Prejudice*. London: Penguin Books, 1972.

———. *Sense and Sensibility*. London: Penguin, 1967.

Bakhtin, Mikhail. *Rabelais and His World*. Trans. Helene Iswolsky. Bloomington: Indiana University Press, 1984.

Barreca, Regina. "Fay Weldon speaks to Regina Barreca." *Belles Lettres* (Sept./Oct. 1987): 7–8.

———. *They Used to Call Me Snow White, But I Drifted: Women's Strategic Use of Humor*. New York: Viking, 1991.

Barreca, Regina, ed. *Last Laughs: Perspectives on Women and Comedy*. Studies in Gender and Culture, vol. 2, series ed. Wendy Martin. New York: Gordon and Breach, 1988.

———. *New Perspectives on Women and Comedy*. Studies in Gender and Culture, vol. 5, series ed. Wendy Martin. New York: Gordon and Breach, 1992.

Beer, Gillian. " 'The Dark Woman Triumphs': Passion in *The Mill on the Floss*." In *George Eliot*, 123–51. Key Women Writer Series, ed. Sue Rose. Brighton, Mass.: Harvester Press, 1986.

Behn, Aphra. *Five Plays*, ed. Maureen Duffy. London: Methuen Drama, 1990.

177

Bergson, Henri. "Laughter: An Essay on the Meaning of the Comic." Trans. C. Brereton and F. Rothwell. London, 1911.

Bizzaro, Patrick. "Global and Contextual Humor in *Northanger Abbey*." *Persuasions: The Jane Austen Society of North America* (7 December 1985): 82–8.

Bloom, Harold. "Introduction." In *Elizabeth Bowen*, ed. Harold Bloom, 1–12. Modern Critical Views. New Haven: Chelsea House Publishers, 1987.

Blyth, Reginald H. *Humor in English Literature: A Chronological Anthology*. 1959. Reprint. Tokyo: The Folcroft Press, 1970.

Blythe, Ronald. Introduction to *Emma* (Jane Austen).

Bold, Alan, ed. *Muriel Spark: An Odd Capacity for Vision*. New York: Vision and Barnes and Noble, 1984.

Boumelha, Penny. "George Eliot and the End of Realism." In *Women Reading Women's Writing*, ed. Suke Rose, 15–35. Brighton, Sussex: The Harvester Press, 1987.

Bowen, Elizabeth. *Collected Impressions*. New York: Alfred A. Knopf, 1950.

———. *The Death of the Heart*. New York: Random House, 1938.

———. *English Novelists*. London: Collins, 1942.

———. *Eva Trout*. New York: Alfred A. Knopf, 1968.

———. "Foothold." In *The Collected Stories of Elizabeth Bowen*, ed. Angus Wilson New York: Alfred A. Knopf, 1981: 297–313.

———. "Green Holly." In *The Collected Stories of Elizabeth Bowen*, ed. Angus Wilson New York: Alfred A. Knopf, 1981: 719–27.

———. *The Heat of the Day*. New York: Alfred A. Knopf, 1949.

———. *The Hotel*. New York: Alfred A. Knopf, 1952.

———. *The House in Paris*. New York: Alfred A. Knopf, 1936.

———. *The Last September*. New York: Alfred A. Knopf, 1952.

———. *The Little Girls*. New York: Alfred A. Knopf, 1964.

———. *To the North*. New York: Alfred A. Knopf, 1950.

Boyd, Zelda. "The Language of Supposing." In *Jane Austen: New Perspectives. Women and Literature*, vol. 3, ed. Janet Todd. New York: Holmes & Meier, 1983.

Bradbury, Malcolm. "Muriel Spark's Fingernails." In *Contemporary Women Novelists*, ed. Patricia Meyer Spacks, 137–149. Englewood, New Jersey: Prentice-Hall, 1977.

Bronte, Charlotte. *Jane Eyre*. London: Penguin Books, 1988.

———. *Villette*. London: Penguin Books, 1980.

———. *Wuthering Heights*. New York: Penguin, 1965.

Brownstein, Rachel M. *Becoming a Heroine: Reading About Women in Novels*. New York: Viking Press, 1982.

———. "Jane Austen: Irony and Authority." In *Last Laughs: Perspectives on Women and Comedy*, ed. Regina Barreca, 57–70. Studies in Gender and Culture, vol. 2, series ed. Wendy Martin. New York: Gordon and Breach, 1988.

Caldwell, Mark. "Fay Weldon's Microwave Voodoo." *Village Voice* (25 September 1984): 52.

Carroll, David, ed. *George Eliot: The Critical Heritage*. New York: Barnes & Noble, Inc., 1976.

Chessman, Harriet. "Women and Language in the Fiction of Elizabeth Bowen." In *Elizabeth Bowen*, ed. Harold Bloom, 123–38. Modern Critical Views. New Haven: Chelsea House Publishers, 1987.

Christ, Carol. "Aggression and Providential Death in George Eliot's Fiction." *Novel: A Forum on Fiction*. 9 (1976): 130–40.

Cixous, Helene. "The Laugh of the Medusa." Trans. Keith Cohen and Paula Cohen. *Signs* 1, no. 4 (Summer 1976): 141–53.

Cixous, Helene and Catherine Clement. *The Newly Born Woman*. Trans. Betsy Wing. Theory and History of Literature, vol. 24, Minneapolis: University of Minnesota Press, 1987.

Clinton, Kate. "Making Light." *Trivia* 1 (1981): 1.

Cohen, Sarah Blacher. "The Jewish Literary Comediennes." In *Comic Relief: Humor in Contemporary American Fiction*, ed. Sarah Blacher Cohen, 172–86. Urbana: University of Illinois Press, 1978.

Daly, Mary. *Gyn/Ecology: The Metaethics of Radical Feminism*. Boston: Beacon Press, 1978.

de Beauvoir, Simone. *The Second Sex*. Trans. H. M. Parshley. New York: Vintage/Random House, 1989.

Doody, Margaret Anne. "Introduction." In *The Female Quixote or The Adventures of Arabella*, by Charlotte Lennox, xi–xxxii. New York: Oxford University Press, 1989.

Douglas, Mary. "Jokes." In *Implicit Meanings: Essays in Anthropology*, 90–114. London: Routledge & Kegan Paul, 1975.

———. *Purity and Danger*. New York: Frederick A. Drager, 1966.

———. "The Social Control of Cognition: Some Factors in Joke Perception." *Man* 3 (1968): 361–76.

Drabble, Margaret. *The Waterfall*. New York: Penguin, 1986.

Dukes, Thomas. "The Unorthodox Plots of Elizabeth Bowen." *Studies in the Humanities* 16, no. 1 (1989): 10–23.

Dunleavy, Janet Egleson and Rachael Lynch. "Contemporary Irish Women Novelists." In *The British and Irish Novel Since 1960*, ed. James Acheson, 93–107. New York: St. Martin's Press, 1991.

Du Plessis, Rachel Blau. *Writing Beyond the Ending: Narrative Strategies of Twentieth-Century Women Writers*. Bloomington: Indiana University Press, 1985.

Eco, Umberto. "Frames of Comic Freedom." In *Carnival!* ed. Thomas Sebeok, 1–9. Berlin: Mouton, 1984.

Eliot, George. *Daniel Deronda*. Baltimore: Penguin Books, 1967.

———. *Middlemarch*. New York: Penguin, 1979.

————. *The Mill on the Floss.* New York: Penguin, 1979.

————. "Silly Novels by Lady Novelists." In *The Essays of George Eliot*, ed. Nathan Sheppard. New York: Funk & Wagnalls, 1883.

————. "The Spanish Gypsy." In *The Complete Works of George Eliot: Poems.* Vol. 1, New York: Harper & Brothers, Publishers, n.d.

Ellman, Mary. *Thinking About Women.* New York: Harcourt Brace and World, 1968.

Farb, Peter. "Speaking Seriously About Humor." *The Massachusetts Review* 22, no. 4 (Winter 1981): 760–76.

Freud, Sigmund. *Jokes and Their Relation to the Unconscious.* Trans. James Strachey. New York: Norton, 1960.

Fullbrook, Kate. "Jane Austen and the Comic Negative." In *Women Reading Women's Writing*, ed. Sue Rose, 39–57. Brighton, Sussex: The Harvester Press, 1987.

Gallagher, Catherine. "Who Was that Masked Woman? The Prostitute and the Playwright in the Comedies of Aphra Behn." In *Last Laughs: Perspectives on Women and Comedy*, ed. Regina Barreca, 23–42. Studies in Gender and Culture, vol. 2, series ed. Wendy Martin. New York: Gordon and Breach, 1988.

Garrod, H. W. "On Austen." In *Critics on Jane Austen*, ed. Judith O'Neill, 21–32. Coral Gables, Florida: Miami University Press, 1970.

Gilbert, Sandra M. and Susan Gubar. *The Madwoman in the Attic: The Woman Writer and the Nineteenth Century Literary Imagination.* New Haven: Yale University Press, 1984.

————. *Sexual Linguistics: Gender, Language, Sexuality.* New Literary History, Vol. XVI #3. Baltimore: The Johns Hopkins Press, Spring 1985.

Gindin, James. "Ethical Structures in John Galsworthy, Elizabeth Bowen and Iris Murdoch." In *Forms of Modern British Fiction*, ed. Allan W. Friedman, 15–41. Austin: University of Texas Press, 1975.

Glendinning, Victoria. *Elizabeth Bowen: A Biography.* New York: Alfred A. Knopf, 1978.

Goreau, Angeline. *Reconstructing Aphra: A Social Biography of Aphra Behn.* Oxford: Oxford University Press, 1980.

Haffenden, John. *Novelists in Interview.* London: Methuen, 1985.

Harding, G. W. "Regulated Hatred: An Aspect of the Work of Jane Austen." In *Twentieth Century Literary Criticism*, ed. David Lodge, London: Longmans, 1972.

Hildebidle, John. *Five Irish Writers.* Cambridge: Harvard University Press, 1989.

Homans, Margaret. "Eliot, Wordsworth and the Scene of the Sisters' Instruction." In *George Eliot's "The Mill on the Floss,"* ed. Harold Bloom, 89–122. Modern Critical Interpretations. New Haven: Chelsea House Publishers, 1988.

———. "Dreaming of Children." In *Female Gothic*, ed. Juliann E. Fleenor, Montreal: Eden Press, 1983.

Hoyt, Charles Alva. "Muriel Spark: The Surrealist Jane Austen." In *Contemporary British Novelists*, ed. Charles Shapiro, 125–43. Carbondale and Edwardsville: Southern Illinois University Press, 1965.

Irigaray, Luce. "When Our Lips Speak Together," *Signs* 6 (Autumn 1980).

Jacobus, Mary. *Reading Women: Essays in Feminist Criticism.* Gender and Culture Series, eds. Carolyn G. Heilbrun and Nancy K. Miller. New York: Columbia, 1986.

———. "The Question of Language: Men of Maxims and *The Mill on the Floss*." In *Writing and Sexual Difference*, ed. Elizabeth Able, 37–52. Chicago: Chicago UP, 1980.

———. "The Question of Maxims and *The Mill on the Floss*." In *George Eliot's "The Mill on the Floss,"* ed. Harold Bloom, 61–76. Modern Critical Interpretations. New Haven: Chelsea House Publishers, 1988.

Janeway, Elizabeth. *The Powers of the Weak.* New York: Alfred A. Knopf, 1980.

Johnson, Claudia. "A Sweet Face as White as Death: Jane Austen and the Politics of Female Sensibility." *Novel: A Forum on Fiction* 22, no. 2 (winter 1989): 159–74.

Johnstone, Peggy Ruth Fitzhugh. "Narcissistic Rage in *The Mill on the Floss*." *Literature and Psychology* 36 nos. 1–2 (1990): 90–109.

Jones, Robin. "The Goblin Ha-Ha: Hidden Smiles and Open Laughter in *Jane Eyre*." In *New Perspectives on Women and Comedy*, ed. Regina Barreca, 201–11. New York: Gordon and Breach, 1992.

Karl, Frederick. *The Contemporary English Novel.* New York: Farrar, Strauss and Cudahy, 1962.

Kemp, Peter. *Muriel Spark.* New York: Barnes and Noble, 1975.

Kermode, Frank. "The Prime of Miss Muriel Spark." *New Statesman* (27 September 1963): 397–98.

———. *The Sense of an Ending.* New York: Oxford University Press, 1967.

Kincaid, James. "Who Is Relieved by the Idea of Comic Relief?" Paper delivered at the December 1991 Modern Language Association Convention, San Francisco.

Kolodny, Anette. "A Map for Rereading; or, Gender and the Interpretation of Literary Texts." In *The (M) Other Tongue: Essays in Feminist Psychoanalytic Interpretation*, eds. Shirley Nelson Garner, Claire Kahane, and Madelon Sprengnether, 241–59. Ithaca and London: Cornell University Press, 1985.

Krause, Agate Nesaule. "Feminism and Art in Fay Weldon's Novels." *Critique: Studies in Modern Fiction* 20, no. 2: (1977) 5–20.

Kuehl, Linda. "Iris Murdoch: The Novelist as Magician/The Magician as Artist." In *Contemporary Women Novelists*, ed. Patricia Meyer Spacks, 92–108. Englewood: Prentice-Hall, 1977.

Langbauer, Laurie. "Romance Revised: Charlotte Lennox's *The Female Quixote*." *Novel: A Forum on Fiction* 18, no. 1 (1984): 29–49.

———. *Women and Romance: The Consolations of Gender in the English Novel.* Ithaca: Cornell University Press, 1990.

Lanser, Susan. "Toward a Feminist Narratology." In *Feminisms: An Anthology of Literary Theory and Criticism*, eds. Robyn R. Warhol and Diane Price Herndl, 610–29. New Brunswick: Rutgers University Press, 1991.

Lee, Hermione. *Elizabeth Bowen: An Estimation.* New York: Vision and Barnes & Noble, 1981.

Lennox, Charlotte. *The Female Quixote, or The Adventures of Arabella.* Boston and Henley: Pandora, 1986.

———. *Henrietta.* Vol. II New York: Garland, 1974.

Lerner, Laurence. *The Truthtellers: Jane Austen, George Eliot, D. H. Lawrence.* New York: Schocken Books, 1967.

Little, Judy. *Comedy and the Woman Writer: Woolf, Spark, and Feminism.* Lincoln: University of Nebraska Press, 1983.

———. "(En)gendering Laughter: Woolf's *Orlando* as Contraband in the Age of Joyce." In *Last Laughs: Perspectives on Women and Comedy* ed. Regina Barreca, 179–92. Studies in Gender and Culture, vol. 2, series ed. Wendy Martin. New York: Gordon and Breach, 1988.

Lodge, David. "Marvels and Nasty Surprises." *The New York Times Book Review* (20 October 1985): 1–4.

———. "The Uses and Abuses of Omniscience: Method and Meaning in Muriel Spark's 'The Prime of Miss Jean Brodie.'" In *Novelist at the Crossroads.* Ithaca: Cornell University Press, 1971.

Lynch, James. "Romance and Realism in Charlotte Lennox's *The Female Quixote*." *Essays in Literature* 14 (1987): 51–63.

Malkoff, Karl. *Muriel Spark.* Columbia Essays on Modern Writers, vol. 36. New York: Columbia University Press, 1968.

Miles, Rosalind. *The Fiction of Sex.* London: Vision Press, 1974.

Mitchell, Carol. "Hostility and Aggression Towards Males in Female Joke Telling." *Frontiers* 3, no. 3 (Fall 1978): 19–23.

Mitchell, Juliet. *Women: The Longest Revolution.* New York: Pantheon Books, 1984.

Morgan, Susan. *Sisters in Time: Imagining Gender in Nineteenth-Century British Fiction.* Oxford: Oxford University Press, 1989.

Newman, Karen. "Can This Marriage Be Saved: Jane Austen Makes Sense of an Ending." *ELH (A Journal of English Literary History)* 50 (1983): 693–710.

Polhemus, Robert. *Comic Faith: The Great Tradition from Austen to Joyce.* Chicago: University of Chicago Press, 1980.

Pullin, Faith. "Autonomy and Fabulation in the Fiction of Muriel Spark." In *Muriel Spark: An Odd Capacity for Vision*, ed. Alan Bold, 71–93. New York: Vision and Barnes and Noble, 1984.

Rich, Adrienne. *On Lies, Secrets, and Silence.* New York: Norton, 1979.

Richmond, Velma Bourgeois. *Muriel Spark.* New York: Frederick Ungar Publishing, 1984.

Rogers, Katharine. "Deflation of Male Pretensions in Fanny Burney's *Cecilia*." In *Last Laughs: Perspectives on Women and Comedy*, ed. Regina Barecca, 87–96. Studies in Gender and Culture, vol. 2, series ed. Wendy Martin. New York: Gordon and Breach, 1988.

Rosenman, Ellen. "Women's Speech and the Roles of the Sexes in *Daniel Deronda*." *Texas Studies in Literature and Language* 31, no. 2 (Summer 1989).

Russ, Joanna. *How to Supress Women's Writing*. Austin: University of Texas Press, 1983.

———. "Somebody Is Trying to Kill Me and I Think It's My Husband: The Modern Gothic." *Journal of Popular Culture* 6 (1973): 666–91.

Russo, Mary. "Female Grotesques: Carnival and Theory." In *Feminist Studies/ Critical Studies*, ed. Theresa de Lauretis, Bloomington, Indiana University Press, 1986.

Satz, Martha. "An Epistimological Understanding of *Pride and Prejudice*: Humility and Objectivity." In *Women and Literature* vol. 3 (1983): 171–86.

Scaldini, Richard. "Les Aventures de Telemaque, or Alienated in Ogygia." In *Locus: Space, Landscape, Decor in Modern French Fiction*, ed. Philip H. Solomon, Yale French Studies 57, 1979.

Shange, Ntozake. "Women Plawrights: Themes and Variations." *The New York Times* (7 May 1989): 1H, 42H.

———. *Nappy Edges*. New York: St. Martin's Press, 1991.

Shaw, Valerie. "Fun and Games with Life-stories." In *Muriel Spark: An Odd Capacity for Vision*, ed. Alan Bold, 44–70. New York: Vision and Barnes and Noble, 1984.

Shershow, Scott Cutler. *Laughing Matters*. Amherst: Amherst University Press, 1986.

Showalter, Elaine. *A Literature of Their Own*. Princeton, New Jersey: Princeton University Press, 1977.

Sochen, June. *Women's Comic Vision*. Detroit: Wayne State University Press, 1991.

Spacks, Patricia Meyer. *Adolescent Idea: Myths of the Young and the Adult Imagination*. New York: Basic Books, 1981.

Spark, Muriel. *The Abbess of Crewe*. New York: Viking Press, 1974.

———. *The Bachelors*. London: Macmillan, 1960.

———. *The Ballad of Peckham Rye*. New York: Putnam, 1960.

———. *Collected Poems* 1. London: Macmillan, 1970.

———. *The Comforters*. New York: Putnam, 1957.

———. *The Doctors of Philosophy*. New York: Alfred Knopf, 1966.

———. *The Driver's Seat*. New York: Putnam, 1970.

———. *The Girls of Slender Means*. New York: Alfred Knopf, 1963.

———. *The Hothouse by the East River*. New York: Viking Press, 1973.

———. "How I Became a Novelist." *John O'London's Weekly* 3 (December 1960): 683.

———. "Keeping it short." Interview. *The Listener* 24 Sept, 1970.

———. *Loitering with Intent*. New York: Coward, McCann and Geoghegan, 1981.

———. *The Mandlebaum Gate*. New York: Alfred Knopf, 1965.

———. "My Conversion." *20th Century* 170 (1961): 58–63.

———. *The Only Problem*. New York: Putnam, 1984.

———. "Portobello Road." In *The Stories of Muriel Spark*, 1–20. New York: J. B. Lippincott, 1985.

———. *The Prime of Miss Jean Brodie*. New York: J. B. Lippincott, 1962.

———. *The Public Image*. London: Macmillan, 1968.

———. *Robinson*. London: Penguin, 1964.

———. "Spirit and Substance." *Vanity Fair* December 1984.

———. *The Stories of Muriel Spark*. New York: E. P. Dutton, 1985.

———. *The Takeover*. London: Macmillan, 1976.

———. *Territorial Rights*. New York: Coward, McCann and Geoghegan, 1979.

———. *Voices at Play*. New York: J. B. Lippincott, 1985.

Spender, Dale. *Mothers of the Novel: 100 Good Women Writers Before Jane Austen*. London: Pandora Press, 1986.

Stanton, Donna. "Difference on Trial." In *The Poetics of Gender*, ed. Nancy Miller. New York: Columbia University Press, 1986.

Stubbs, Patricia. *Muriel Spark*. London: British Council, Longman Group, 1973.

Thompson, Sharon. "The Canonization of Muriel Spark." *Village Voice Literary Supplement* (October 1985):

Toth, Emily. "Forbidden Jokes and Naughty Ladies." *Studies in American Humor* 1–2 (1985): 6–18.

———. "Female Wits" *Massachusetts Review* 22, no. 4 (Winter, 1981): 783–93.

Updike, John. "Between a Wedding and a Funeral." *New Yorker* (14 September 1961): 192.

Walker, Nancy. *A Very Serious Thing: Women's Humor and American Culture*. Minneapolis: University of Minnesota Press, 1988.

———. "Do Feminists Ever Laugh? Women's Humor and Women's Rights." *International Journal of Women's Studies* 4, no. 1 (January/February 1981): 1–9.

———. "Humor and Gender Roles: The 'Funny' Feminism of the Post-World War II Suburbs." *American Quarterly* 37 (1985): 98–113.

———, and Zita Dresner, eds. *Redressing the Balance: American Women's Literary Humor from Colonial Times to the 1980's*. Jackson and London: University Press of Mississippi, 1988.

Wander, Michelene, "Me and My Shadows." In *On Gender and Writing*, ed. Michelle Wander. London: Pandora Press, 1983.

Warren, Leland E. "Of the Conversation of Women: *The Female Quixote* and the Dream of Perfection." *Studies in Eighteenth-Century Culture* 11 (1982): 367–80.

Waugh, Evelyn. Review of *The Comforters*. *The Spectator* (22 February, 1957): 256.

———. "Threatened Genius." *The Spectator*. (7 July, 1961): 28.

Weldon, Fay. *Darcy's Utopia*. New York: Viking, 1991.

―――. *Down Among the Women*. Chicago: Academy Chicago Publishers, 1984.

―――. *The Fat Woman's Joke*. London: Coronet, 1982.

―――. *Female Friends*. New York: St. Martin's Press, 1974.

―――. *Heart of the Country*. New York: Viking Penguin, 1990.

―――. *Letters to Alice: On First Reading Jane Austen*. London: Hodder and Stoughton, 1977.

―――. *The Life and Loves of a She-Devil*. New York: Pantheon Books, 1984.

―――. *Little Sisters*. London: Hodder and Stoughton, 1977.

―――. *Praxis*. New York: Summit Books, 1978.

―――. *The President's Child*. New York: Doubleday, 1983.

―――. *Remember Me*. New York: Random House, 1976.

―――. "Thoughts We Dare Not Speak Aloud." *The Daily Telegraph* (2 December 1991).

―――. *Watching Me Watching You*. Great Britain: Hodder and Stoughton Ltd., 1981.

―――. *Words of Advice (Little Sisters)*. New York: Random House, 1977.

Whittaker, Ruth. "'Angels Dining at the Ritz': The Faith and Fiction of Muriel Spark." In *The Contemporary English Novel*, 157–179. Stratford Upon Avon Studies 18. New York: Holmes and Meier, 1980.

Wilt, Judith. "The Laughter of Maidens, the Cackle of Matriarchs: Notes on the Collision Between Humor and Feminism." In *Gender and the Literary Voice*, ed. Janet Todd, New York: Holmes and Meier. 1980: 1 74.

Wittig, Monique. "The Mark of Gender." In *The Poetics of Gender*, ed. Nancy K. Miller, 59–73. New York: Columbia University Press, 1986.

Woolf, Virginia. "George Eliot." In *Collected Essays*, ed. Leonard Woolf, 162–72. London: Chatto & Windus, 1966–67.

―――. *A Room of One's Own*. New York and London: Harcourt Brace and Jovanovich, 1957.

―――. *Three Guineas*. New York: Harcourt, Brace and World, 1963.

―――. *The Voyage Out*. New York: Signet/Penguin, 1991.

Yeager, Patricia. *Honey Mad Woman: Emancipatory Strategies in Women's Writing*. New York: Columbia University Press, 1988.

Index

Books in the Humor in Life and Letters Series